JUDGEMENT AND SENSE IN MODERN FRENCH PHILOSOPHY

This book proposes a radical new reading of the development of twentieth-century French philosophy. Henry Somers-Hall argues that the central unifying aspect of works by philosophers including Sartre, Foucault, Merleau-Ponty, Deleuze and Derrida is their attempt to provide an account of cognition that does not reduce thinking to judgement. Somers-Hall shows that each of these philosophers is in dialogue with the others in a shared project (however differently executed) to overcome their inheritances from the Kantian and post-Kantian traditions. His analysis points up the continuing relevance of German idealism, and Kant in particular, to modern French philosophy, with novel readings of many aspects of the philosophies under consideration that show their deep debts to Kantian thought. The result is an important account of the emergence, and essential coherence, of the modern French philosophical tradition.

HENRY SOMERS-HALL is Reader in Philosophy at Royal Holloway, University of London. He is author of *Hegel, Deleuze, and the Critique of Representation* (2012) and *Deleuze's* Difference and Repetition (2013), and co-editor of *The Cambridge Companion to Deleuze* (with Daniel W. Smith, Cambridge University Press, 2012) and *A Thousand Plateaus and Philosophy* (with Jeffrey A. Bell and James Williams, 2018).

T0382157

Titles published in the series

JUDGEMENT AND SENSE IN MODERN FRENCH PHILOSOPHY

A New Reading of Six Thinkers

HENRY SOMERS-HALL

Royal Holloway, University of London

CAMBRIDGE
UNIVERSITY PRESS

Shaftesbury Road, Cambridge CB2 8EA, United Kingdom

One Liberty Plaza, 20th Floor, New York, NY 10006, USA

477 Williamstown Road, Port Melbourne, VIC 3207, Australia

314–321, 3rd Floor, Plot 3, Splendor Forum, Jasola District Centre, New Delhi – 110025, India

103 Penang Road, #05–06/07, Visioncrest Commercial, Singapore 238467

Cambridge University Press is part of Cambridge University Press & Assessment,
a department of the University of Cambridge.

We share the University's mission to contribute to society through the pursuit of
education, learning and research at the highest international levels of excellence.

www.cambridge.org
Information on this title: www.cambridge.org/9781009048637

DOI: 10.1017/9781009047920

First published 2022
First paperback edition 2024

A catalogue record for this publication is available from the British Library

Library of Congress Cataloging-in-Publication data
NAMES: Somers-Hall, Henry, author.
TITLE: Judgement and sense in modern French philosophy / Henry Somers-Hall, Royal
Holloway, University of London.
DESCRIPTION: Cambridge, United Kingdom ; New York, NY, USA : Cambridge University
Press, 2021. | Series: Modern European philosophy | Includes bibliographical references and
index.
IDENTIFIERS: LCCN 2021024847 (print) | LCCN 2021024848 (ebook) | ISBN 9781316517901
(hardback) | ISBN 9781009047920 (ebook)
SUBJECTS: LCSH: Philosophy, French – 20th century. | BISAC: PHILOSOPHY / History &
Surveys / Modern | PHILOSOPHY / History & Surveys / Modern
CLASSIFICATION: LCC B2421 .S66 2021 (print) | LCC B2421 (ebook) | DDC 194–dc23
LC record available at https://lccn.loc.gov/2021024847
LC ebook record available at https://lccn.loc.gov/2021024848

ISBN   978-1-316-51790-1   Hardback
ISBN   978-1-009-04863-7   Paperback

Contents

Acknowledgements

I owe special thanks to Jeff Bell, Emily Harding, and Nathan Widder, who were all kind enough to comment on an earlier draft of this book. I would also like to thank the two anonymous reviewers at Cambridge University Press for their careful reading of the manuscript. It is difficult to keep track of all of the encounters and influences on a project such as this, which was many years in the making, but I would like to thank the following friends and fellow travellers in particular for their generosity, and for their dialogue: Brent Adkins, Michael Bacon, Anthony Bruno, Helen Darby, Neil Gascoigne, Sacha Golob, Tom Greaves, Joanna Hodge, Stephen Houlgate, Wahida Khandker, Leonard Lawlor, Beth Lord, Craig Lundy, Emma McNally, Paul Patton, Erin Plunkett, Dave Preston, John Protevi, Scott Revers, John Sellars, Corry Shores, Alan Schrift, Janae Sholtz, Dan Smith, Ed Thornton, David Ventura, Daniela Voss, Judith Wambacq, Thomas Waterton, Daniel Whistler, and James Williams. I would like to thank Emma McNally further for allowing me to use one of her drawings for the cover image. Her work, as Merleau-Ponty would say, gives visible existence to what profane vision believes to be invisible, and traces out something of the texture of thought I have tried to give expression to myself in this work. Thanks also to my family: dearest Nell, Lutalo, Helena, Arrietty, and Persephone. This book is dedicated to my daughter, Helena.

Finally, thanks to Hilary Gaskin of Cambridge University Press for her support throughout this project, and to Sally Evans-Darby for her numerous corrections and improvements to the text.

Some of the material in this book has been published previously. I am grateful for permission to use material previously published in 'Bergson and the Development of Sartre's Thought', *Research in Phenomenology*, 47 (2017), 85–107, which appears in Chapters 2 and 3, and material previously published in 'Merleau-Ponty's Reading of Kant's Transcendental Idealism', *Southern Journal of Philosophy*, 57:1 (2019), 103–31, which appears in Chapter 4.

I was only able to write *Judgement and Sense in Modern French Philosophy* because of a fellowship awarded to me by the Arts and Humanities Research Council (AHRC) which freed me from teaching and administrative responsibilities to let me work through the groundwork for the project. I would like to thank the AHRC for supporting this project.

Introduction

At the heart of this enquiry is the question of what it means to think, and how this question has been answered within the French tradition. This book addresses the question of what unifies the French philosophical tradition across the twentieth century by exploring these two questions. Kant claimed that the structure of experience mirrored the categories of thought because the cognitive faculties of the subject played a constitutive role in structuring experience. As such, the structure of thought for Kant is fundamentally tied to the nature of metaphysics. In developing his account of what thinking entailed, Kant took judgement, the attribution of a predicate to a subject, to be the paradigm act of thinking. Throughout the nineteenth century, efforts to move beyond Kant's model of thinking as judgement centred on the attempt to augment that model. For instance, Hegel saw Kant's account of judgement as an essentially fixed form of the true nature of thinking, and therefore developed a more processual account of thinking. His account still ultimately operates by putting judgement into motion, however, rather than rejecting the model of thinking as judgement itself. Conversely, philosophers such as Schelling who do not understand thinking solely in terms of judging often retreat into an indeterminate mysticism, thus retaining the idea that anything positive that can be said about thought must take judgement as a model.

The twentieth-century French tradition can be characterised in contrast by an attempt to replace, rather than augment, judgement as the paradigm case of thinking. This can be seen in the effort to develop an account of perception and cognition as perspectival rather than object-centred which we find in the phenomenological work of Sartre and Merleau-Ponty, and Bergson's rejection of accounts of thinking which take their central metaphor from space. In both cases, the subject-predicate account is considered an abstraction from the inherently contextual and temporal nature of thinking. Foucault's methodology can also be seen as his own rejection of classical models of thought. In particular, he claims that what he calls the 'juridico-discursive' understanding of the world can only explain the determination of objects, rather than their constitution. Consequently, he develops an alternative non-object-centred logic to that of the early phenomenologists. Deleuze and Derrida's attempts to formulate a new concept, or quasi-concept, of difference derive directly from the limitations they see in Kant's account of thought in the *Critique of Pure Reason*. That is, it is by understanding how something is determined without relying on negation that they develop a new way of understanding difference, and with it, thought. All of these projects share a concern to provide an alternative model of cognition, and thereby to overcome the limitations of the Kantian project. When viewed from this perspective, it becomes clear that each of these philosophers is in a dialogue with the others, and that the French tradition can be seen as a unified attempt to maintain the radicality of the transcendental project while moving away from its account of the nature of thinking.

By bringing these different accounts into relation with each other, this work develops a novel genealogy of twentieth-century French thought. It also investigates French philosophy as a coherent research project analysing problems that are central to the philosophical tradition, and allows the re-evaluation of French thought as a rich and rigorous philosophical movement. I focus on the problem of how one understands thinking, and hence we will evaluate some more general claims about the nature of thought, and formulate and assess the arguments which support the move away from models of thought as judgement and their broader implications. While in this work the focus is very much on the model of thinking and what this account of thinking tells us about the nature of the world, such concerns have implications beyond the purely theoretical, and we can see that these alternative models bring with them the kinds of radical changes to how we orientate ourselves in the world introduced by the existentialists and the post-structuralists.

This is not the first work to deal with the development of French philosophy. The majority of these organise the development of French thought chronologically, rather than around a problem (see, for example, Gutting 2001, Schrift 2006, or Descombes 1980). While these approaches are vitally important for a full understanding of the connections between French philosophers, they are inevitably less able to present the problem-centred approach found in this work. Mullarkey (2006) does relate a series of thinkers in the French tradition by looking at their various philosophical claims. In particular, Mullarkey argues that the second half of the twentieth century is dominated in the French tradition by attempts to develop a non-reductive account of the nature of life while avoiding the category of transcendence. This is certainly an important theme in the second half of the twentieth century: a focus on immanence emphasises the rupture between the pre-war and post-war periods, as it breaks with phenomenology's concern with the transcendence of intentionality, and hence prevents us from using the resources of the phenomenological tradition to clarify and explicate later thought. Lawlor (2011) provides an account of early French philosophy that has an awareness of their role in founding later French philosophy, focusing on the notion that French philosophy is governed by the desire to reverse Plato, but as the title suggests, it does not draw out these implications, and concludes with Foucault's early work. McCumber (2014) develops an account of continental philosophy more generally on the basis of its incorporation of time. While this is an important theme, McCumber does not distinguish between the seemingly incongruent modes of history and becoming, risking the possibility of resting the unity of the discipline on an equivocation.

Presenting a different vision of the interrelation of philosophies does not entail rejecting the interpretation offered by others, just as the contours of the constellations of the same stars do not falsify other potential constellations. Difference here does not therefore necessarily entail negation. As such, by seeing the tradition as centred on freedom, the reversal of Plato, and immanence and transcendence, each enriches our understanding of French philosophy. We can perhaps here take up Bergson's example of the concept of colour, which is not formed by the removal of what is particular about each colour, but by passing each colour through a converging lens to constitute a light which contains them all. We should note that every interpretation similarly is only partial, since traditions always incorporate heterodox figures and radical divergences. The reading in this work does not account, for instance, for a figure such as Léon Brunschvicg, against whom many of the phenomenologists reacted, and who explicitly affirms the place of judgement (and other examples could be given), or Jean-Luc Nancy's greater proximity to Hegel than those we encounter in this work. Nonetheless, the six figures presented in this work present a broad range of approaches present within the French tradition, and together show why the concepts of thought, sense, and judgement form such a pervasive and vital problem.

There are a number of interrelated claims that I derive from this reading of the French tradition. First, as we have noted, there is the rejection of the claim that thinking is judging. As we will see in Chapter 1, this assumption is at the heart of the German idealist tradition, where determination in

general is understood in terms of predication. Where judgement does not
hold, as in Hölderlin's conception of being, for instance, we have an
absence of determination, and where we move beyond the normal model
of the understanding, as in Hegel's work, we do so through the augmentation of predicative structures to cover over its limitations. Bergson's
recognition of a difference between the representation of time and the
way time is actually lived opens the way to this rejection of the paradigm of
thinking as judging, and this interplay of thinking and the representation
of thinking as judging, with a difference in kind between the two, will be
a theme amongst all of the philosophers we consider. For Sartre, this will be
through a distinction between knowledge and consciousness that leaves
philosophy open to paralogism. For Merleau-Ponty, this is through the
conflation of perspective with the representation of perspective. For each of
the post-war thinkers, Derrida, Foucault, and Deleuze, we similarly find
that the nature of thinking, whether characterised by *différance*, power, or
intensity, is overwritten by the structures of judgement which differ in kind
from thinking itself.

Together with this movement away from judgement comes a recognition
of the centrality of Hegel, but Hegel as the founder of a model of thinking to
be avoided. We find therefore the recognition of the pressing need to
develop a non-dialectical model of thought. Hence, the 'generalised anti-
Hegelianism' that Deleuze recognises in 1968 extends back from Bergson's
claim that one cannot reconstitute the concrete from abstract elements,
through Sartre's criticism of Hegel's 'optimism' to Merleau-Ponty's rejection of Hegel's account of indeterminacy. We find it in Derrida's claim,
echoing Sartre, that the Hegelian *Aufhebung* is a false resolution, and
Foucault's move to understanding the transitions between historical epochs
in terms of contingency rather than dialectical necessity.

This attempt to move away from Hegel is intertwined with another
shared trait amongst all of the philosophers we will look at: the return to
Kant in order to find an alternative model to the dialectic. We can
recognise two important aspects of this. First, a number of the philosophers
we will look at take up Kant's distinction between concepts and intuitions,
noting that here Kant introduces a difference in kind between the two
forms of organisation that will be instrumental for their own attempts to
develop a novel account of thinking. While for Kant this difference in kind
is understood in terms of an active faculty of understanding and a passive
faculty of intuition, figures such as Merleau-Ponty and Deleuze will
disrupt the active–passive distinction in order to see in perception, or
beneath perception, a novel mode of synthesis that does not rely on

judgement. Second, throughout the tradition, we find a return from Hegel's speculative dialectic to Kant's transcendental dialectic. Here, instead of seeing the antinomies that appear within representation showing the presence of contradiction in the world, and the need to augment our account of judging to encompass contradiction, they point to the necessity of recognising an element that falls outside of representation. Thus, we will find throughout the work explored in this volume recourse to Kantian notions such as paralogisms, transcendental ideas, and illusions. It is this Kantian claim that reason naturally falls into illusions when operating on its own that allows these thinkers to explain how it is that thinking should not be equated with judging, but how it is that this equation has traditionally been made. I will argue that this notion of transcendental illusion is extended throughout the French tradition to argue that Kant himself falls into error when he fails to distinguish the way in which we represent thinking from thinking itself.

Finally, in rejecting judgement, we have the introduction of a new model of thinking. In essence, the French tradition considered in this volume can be seen as attempting to discover a new way of understanding organisation that does not rely on judgement, or notions such as subjects or predicates. This model of thinking has a number of characteristics running through the tradition. First, this logic tends to be a logic of sense that seeks to explain how we encounter a world that is meaningful. We will find that all six of the philosophers we will be dealing with present arguments to show that sense cannot be grounded in judgement for the reason that everything resembles everything else to some degree, and hence once we are dealing with the discrete elements that make up a judgement, it is impossible to distinguish meaningful and coincidental relations. As such, we need an account of the constitution of the elements of judgement that a model of thinking as judging presupposes as simply given. Rather than the logic of association that we find in, for instance, empiricism, this logic will be responsible for constituting a field of elements with relationships of sense. It will operate within a field that is itself not atomic in structure. The relationship between thinking and its representation in terms of judgement will thus be one that involves a transposition between elements that differ in kind. We can see these relationships played out between Bergson's two multiplicities, Merleau-Ponty's account of perception and objective thought, and, to take one more example, Foucault's account of power, and its constitution of a domain of discourse. In each of these cases, therefore, we have a movement beyond what would be possible for Kant through the recognition that we do not simply have to have indeterminacy outside of representation, but that there could be a model of organisation that differs in kind from it.

I.1   Outline

We will be looking at six French philosophers over the course of this volume, and while the sequence of presentation is chronological, the aim will be to explore the way each of the philosophers we are considering develops their philosophy in relation to a set of concerns shared by them all. By focusing on a shared problematic, we will be able to mitigate a common problem, particularly in the continental tradition, of different philosophers developing their own technical vocabularies within which to present their ideas, or more seriously, the shifts in meaning of the same terms between different philosophers. By focusing on their arguments and shared problems, I also hope to mitigate the common desire of philosophers to emphasise their differences from their contemporaries and immediate predecessors and instead to demonstrate lines of continuity within the tradition. The aim will be to reconstruct each philosopher's philosophical position on the basis of their accounts of the nature of thought, and to see how their accounts can be read as responses to problems emerging from the German idealist tradition. For this reason, the first chapter will present an overview of the place of judgement in Kant's thought and that of his successors.

The opening chapter looks at the role of judgement in Kant's *First Critique*, focusing on the way in which the legislative function of the understanding is central to transcendental idealism. I will go on to show how Kant associates determination with judgement, and how this association is maintained in Hölderlin and Schelling's efforts to resolve certain aporias in the Kantian system, with being understood as indeterminate because it differs from the world of judgement. I conclude by showing how Hegel resolves difficulties presented by Hölderlin's distinction between judgement and being by seeing judgement as an abstraction from a richer process of reason. As such, I demonstrate the centrality of judgement in the German idealist tradition.

In Chapter 2, I introduce Bergson's claim that thinking has a processual character that distinguishes it from judging. I analyse Bergson's claim in *Time and Free Will* that the structure of our mental lives is different in kind from the way we understand the external world. I show how Bergson's later work develops an account of the interrelations of durational thinking and judging. Drawing on Bergson's early untranslated lectures on Kant, I show

how Bergson pinpoints a lacuna in Kant's account of the imagination, and attempts to argue that it is only by understanding thinking as operating through a process of dissociation, rather than the synthetic association of Kant's model of the imagination, that we can understand the emergence of a meaningful world.

The third chapter explores Sartre's account of thinking, focusing on his relatively neglected early work on the imagination. I take up Sartre's largely unacknowledged debt to Bergson, showing that despite Sartre's move to phenomenology, his account of the difference between imagining and perceiving relies on Bergson's logic of multiplicities. I argue that this influence carries on into *Being and Nothingness* where Sartre's account of the situation as the process that makes judgement possible relies on a pre-juridical moment that inverts Bergson's account of free will while remaining true to the categories underlying it. I analyse Sartre's account of why we falsely understand consciousness as juridical, which reworks Kant's own arguments in the paralogisms before showing how his account of consciousness ultimately fails to provide the positive account of the constitution of a situation that he requires.

Chapter 4 develops Merleau-Ponty's perspectival account of experience. I show how Merleau-Ponty's claim that perception has a different structure to what he calls 'objective thought' can be derived from his interpretation of Kant's paradox of symmetrical objects. I look at how this difference in structure leads to Merleau-Ponty's distinctive accounts of perspectival depth and orientation in space, before returning to Kant to show how Merleau-Ponty's account of perception as having a figure-background structure leads to substantial divergences from Kant's account of the constitution of the object (in doing so, I reconstruct a sustained argument against Kant's transcendental deduction from fragmentary comments throughout Merleau-Ponty's work). I also show that the model of determination developed by Merleau-Ponty, while relying on context, differs significantly from Hegel's account of determination, and supplements deficiencies in Sartre's account.

Chapter 5 explores Derrida's analysis of the problem of judgement through an extended exploration of Derrida's analysis of presence and *différance*. I analyse three of Derrida's readings of other philosophers: Plato, Hegel, and Husserl, with the aim of showing how in each case Derrida believes that the priority of presence (and hence judgement) rests on a transcendental idea that exceeds the given. I argue that despite Derrida's apparent hostility to the phenomenological tradition, his work is indebted to Sartre, and echoes Bergson's analysis of resemblance.

Chapter 6 turns to Michel Foucault, looking at both his early archaeo-logical work and his introduction of power in the later genealogical writings. I focus on how his early work examines the rules which precede and make possible judgements. We will see that Foucault derives the term and method of archaeology from Kant's own work, though Foucault develops his own non-juridical logic of it. I then show how this attempt to understand thinking as different from judging carries on into Foucault's later genealogical work with his notion of biopower as an attempt to provide an alternative model of power to what we find in the juridico-discursive model that he argues typifies traditional understandings of it.

Our final chapter begins by returning to Hölderlin's account of the relationship between being and judgement. I argue that central to Deleuze's philosophy is the introduction of an account of determination that operates differently from the subject-predicate determination discovered in judge-ment. The chapter draws on Chapter 4's account of depth to show how Deleuze takes up then expands Merleau-Ponty's account of our perspectival relationship to the world. It further develops Kant's notions of transcendental illusion to show why we tend to misunderstand the nature of thinking and the transcendental ideas to illuminate Deleuze's account of how thinking produces sense prior to the introduction of judging.

Judgement and the German Idealists

1.1 Introduction

In this opening chapter, I want to explore why judgement was taken up as the model for thinking in the German idealist tradition. We will begin with the work of Immanuel Kant, as it is Kant who sets the agenda for the development of German idealism. As we shall see, Kant's revolution in philosophy involves moving from seeing thinking as a correspondence between subject and object to seeing thinking as legislating for experience. I will begin with the justification for this move before exploring what its implications might be for our conception of experience. I want to then look at why judgement plays a central role in Kant's conception of experience. For the remainder of the chapter, I will consider some of the responses to Kant's account of thinking and experience in the German idealist tradition, focusing on Hölderlin, early Schelling, and Hegel. My claim is that the general trend of German idealism was to see thinking in terms of judgement. Even where an alternative account was developed, as in the case of Hegel, this took the form of an augmentation of judgement, rather than a rejection of it.

1.2 Kant's Conception of Judgement

Kant is not the first philosopher to accord a central place to judgement in his account of our relationship to the world. For Leibniz, for instance, all propositions can be understood in terms of the attribution to a subject of a property. As he writes in his notes on logical reasoning, '[i]n every categorical proposition (for from them I can show elsewhere that other kinds of propositions can be dealt with by changing a few things in the calculus) there are two terms, the subject and the predicate' (Leibniz 1989: 11). The role of judgement in Kant's transcendental idealism is just as pervasive, given the legislative function of the understanding in constituting the experience of the subject. As we shall see, in attempting to determine the categories through which being is thought, Kant, as Hegel notes, 'turn[s] metaphysics into logic' (Hegel 1989: 51), and by doing so makes understanding the nature of judgement integral to his project.[1] He writes, for instance, that 'we can reduce all acts of the understanding to judgements, and the understanding may therefore be represented as a faculty of judgement' (Kant 1929: A69/B70). Béatrice Longuenesse notes that Kant in fact provides a number of different definitions of judgement, each of which develops a complementary aspect of his account of it.[2] In this section, I want to work through some of the characteristics of judgement. At the opening of the 'Analytic of Concepts', Kant gives a brief account of the nature of judgement:

> In every judgement there is a concept which holds of many representations, and among them of a given representation that is immediately related to an object. Thus in the judgement, 'all bodies are divisible', the concept of the divisible applies to various other concepts, but is here applied in particular to the concept of body, and this concept again to certain appearances that present themselves to us. These concepts, therefore, are mediately represented through the concept of divisibility. Accordingly, all judgements are functions of unity among our representations; instead of an immediate representation, a *higher* representation, which comprises the immediate representation and various others, is used in knowing the object, and thereby much possible knowledge is collected into one. (Kant 1929: A68–9/B93–4)

The first point to make about this definition is that it asserts that judgements involve the unification of diverse representations. In this case, the diverse representations of a body and divisibility are brought together in the judgement itself. As we shall see, this ability to give unity to a multiplicity will be an essential aspect of judgement's legislative role in the constitution of a field of objects for a subject. We can also note that it does so by being a 'function of unity', implying that judgement is not simply a passive collection of elements, but is itself a task or process by which the elements of diversity are brought together. Judgement is thus an activity.

There are many ways in which a multiplicity can be brought into the form of a unity, and so if we are going to understand Kant's conception of judgement, we need to explore further how the different representations

---

[1] For Hegel's interpretation of Kant's philosophy as a logic, see Longuenesse 2007: 15–18.
[2] Longuenesse 1998: 81. I will for the most part be following Longuenesse's excellent account of Kant's analysis of judgement in this section, with some changes of emphasis reflecting themes of particular importance to the twentieth-century French tradition.

that make up a judgement are connected together. The first point to note is that a judgement contains two predicates – in this case, the predicate 'body' and the predicate 'divisibility' – and so Kant's conception of judgement appears to be more complex than that which we find in Leibniz. For Kant, we have a situation where judgement is a relation between representations: the second, 'body', related immediately to the object that judgement relates to, in effect picking out the object for the judgement, and the first, 'divisibility', related mediately through the concept of body. In fact, this idea that judgement contains a reference to objects is a fundamental feature of its structure. Later in the *Critique of Pure Reason*, Kant explicitly distinguishes the kind of unity found in judgement from that which might be gained by, for instance, a Humean conception of association, by introducing the concept of the object:

> But if I investigate more precisely the relation of the given cognitions in any judgment and distinguish it, as belonging to the understanding, from the relation according to laws of reproductive imagination, which has only subjective validity, I find that a judgement is nothing but the manner in which given cognitions are brought to the objective unity of apperception. (Kant 1929: B141)

The notion of objective unity in this claim does not mean that Kant believes that all judgements, by virtue of their form, correlate with the world, and are hence true,[3] since such a claim would be absurd, given the possibility of contingent empirical judgements. Rather, the claim, as Henry Allison succinctly puts it, is that 'every judgement involves a synthesis or unification of representations in consciousness, whereby the representations are conceptualised so as to be referred or related to an object' (Allison 2004: 87). As such, the notion that judgements relate to objects is a constitutive feature of judgement itself.[4]

A further consequence of this is that the connection between representations in a judgement results in a structure that is truth functional – a judgement can either correctly or incorrectly characterise an object or objects that it relates to. In both of these dimensions, judgement differs from

---

[3] See Allison 2004: 88 and Longuenesse 1998: 82.

[4] This applies to both what Kant calls in the *Prolegomena* judgements of perception and judgements of experience (Kant 1997: §20). In the former, we have judgements which are fundamentally tied to our perception of the nature of the world (such as Kant's example of 'If the sun shines on the stone, it becomes warm'), and judgements of experience, which assert claims that the understanding considers to have necessary validity (such as the claim that 'the sun warms the stone'). What the two cases have in common is that both are made possible by relating representations through the concept of an object.

the kind of unity that is developed by the imagination. The reference to an object within the structure of judgement ensures that what is aimed at by a judgement is something that transcends the particular situation and impressions of a given subject. For the imagination, operating without the concept of an object, we simply have a collection of representations not related together by objective functions, but by principles such as resemblance, contiguity, and association. A unity governed by association (such as Allison's example of the association of heat with the thought of the sun [2004: 88]) is not truth functional, and merely rests on the habitual interrelation of representations with one another. We can also note that in the case of an imaginative unity, the relationship between representations is flat – representations are simply coordinated with one another. As we saw in the case of the divisibility of bodies, however, there is a relationship of containment or subordination between the representations in the judgement. Divisibility is subordinated to the concept of body in such a manner that whatever is considered to be a body is necessarily also considered to be divisible. This relationship of subordination at the heart of judgement suggests important connections with syllogistic inference which Kant himself will draw out in the transcendental dialectic. For now we can note, however, that the ordered, object-centred, and active characteristics of judgement mean that it will play a central role in Kant's attempt to replace a philosophy of correspondence with one of legislation.

1.3   The Aims of Kant's Project

Kant's claim that 'the proper problem of pure reason is contained in the question: How are synthetic *a priori* judgements possible?' (Kant 1929: B19) reinforces the centrality of judgement. His question opens out onto a more substantial role for judgement than the mere formulation of claims about the world. Kant's claim here draws together two distinctions that are central to our understanding of judgements. The first is between analytic and synthetic judgements. For analytic judgements, 'the predicate B belongs to the subject A as something which is (covertly) contained in this concept A' (Kant 1929: A6/B10). For synthetic judgements, 'B lies outside the concept A, although it does indeed stand in connection with it' (Kant 1929: A6/B10). As Kant clarifies, analytic judgements provide knowledge in a manner that is explicative – they allow us to draw out connections implicit in a concept that we may have only understood in a confused manner. Synthetic judgements are ampliative, which means that they actively extend our knowledge by telling us something novel about the subject at hand. This distinction is combined with a distinction between a priori and a posteriori judgements. A priori knowledge is knowledge that is 'absolutely independent of all experience' (Kant 1929: B5), whereas a posteriori knowledge is knowledge gained through experience itself. This independence from experience for Kant implies that a priori truths are necessary truths, since 'experience teaches that a thing is so and so, but not that it cannot be otherwise' (Kant 1929: B3). Synthetic a priori knowledge is thus knowledge which is not derived from experience, and yet is ampliative, or that tells us something genuinely novel about the world. Kant's ostensive project is thus to understand how judgements such as that every event has a cause (a claim which goes beyond anything contained within the concept of an event) can be known with certainty. This claim in particular is one of the principal targets of Hume's scepticism.

The question of how synthetic a priori judgements are possible opens out onto the broader question of the nature of experience, and the relationship of the subject to the object. The *First Critique* seeks to address the failure of metaphysics to answer this question, and Kant begins with the broad claim that 'hitherto it has been assumed that all our knowledge must conform to objects. But all attempts to extend our knowledge of objects by establishing something in regard to them *a priori*, by means of concepts, have, on this assumption, ended in failure' (Kant 1929: Bxvi). Kant's claim, therefore, is that despite the apparent divergences between approaches to metaphysical questions, there is a shared set of assumptions underlying the different approaches. In the introduction to the *First Critique*, Kant's account of this common-sense view is quite brief, but he discusses it in greater detail in the paralogisms, where he defines the standard metaphysical position as transcendental realism:

> [Transcendental realism] regards time and space as something given in themselves, independently of our sensibility. The transcendental realist thus interprets outer appearances (their reality being taken as granted) as things-in-themselves, which exist independently of us and of our sensibility, and which are therefore outside us – the phrase 'outside us' being interpreted in conformity with pure concepts of understanding. It is, in fact, this transcendental realist who afterwards plays the part of the empirical idealist. After wrongly supposing that the objects of the senses, if they are to be external, must have an existence by themselves, and independently of the senses, he finds that, judged from this point of view, all our sensuous representations are inadequate to establish their reality. (Kant 1929: A369)

At the heart of this definition is the claim that for the transcendental realist, the reality of objects is defined independently of our manner of relating to them. Once we make this assumption, the question of how we can make judgements which are necessary but also contentful becomes dependent on our justification of the correspondence between our representations of the world and the world itself. This question arises for both the rationalist and the empiricist. For the rationalist, the question becomes how our innate ideas about the world can be justified as conforming to the nature of the world itself. Descartes' solution to this problem is to posit God as the guarantor of the natural light of reason, a solution also adopted by Leibniz in asserting that God guarantees the correspondence between the monads. While the empiricist rejects the belief in innate ideas, they still begin with a conception of the object that sees it as external to the subject. For the empiricist, the key question is the relationship between our sense impressions and their causes. For Locke, for instance, sense impressions are signs of things themselves, and bear a relationship of resemblance to them:

> [S]imple ideas are not fictions of our fancies, but the natural and regular productions of things without us, really operating upon us; and so carry with them all the conformity which is intended; or which our state requires: for they represent to us things under those appearances which they are fitted to produce in us . . .. Thus the idea of whiteness, or bitterness, as it is in the mind, exactly answering that power which is in any body to produce it there, has all the real conformity it can or ought to have, with things without us. (Locke 1975: 4.iv.4)

As we know, this correspondence between impressions and things is criticised, particularly by David Hume, but Kant's point is that even when the connection between our sense impressions and the object itself is thrown into doubt, the account of knowledge which our scepticism criticises is still understood on the basis of the criterion of correspondence between our categories of thinking and the things themselves.

Henry Allison describes this transcendental realist conception of metaphysics as a 'theocentric model of knowledge' (2004: 27), to the extent that it assumes that knowledge of the world is equated with the kind of direct access to the nature of the world that we might associate with God's knowledge of the world. This does not mean that knowledge is equivalent to God's knowledge, but rather, as was the case with Leibniz, as our knowledge of the world becomes more adequate, it approaches the kind of intellectual intuition of the world we associate with God. A further consequence of this is that transcendental realism does not develop a sharp distinction between our rational understanding of the world and the manner in which the thing is given to us. In this sense, spatial and temporal properties are seen as properties of things themselves, and as knowledge is understood as correspondence of our representations with objects themselves, the spatial and temporal aspects of our representations of things are collapsed into the conceptual relationships with things. For Leibniz, space and time are merely inadequate ways of understanding what are in reality conceptual determinations.[5] For the empiricists, our ideas ultimately differ from our sense impressions merely in degree, rather than in kind. As we shall see, the claim that there is a difference in kind between the organisation of intuition and concepts will be crucial both in the formulation of transcendental idealism and in the work of many of the French philosophers who come after Kant.

As Deleuze notes, we can see Kant's revolution as involving a move from seeing knowledge in terms of a correspondence of concepts with objects to seeing knowledge as involving a legislative function in regard to objects (Deleuze 1984: 58). In essence, Kant's claim is that rather than presupposing that the notion of an object is something that pre-exists our epistemic relationship to the world, leading either to dogmatism or scepticism, we should consider the possibility that our concept of an object may be a principle that we use to organise our experience ('We must therefore make trial whether we may not have more success in the tasks of metaphysics, if we suppose that objects must conform to our knowledge' [Kant 1929: Bxvi]). By seeing consciousness as conditioning experience, such that it conforms to our categories of understanding, we no longer make the unwarranted theocentric assumption of a pre-established harmony between our categories of thought and the objects of the world. As such, Kant no longer holds to a transcendentally real conception of objects, and in this sense he is an idealist. For the transcendental realist, a belief that knowledge was a form of correspondence between our representations and a transcendent realm of objects led to scepticism, and empirical idealism, to the extent that we were limited to understanding the world in terms of representations for which we couldn't prove objective reality. For Kant, on the contrary, once the concept of an object is recognised as something that is legislated by the subject, the fact that we ourselves constitute a world composed of objects means that we can guarantee that our conception of an object will be instantiated in experience. As such, Kant's project combines an idealism on a transcendental level with an empirical realism.

---

[5] 'As for my own opinion, I have said more than once that I hold space to be something purely relative, as time is – that I hold it to be an order of coexistences, as time is an order of successions. For space denotes, in terms of possibility, an order of things that exist at the same time, considered as existing together, without entering into their particular manners of existing' (Leibniz and Clarke 2000: 15).

As we shall see in the next section, in order to develop this constitutive account of experience, Kant gives a prominent role to judgement in his system.

1.4   Functions and Categories

Even though objects conform to our knowledge of them for Kant, this does not mean that we simply have a radical idealism, such as that of Berkeley. While we may organise what is given to us, there is still a given. Our intuition of space and time is essentially receptive, while our cognitive faculties are active. This brings us to the central problem of the *First Critique*. As we saw earlier, transcendental realism posits a difference in degree between concepts and intuitions, which allows it to claim that our own perception of the world is analogous to the God's-eye view that it is supposed to correspond to. For Kant, there is a difference in kind between our receptive intuition of the world and the active faculty that organises experience. Deleuze puts the problem as follows:

> We have seen that [Kant] rejected the idea of a pre-established harmony between subject and object; substituting the principle of a necessary submission of the object to the subject itself. But does he not once again come up with the idea of harmony, simply transposed to the level of faculties of the subject which differ in nature? (Deleuze 1984: 19)

In other words, although the fact that we constitute objects and our representations of them allows us to solve Hume's problem of the external world, Kant has introduced a new, internal problem. How can two faculties which are different in kind relate to each other? Kant himself raises this difficulty. He begins by arguing that knowledge involves a form of synthesis. That is, making a statement involves bringing together different concepts into a unity. He then notes that 'appearances might very well be so constituted that the understanding should not find them to be in accordance with the conditions of its unity' (Kant 1929: A90/B123). There could, therefore, be nothing in intuition to which the understanding can apply itself. This problem of how the faculties relate to one another is the problem that required a reworking of his initial formulation of transcendental idealism in his inaugural dissertation, and was responsible for the delays in the publication of the *First Critique* itself.[6]

---

[6] Allison 2015: chapter 3 is a good source for Kant's development between the dissertation and the *First Critique*.

Kant's solution to this difficulty involves arguing that conceptual thought plays a necessary organising role in experience. We can draw a distinction between perception, which simply involves us being presented with appearances, and experience. Kant argues that the difference between perception and experience is that whereas perception simply requires intuition, experience also involves the notion that we experience a world of objects.[7] When we look at our experience of the world, Kant argues that we can see that the notion of an object is not directly given in intuition. Instead, our experience of a world made up of things rather than, for instance, sensations *presupposes* a conception of an object, or objecthood. The question of the *First Critique* can therefore be reformulated as: what is it that allows us to experience a world of objects, rather than simply appearances? Kant addresses this claim in a section of the *First Critique* titled the 'Transcendental Deduction'. The claim that the transcendental deduction makes is that it is the understanding, which is the faculty of concepts (or, as we shall see, rules), that gives us the concept of an object. As such, the understanding plays a necessary role in experience, and the gap between the different faculties has been bridged:

> The question now arises whether *a priori* concepts do not also serve as antecedent conditions under which alone anything can be, if not intuited, yet thought as object in general. In that case all empirical knowledge of objects would necessarily conform to such concepts, because only as thus presupposing them is anything possible as *object of experience*. (Kant 1929: A93/B126)

Kant's attempt to justify this response has two moments to it. First, Kant argues that if there are categories of the understanding that unify experience under the form of the object, then these must be related to the functions of understanding that give unity to judgements. This first stage of Kant's argument is normally referred to as the metaphysical deduction. This stage is followed by the transcendental deduction, where Kant shows that the categories of the understanding do in fact unify experience. In the following sections, I want to work through these two sections of the *First Critique*, focusing on the transcendental deduction as developed in its first edition. These sections are both controversial; particularly in the case of the transcendental deduction, the structure of the argument, and even its aims, are still much debated.[8] My aim in working through them here will not be

---

[7] Cf. for instance Kant 1929: A93/B126: '[A]ll experience does indeed contain, in addition to the intuition of the sense through which something is given, a *concept* of an object as being thereby given, that is to say, as appearing.'

[8] See Guyer 1992 and Allison 2004: chapter 7 for summaries of some of the major issues governing the interpretation of the transcendental deduction.

to present a rigorous reading of Kant's argument, but rather to show why Kant believes that there is a necessary connection between judgement, synthesis, objecthood, and experience.

1.5   The Metaphysical Deduction

So far in this chapter, we have focused on the programmatic aspects of Kant's project and his account of judgement. Kant's analysis of the nature of judgement forms a part of what he calls 'general logic', which is the analysis of 'the form of thought in general' (Kant 1929: A55/B79). For Kant, the subject has a constitutive role in producing the field of objects to which judgements relate. In this sense, as well as the general logic, there is also the possibility of a logic that governs the legislative rules by which the subject constitutes objects that are taken up into judgements. This second logic, which Kant calls transcendental logic, therefore deals with 'the origin of the modes in which we know objects, insofar as that origin cannot be attributed to the objects' (Kant 1929: A55/B80). The metaphysical deduction aims to determine what categories are responsible for determining the structure of experience. The metaphysical deduction is titled 'the clue to the discovery of all pure concepts of the understanding', and this clue derives from the synthetic nature of judgement itself. If transcendental logic is going to explain how the kinds of objects that are compatible with judgement can be constituted, it is a reasonable assumption that the categories themselves will be analogous to the functions of judgement. Kant argues, therefore, that our starting point should be the table of possible functions of judgement. This details all of the possible ways in which representations can be united together in a judgement (such as the difference between 'all bodies are divisible', 'some bodies are divisible', 'if something is a body, then it is divisible', etc.). The table of judgements lists four headings (quantity, quality, relation, modality), each containing three kinds of judgement that exhaust the respective characteristics of a judgement. For example, in terms of quantity, a judgement can relate to 'all x's', 'some x's', or 'this x'. What transcendental logic requires is a set of concepts that are both related to judgement and have some reference to intuition. This combination of an analogous structure to the functions of judgement on the one hand and a reference to intuition on the other defines the categories. As an anticipation of Kant's future argument, we can see here that if Kant is able to show that the categories do play a role in organising intuition, then he will have shown how judgement is able to relate to the objects of experience. The central claim is the following:

> The same function which gives unity to the various representations *in a judgement* also gives unity to the mere synthesis of various representations *in an intuition*; and this unity, in its most general expression, we entitle the pure concept of the understanding. The same understanding, through the same operations by which in concepts, by means of analytical unity, it produced the logical form of judgement, also introduces a transcendental content into its representations, by means of the synthetic unity of the manifold in intuition in general. (Kant 1929: A79/B104–5)

By positing an isomorphism between the functions that constitute the object of experience and the functions of judgement, Kant guarantees that judgements will accord with the structure of the object, as the object is constituted from the outset to accord with judgement.

1.6   The Transcendental Deduction

The aim of the transcendental deduction is to demonstrate that the categories do in fact play a role in the constitution of experience. Kant's claim is that experience rests on a threefold synthesis, which in turn requires us to posit a subject and an object, leading us to introduce the categories as rules which relate to the constitution of objects. In this section, I want to go through these various syntheses quickly in order to give a sense of the role of judgement in Kant's account of the world. I will focus on the version of the transcendental deduction given in the first edition of the *First Critique* (known as the 'A' deduction), principally because of the greater emphasis it places on the different moments of synthesis, over the more formal 'B' deduction.[9]

The first condition for the possibility of experience is what Kant calls a 'synthesis of apprehension', performed by intuition, the faculty responsible for giving us the spatial and temporal manifolds within which experience takes place. Although everything we experience in the external world occurs in space, Kant here concentrates on time, as he claims that even non-spatial phenomena, such as mental states, occupy a position in time. Thus, if he can ultimately show that the categories are responsible for temporal experience, he will have shown that the categories are responsible for all experience. This condition relates to our understanding of experience as essentially temporal and involving a manifold or diversity of different moments. In order for us to be able to experience the world, we

---

[9] Given the focus of this book on French thought, my aim here will not be to justify Kant's argument, but rather to show how the various syntheses he presents provide an account of the constitution of experience.

have to somehow be able to order these experiences. That means that we have to apprehend the different temporal moments of experience as forming a sequence. We need a unifying synthesis of time, since otherwise we would simply encounter a series of moments without relation to one another, rendering experience impossible. This first synthesis therefore gives us a unified temporal framework by '[running] through and [holding] together' (Kant 1929: A99) the various moments of time. We can note here that even if what is given to us is a well-ordered temporal sequence, we still need some kind of synthesis on the part of the subject to take up this temporal sequence and recognise it as well ordered.

The synthesis of apprehension on its own clearly does not give us our conception of experience of objects. In order for the synthesis of apprehension to be possible, we need a further synthesis. The synthesis of apprehension allows us to recognise different moments as belonging to the same temporal sequence. Kant notes that when we contract habits, for instance, we make use of the imagination's associative principles, and if we hear a melody, or see a pattern often enough, we come to expect the next note or sign on the basis of what we have already heard or seen. This ability to expect the future is an empirical synthesis on the part of our imagination, to the extent that our particular habits themselves are not conditions for the possibility of experience. The possibility of contracting a habit *does* imply a transcendental synthesis on the part of the subject, however, as habits rely on the existence of regularities within the world:

> If cinnabar were sometimes red, sometimes black, sometimes light, sometimes heavy, if a man changed sometimes into this, sometimes into that animal form, if the country on the longest day were sometimes covered with fruit, sometimes with ice and snow, my empirical imagination would never find opportunity when representing red colour to bring to mind heavy cinnabar. (Kant 1929: A100–1)

The empirical synthesis whereby we recognise regularities in the world therefore relies on a transcendental synthesis that makes this recognition possible. This synthesis is the synthesis of production in the imagination. Kant introduces the example of drawing a line to explain this transcendental synthesis. Kant claims that in order for us to associate various representations with one another, they must have an 'affinity' (Kant 1929: A122) with one another: they must be associable. That is, as well as being brought together, as the first synthesis shows, they must be related to one another in such a way that they have some coherence to each other. If I draw a line in thought, to use Kant's example, it must be the case that I can reproduce the previous moments as being contiguous with the present one in order for the thought to be complete.

This synthesis implies a further synthesis, since we do not simply need different moments of experience to have an affinity with each other, but these different moments also need to be related together as a unity for consciousness itself. In the 'B' deduction, Kant puts this point as follows:

> It must be possible for the 'I think' to accompany all our representations; for otherwise something would be represented in me that couldn't be thought at all, and that is equivalent to saying that the representation would be impossible, or at least would be nothing to me. (Kant 1929: B131–2)

Now, when we think of a process such as listening to a melody, all of the different notes of the melody need to be related to the same consciousness, and recognised as belonging to the same consciousness. Otherwise, we would have a sequence of moments that were unconnected with one another, rather than the unity of a melody. Likewise, the process of counting requires us to recognise that each individual number relates to a unified notion of the total. When we analyse the process of counting, or listening to a melody, then we can note that neither the total nor the melody itself is given as an appearance. If we introspect, then all we have is a series of notes in the latter case, or a procession of numbers in the former.

We can make a similar claim about the relationship between the different moments of our experience of external objects. If we walk around a building, for Kant, this building is presented to us through a series of different perspectives of it. A condition of seeing these different perspectives as being perspectives of the same building, however, is that I am able to relate them together as being *my* perceptions of the building. Without this, we would simply have a series of fragmentary appearances. Without the unity of consciousness, these perspectives would not even be perspectives of different buildings. Rather, they would be appearances without any relation to anything, since they would be without any kind of unity whatsoever.

So material objects unite appearance in an analogous way to how melody unites the individual notes that relate to it. In a similar way, the notion of a material object is not itself discovered in experience. Rather, it is that which allows a series of appearances to be conceived as forming a unity. In order for experience to be possible, we need to be able to see the series of appearances as relating to the same subject. This, in turn, means that the appearances themselves need to exhibit unity. It is the concept of the object that gives all of these moments of appearance a unity, as it is by seeing all moments of appearance as referring to an underlying object that we are able to unify them. What makes the unity of consciousness possible is therefore the unity of appearances granted by the concept of an object.

If the subject is going to be able to unify experience, then we need to ask what Kant thinks this self is. Kant takes it as a fundamental assumption that 'I think' must be able to accompany all of our representations. This does not imply that our conscious experience must always be accompanied by a reference to ourselves ('I see a building', 'I am counting', etc.), and we are often directly engaged with the world without explicitly thematising our relationship with it ('there is a building', 'the total is x'). The 'I think' cannot therefore be the foundation of experience, since it is not always present. Rather, it is a mark that the kind of synthesis which gives unity to our representations has taken place. Similarly, if we introspect, we do not find a self, but rather simply a series of related impressions – 'no fixed and abiding self can present itself in this flux of inner appearances' (Kant 1929: A107). The situation here is rather like the case of the imagination. The fact that we were able to discover affinities between appearances presupposed a deeper synthesis whereby the imagination produced these affinities. Here it is the case that the 'I think' is made possible by a prior, transcendental synthesis.

This condition which makes possible the 'I think' has what appears to be a faintly paradoxical nature in Kant's account. It is transcendental because it is a condition of the possibility of experience. As such, it doesn't occur within experience itself. This means that it is not something that we can have knowledge of, but something we must presuppose as a foundation for experience. If we return to the distinction Kant made between perception and experience, we can see that our relationship with the transcendental unity of apperception is even more limited. Experience relates to objects that we can make judgements about, whereas perception just gives us a manifold of appearances. If the transcendental unity of apperception, as Kant calls it, is prior to experience, then it is also not the kind of thing we can make judgements about. While we can say, following Descartes, that 'I think, therefore I am', we cannot say what this 'I am' consists in. Substance is a category, and as the transcendental unity of apperception is supposed to be the ground for our use of the categories, we cannot even judge the self to be a substance. Nevertheless, Kant's deduction shows that we need to posit some such subjective unity if experience is going to be possible.

We can say something similar about the object. It cannot be given in experience, and rather is a condition for the possibility of experience. It is really simply a way of allowing the various appearances that are given to us to be united in a rule-governed manner. Essentially, it allows appearances to refer to something beyond themselves, and thus, like musical notes that refer beyond themselves to a melody, to form the kind of unity that we need in order to apply the 'I think' to our representations. As Kant puts it, '[i]t is easily seen that object must be thought only as something in general = x, since outside our knowledge we have nothing which we could set over against this knowledge as corresponding to it' (Kant 1929: A104). The conclusion of this, therefore, is that both a transcendental subject and a transcendental object are necessary for Kant in order for us to move from perception to experience. If these are necessary, then one further question we need to ask is, what makes possible the subject and object?

For Kant, each of these makes the other possible. The subject makes the object possible, since it is the transcendental unity of apperception that allows the 'I think' to accompany all of our representations. In unifying representations, the subject grounds the transcendental object, which simply is the formal unity of representations. The object in turn grounds the subject, as since the subject cannot be given in intuition, it discovers itself through the synthesis of the manifold. In being able to draw a distinction between a representation and an object itself, the subject can know its representations *as* representations. Without this distinction, representations would simply 'crowd in upon the soul' (Kant 1929: A111). The concept of an object allows the subject to recognise representations as representations of the object, and thus to distinguish itself from them. In recognising itself through this synthesis of unification of representations into an object, consciousness recognises itself as a spontaneous consciousness.

1.7 The Resolution of Kant's Dilemma

To return to our earlier question, how are the different faculties able to relate to each other? For experience to be possible, the subject needs to synthesise appearances into objective unities. As we saw, what was integral to the structure of judgement was that it was an active process, and that it involved the relation of properties to the concept of an object. The categories share the structure of judgement, but also contain a reference to intuition. They thus give us the essential characteristics of what it is for something to be an object (to be a substance, to have properties, etc.), and so Kant argues that the categories of the understanding provide the rules for this synthesis. Thus we have a situation whereby appearances are synthesised into experience by relating them to the notion of an object, and in order to relate appearances to the notion of an object, we need rules governing objects in general, and these are the categories.

Kant's approach here is important because it shows the interrelations between a number of concepts, such as judgement, the object, synthesis, and consciousness. Conscious synthesis takes the form of a judgement. When I count, or bring together the moments of a judgement ('the table is red'), it is I who actively relates these representations to one another. In a sense, the spontaneity of my ego is what holds together the passive determinations, 'table' and 'redness'. In taking this kind of synthesis as the model for synthesis more generally, Kant develops a conception of experience that implies the relationship of a subject to an object – one that characterises the world in terms of properties. As we shall see in the following chapters, much of French philosophy will accept Kant's discovery of the rich web of interrelations between these concepts. A result of this is that an attempt to diverge from any of Kant's core concepts will necessitate a broader set of revisions to all of these concepts. This will involve a rejection of judgement as the paradigmatic model of thinking. For the remainder of the chapter, however, I want to sketch some of the key lines of response to Kant in the German tradition. Here, I will claim, the response to Kant takes the form of an attempt to rework the notion of judgement to allow a broader metaphysical project to develop.

1.8 Absolute Idealism

As we have just seen, Kant designated his idealism transcendental idealism, in that it saw the subject as responsible for legislating certain aspects of experience, notably the fact that we encounter a spatio-temporal world of objects. In that the subject plays a conditioning role in experience, Kant also designated his idealism formal idealism (Kant 1929: B519). The idea that the subject plays a synthetic role within the constitution of experience is one also taken up by Kant's successor, Johann Gottlieb Fichte, although Fichte also attempts to systematise and correct some deficits in Kant's account. After Fichte, however, transcendental idealism was superseded by the absolute idealisms of Hölderlin, Schelling, and Hegel. For the remainder of this chapter, I want to discuss this series of philosophers who emerged after Kant and developed a series of differing approaches to Kant's thought. These approaches share a diagnosis of some of the central problems of Kant's thought, but differ dramatically in the way they seek to address these problems. The label 'absolute idealism' emerges in that they take issue with the subjective character of Kant's method. We can get a sense of the programmatic intentions of absolute idealism by looking at Hegel's criticism of Kant:

> The critical philosophy had, it is true, already turned metaphysics into logic but it, like the later idealism, as previously remarked, was overawed by the object, and so the logical determinations were given an essentially subjective significance with the result that these philosophies remained burdened with the object they had avoided and were left with the residue of a thing-in-itself, an infinite obstacle, as a beyond. (Hegel 1989: 51)

Absolute idealism seeks to rectify what it sees as a too subjective approach to the categories. At the heart of the absolute idealists' projects was a recognition that while Kant had inaugurated a new era in philosophy, his own account suffered from a number of arbitrary claims and ungrounded distinctions. The first of these was the distinction between intuition and concepts, which, as we saw, led to the central problem of the *First Critique*: the relation of the faculties. In the introduction to the *First Critique*, Kant speculated about a single origin of the faculties, suggesting that 'there are two stems of human knowledge, namely *sensibility* and *understanding*, which perhaps spring from a common, but to us unknown, root' (Kant 1929: A19/B29). As we saw, Kant shows in the transcendental deduction that the categories have a necessary role to play in the organisation of experience, and hence that we are justified in applying conceptual determinations to the objects of experience. If we return to the initial aim of the *First Critique*, it was precisely this: to determine how a given type of judgement about the world, synthetic a priori judgement (and, in fact, judgement more generally), was possible. In relation to this, we can note that the term deduction used by Kant in his transcendental deduction does not refer to deduction as logical inference. Rather, it has its origin in German legal language, and signifies a kind of genealogy that could be drawn up to show the validity of a legal claim of a ruler of one of the relatively independent territories of the Holy Roman Empire (Henrich 1989). In taking up this conception of deduction, it becomes clear that Kant does not need to trace the origins of the faculties beyond the point where he has established the validity of his initial claim, just as we do not need to trace back the history of ownership of a property beyond what is needed to resolve a particular dispute. Thus, the origin of the faculties does not need to be discovered to justify our ability to apply synthetic a priori judgements to the world. Nonetheless, both Fichte and the absolute idealists who came after him sought to develop an account of the origin of this distinction. Similarly, the distinction between the phenomenal and the noumenal became problematised. In presenting the constitution of experience purely in terms of the subject, Kant appeared to rule out any possibility of making claims about the thing-in-itself. Nonetheless, Kant's transcendental idealism appeared to rely on the notion that the subject is affected by something that provides the content of intuition in order to get off the ground. Kant's contemporary, Jacobi, summed up Kant's dilemma succinctly by noting that without the concept of the thing-in-itself, he could not get into Kant's system, and with the concept of the thing-in-itself, he could not stay within it.[10] For Hegel at least, these two distinctions mutually implied each other to the extent that it was the mediating role of intuition that prevented us from seeing the categories as relating to real objects.[11]

Finally, Kant's derivation of the categories in the metaphysical deduction was taken to be problematic. Here, Kant attempts to provide a derivation of the categories that make experience of a world of objects possible. Nonetheless, the derivation of the categories from the functions of understanding, as well as the claim that the list of twelve categories was complete, were both considered to be weak claims by Kant's successors. Kant's himself denied the possibility of further explanation:

> This peculiarity of our understanding, that it can produce *a priori* unity of apperception solely by means of the categories, and only by such and so many, is as little capable of further explanation as why we have just these and no other functions of judgement, or why space and time are the only forms of our possible intuition. (Kant 1929: B145–6)

The absolute idealists sought to develop a more sophisticated derivation of the categories than Kant had thought possible.

Horstmann (2000: 117) sums up these different aspects of absolute idealism by arguing that there were three claims that the absolute idealists held to: (1) they were all convinced that Kant had succeeded in establishing the most resourceful philosophical system to be found in modern times, a system that was deeply committed to the idea of the unity of reason and that permitted a coherent picture of the world in all its different aspects. It was this claim that made them followers of Kant, or Kantians; (2) at the same time, however, they were also convinced that Kant had not succeeded in developing adequately his systematic approach because he was hopelessly entangled in a dualistic mode of thinking which was fundamentally at odds with his proclaimed goal of unity. This conviction made them opponents of Kant; (3) they all shared the opinion that, in order to avoid Kant's dualism, one has to supplement his philosophy with a monistic basis

---

[10] See Henrich 2003: 78.   [11] See Guyer 2000: 46–9.

and accept that monism is the only viable alternative to dualism. It is this belief that made them German idealists.

In exploring the relationship between absolute idealism and judgement, I want to look at three key figures. The first of these is Friedrich Hölderlin, whose short note on judgement and being sets out many of the central tenets of absolute idealism. The second is F. W. J. Schelling, where we will focus on his attempts to move beyond Fichte in developing his philosophy of identity. The third is G. W. F. Hegel, where we will focus on his account of the method of dialectic, and the speculative proposition. The aim will not be to provide an exhaustive account of absolute idealism, but rather to provide support for the claim that judgement remains the paradigmatic model for what it is to think for the post-Kantian German idealists.

1.9   Hölderlin: Judgement and Constitution

Friedrich Hölderlin plays an important role in the development of absolute idealism. Hölderlin was a friend to both Schelling and Hegel, and his brief note, *Judgement and Being*, sets out with remarkable economy a path for idealism beyond the limitations of Kant and Fichte's transcendental idealism. To understand the development of Hölderlin's absolute idealism, we need to begin with Fichte's attempt to develop a coherent foundation for Kant's transcendental idealism (Horstmann 2000: 123). In order to develop a response to the sceptical attacks on Kant's system (and the systematisation of it by Kant's disciple, Reinhold), Fichte attempted to prove that transcendental idealism could be developed systematically from a single principle. In line with Kant's account, Fichte took the first principle of his account to be subjective. Beginning with judgements of which were empirically certain, such as the judgement, 'A is A', Fichte claimed that we can develop a deduction that shows the necessity of self-consciousness as a first principle. In essence, Fichte begins by claiming that the proposition 'A is A' can be reformulated as the claim that 'if A exists, then A exists'. Fichte's argument is that such a proposition requires a self-consciousness in order to posit the existential claims that make up the proposition. This empirical principle has a transcendental basis. If the I is able to posit the existence of A in forming the judgement, 'A is A', then we need to ask what the basis of the 'I' itself is. Fichte's response is that the self-consciousness that forms the basis for transcendental idealism is able to posit itself. In other words, the I grounds itself since, through its own activity, it posits its own existence. The 'I' for Fichte is therefore both an activity and the result of that activity. As he puts it, the I 'is at once the agent and the product of action; the active, and what the activity brings about; action and deed are one and the same' (Fichte 1982: 97). By making the fundamental principle of transcendental idealism the self-positing movement of consciousness, Fichte solves the problem of demonstrating the necessity of this first principle. Such a principle is a unity that is presupposed in all of our acts of empirical consciousness, but is not simply a fact that could in turn require further justification. It is also the action which generates that fact reflexively. Fichte claims that just as the principle 'A is A' can be traced back to the I, we can provide similar justifications for the other categories of thought. He therefore appears to overcome the limitations of Kant's account.

In a letter to Hegel written in January 1795, Hölderlin describes Fichte as '[standing] very much at the crossroads' (Hölderlin 1988b: 125). Hölderlin notes in this letter that Fichte's attempt to ground transcendental idealism in a fact of consciousness is illegitimate. His criticism of Fichte appears in compressed form as follows:

> [H]is absolute 'I' (=Spinoza's Substance) contains all reality; it is everything, and outside of it there is nothing; hence there is no object for this 'I', for otherwise not all reality would be within it; however, a consciousness without object cannot be thought, and if I myself am this object, then I am myself necessarily restricted, even if it were only within time, hence not absolute; therefore, within the absolute 'I', no consciousness is conceivable; as absolute 'I' I have no consciousness, and insofar as I have no conscious-ness I am (for myself) nothing, hence is the absolute 'I' (for me) nothing. (Hölderlin 1988b: 125)

Hölderlin's claim here is that Fichte's account relies on a notion of subjectivity that it cannot justify. Fichte's account of consciousness relies on the fact that to be conscious is to be conscious *of* something. The claim is that in order to be conscious of something in a determinate manner, I must be able to oppose it to something that it is not.[12] This principle is central to Fichte's account, and even applies to consciousness' reflection on itself. It is this principle that also allows Fichte to derive the world as non-ego from the ego. Consciousness therefore requires a relation to an object that it is not, in order to become determinate. If the absolute 'I' is a genuine first principle, however, then there can be no other object for it to relate to. As such, the absolute 'I' cannot be understood as conscious, and hence it is illegitimate to describe the first principle of philosophy as a subjective principle.

---

[12] Cf. Beiser 2002: 387–8 for a more detailed analysis of this argument.

In fact, the claim that for something to be determinate it must be opposed to another object means that the first principle cannot be determined as an objective principle either. Given the unitary structure of the first principle, no determinations of it are possible at all. In *Judgement and Being*, Hölderlin outlines the implications of his critique of Fichte. In this note, Hölderlin takes up one of Kant's key claims in the transcendental deduction: that we cannot make sense of a subject without an object, and vice versa. He argues, however, that if we are to properly understand the grounds of judgement, they cannot be discovered through a simple repetition of the functions of the understanding at a higher level. Thus, if we are to understand the grounds of judgement, we need to move to a position where the subject and object are *not* separated from one another. Given the significance of his account, it is worth quoting Hölderlin's description of judgement at length:

> Judgement [*Urteil*], in the highest and strictest sense, is the original separation of object and subject which are most deeply united in intellectual intuition, that separation which alone make subject and object possible, the original-separation [*Urteilung*]. In the concept of separation, there lies already the concept of reciprocity of object and subject, and the necessary presupposition of a whole of which object and subject form the parts. (Hölderlin 1988a: 37, translation modified)

Hölderlin's point here is that one of the conditions for judgement is that we are able to understand the subject as separated from the object. As we saw in Kant's transcendental deduction, judgement is a structure of experience that relates a subject to an object, and as such it requires a separation of the two terms. For Hölderlin, the German term for judgement, *Urteilung*, implies etymologically this notion of an original (*Ur*) separation (*Teilung*). As Kant showed, it is this separation that makes possible the determinate nature of the world. As such, in separating out the world, it is judgement that makes possible determination in general. It is in this sense that the Fichtean 'I am I' cannot be the foundation of idealism. In recognising myself as myself, I do indeed in a sense recognise myself as self-identical, but this self-identity cannot be understood through the notion of the 'I' alone. The 'I am I' is a moment of self-identity only on the basis of the fact that the structure of judgement (the original separation) is already in place.[13] It is only on condition of this separation that the 'I' can take itself as an object. In effect, the first principle of Fichte's system therefore turns out not to be self-consciousness,

---

[13] Fichte 1982 makes the juridical nature of 'I am I' clear on pp. 97–8.

but rather judgement, understood as the separation of the self and object that makes possible self-consciousness. If judgement requires this notion of separation, we are going to have to seek its ground in something which is unseparated. Otherwise, we will just repeat the structure of judgement at a higher level, meaning that we will not have really explained how objects are possible. Hölderlin describes this higher level in the second part of this fragment, which deals with Being:

> Being expresses the connection between subject and object. Where subject and object are united altogether and not only in part, that is, united in such a manner that no separation can be performed without violating the essence of what is to be separated, there and nowhere else can be spoken of *Being proper*. (Hölderlin 1988a: 37)

Hölderlin's first 'principle' is therefore prior to the kind of unity we find in consciousness, and in judgement, and for this reason we have the transition to absolute being. Without the opposition of subject and object, there is no way to make sense of being as subjective, or indeed as objective. In fact, as Being contains no oppositions at all (it contains no separations), it can contain no determinations whatsoever. As Larmore (2000: 148) notes, this first term of philosophy, which Hölderlin calls Being, is better described as a ground than a principle, as without determinations it cannot be thought. In this sense, from the position of judgement, Being is entirely unknowable.

While showing that the foundations of judgement cannot be understood in terms of judgement itself, Hölderlin in fact perpetuates the priority of judgement we find in Kant. As Beiser notes,[14] Hölderlin attempted to develop an account of a relation to being that did not operate through judgement, but instead had its grounds in aesthetic experience, but his development of such a model was only tentative. At root, for Hölderlin, all determination operates in terms of judgement, and that which is outside of judgement must be seen as indeterminate. As Deleuze puts it when talking of the philosophical tradition more generally, 'what is common to metaphysics and transcendental philosophy is, above all, this alternative they impose on us: *either* an undifferentiated ground, a groundlessness, formless nonbeing, or an abyss without differences and

---

[14] Cf. Beiser 2002: 391–7. As Beiser notes, Hölderlin's conception of aesthetic sense is troubled by the paradox that either it remains a purely indeterminate intimation of the absolute, or it collapses back into the determinacy of rational discourse, and hence becomes subject to the modes of determination that make thinking the absolute impossible. Hölderlin's eventual solution is to argue that the absolute is expressible in mythical language, which combines the immediacy of our intuitions with the determinacy of language.

without properties, *or* a supremely individuated Being and an intensely personalised Form' (Deleuze 1990: 105–6). Once the assumption has been made that all determination has to be understood in terms of judgement, we seem forced to make a sharp distinction such as Hölderlin's between the indeterminate grounds of judgement and the determinate world of judgement itself. The immediate problem with such an approach is that it fails to provide any account of why an undifferentiated being originarily divides itself into the opposition of subject and object. Without any distinctions in Being at all, any attempt at a deduction such as Fichte's now seems impossible. As we shall see, one of the central concerns of the French tradition will be to develop an account of determination that does not understand it purely in terms of the separation of the world into subjects and objects presupposed by judgement. As such, it will restore the possibility of understanding how a world of subjects and objects becomes constituted in the first place. For the remainder of this chapter, I want to explore two responses to the dilemma instituted by Hölderlin that emerged within absolute idealism itself: those of Schelling and Hegel.

1.10 Schelling and the Question of the Absolute

Exploring the role of judgement in Schelling's thought is complicated by the apparent lack of systematic development of his views. While some commentators are correct to note thematic connections running through his work as a whole,[15] there is still a great deal of truth to Hegel's assertion that 'Schelling worked out his philosophy in view of the public. The series of his philosophic writings also represents the history of his philosophic development and the gradual process by which he raised himself above the Fichtian principle and the Kantian content with which he began. It does not thus contain a sequence of separately worked-out divisions of Philosophy, but only successive stages in his own development' (Hegel 1995: 513). Schelling's earliest work is easily interpreted as operating within the framework of Fichte's philosophy,[16] though beginning with his philosophy of nature, and then more openly with his identity philosophy, Schelling breaks with Fichte. The identity philosophy meets Horstmann's three criteria for absolute idealism that I outlined earlier in this chapter,

---

[15] Cf., for instance, Heidegger's comment that 'The truth is that there was seldom a thinker who fought so passionately ever since his earliest periods for his one and unique standpoint' (Heidegger 1985: 7).

[16] See Snow 1996: 45–55 for a reading that complicates this view by focusing on the importance of Spinoza for Schelling's development.

and so we will focus on exploring the way in which judgement is conceived of in this system.

Schelling's earliest works appeared from 1794, when Schelling was nineteen years old. These works, which made his name, led in 1798 to a professorship at Jena, where he worked closely with Fichte. Schelling was close friends with Hölderlin, and as Beiser notes (2002: 478), Hölderlin would have made Schelling aware of his criticisms of Fichte as early as July 1795. In spite of this, it was not until around 1800 that the relationship between Fichte and Schelling broke down into one of mutual suspicion. We can see the origins of this final breakdown of relations in Schelling's development of *Naturphilosophie*. Schelling's aim in this work is to develop a systematic account of nature that goes beyond mechanism. Central to this effort is Schelling's incorporation of the categories of organicism into our account of the world.[17] Rather than seeing the world in terms of the mechanical interactions of atoms, Schelling takes up the notion that Kant develops in the *Critique of Judgement* that we can understand nature in terms of unities with purposes and ends. Kant held that the kinds of teleological categories we use to understand organic life had only a heuristic function. That is, while they were of use in explaining the world, we were not justified in claiming that purposive principles were actually at work in nature itself. As Kant puts it,

> It is a mere consequence of the particular constitution of our understanding that we represent products of nature as possible only in accordance with another kind of causality than that of the natural laws of matter, namely only in accordance with that of ends and final causes, and that this principle does not pertain to the possibility of such things themselves (even considered as phenomena) in accordance with this sort of generation, but pertains only to the judging of them that is possible for our understanding. (Kant 1987: 5:408)

Schelling in his *Naturphilosophie* claims that the categories of the organic have a constitutive role in the structure of nature. As such, Schelling considers nature as a whole as a self-organising entity. The grounds for this move come from Schelling's consideration of the role of the subject in organising experience. As Horstmann notes, while Schelling's argument on this point is somewhat confusing, it ultimately rests on the fact that knowledge seems to require that our understanding has a structural counterpart to it in the world itself (Horstmann 2000: 122–3). On the surface, this kind of claim fits well with Fichte's transcendental idealism. If we

---

[17] For more on Schelling's organicism, see Horstmann 2000: 127–35 and Snow 1996: 67–92.

derive our philosophy from one single principle, it seems clear that all of the content of our theory will come from that principle. For Fichte, the external world is derived from the nature of consciousness. If properties only become determinate in relation to their opposites, then the ego needs a moment of non-ego to know itself. This moment of non-ego is the world. As such, the world is a product of consciousness itself. Initially, Schelling takes this claim to mean that the study of nature is itself a project that takes place inside Fichte's *Wissenschaftslehre*. As such, the study of nature is another way of understanding the nature of the self:

> [W]hat the soul intuits is always its own self-developing nature .... Thus through its own products the soul reveals the pathway, imperceptible for common eyes but clearly and distinctly visible to the philosopher, along which it gradually travels towards self-consciousness. The external world lies open before us in order that we may rediscover the history of our own spirit.[18]

The purposiveness that we encounter in nature is therefore initially understood as a result of the purposiveness of the subject, who is also expressed in nature.

In 1799, Schelling takes a step beyond this initial consideration of nature as a subordinate moment within Fichte's philosophy of consciousness. In his *Introduction to the Outline of a System of the Philosophy of Nature*, Schelling instead argues that the *Naturphilosophie* and Fichte's transcendental idealism comprise two parallel disciplines, neither of which has any priority over the other:

> Now if it is the task of transcendental philosophy to subordinate the real to the ideal, it is, on the other hand, the task of the philosophy of nature to explain the ideal by the real. The two sciences are therefore but one science, differentiated only in the opposite orientation of their tasks. Moreover, as the two directions are not only equally possible, but equally necessary, the same necessity attaches to both in the system of knowledge. (Schelling 2004: II, 272–3)

As Schelling notes, transcendental philosophy and the philosophy of nature approach the world from different perspectives, with Schelling calling the philosophy of nature 'the Spinozism of physics' (Schelling 2004: II, 273).[19] In this sense, the philosophy of nature becomes a system whereby we see the development of consciousness itself out of the

---

[18] Schelling, *Samtliche Werke I*: 123, quoted in Sturma 2000: 218.
[19] As Beiser notes (2002: 530), this Spinozism gives a real place to final causes within the world, a claim Spinoza himself would reject.

structures of the natural world. From this perspective, therefore, nature is not a reflection of the ego, but rather the ego is a moment of nature:

> [T]here is no place in this science for idealistic methods of explanation, such as transcendental philosophy is fitted to supply, since for it Nature is nothing more than the organ of self-consciousness, and everything in Nature is necessary merely because it is only through the medium of such a Nature that self-consciousness can take place. (Schelling 2004: II, 273)

With this move, the *Naturphilosophie* is no longer seen as operating within the framework of Fichte's transcendental idealism, as it requires us to posit an actual dynamic principle within matter itself. Given the disparity between the two methods of Schelling's philosophy, it should be clear that this parallelism between the philosophy of nature and his transcendental idealism was unsustainable. It is in order to reconcile these disparate approaches to understanding consciousness and the world that Schelling moves to his philosophy of identity, a form of absolute idealism.

1.11   Schelling's Absolute Idealism

In Schelling's *Presentation of My System of Philosophy*, he claims that from the beginning he has attempted to present 'one philosophy that I know to be true from two wholly different sides' (Schelling 2012b: 141). As has been noted,[20] Schelling's claims to have been formulating a consistent position throughout his work must be taken with a degree of scepticism. Nonetheless, the *Presentation* shows a development of themes from Schelling's earlier work. How does Schelling distinguish his absolute idealism from his earlier commitments to Fichte? Schelling's account of this difference is rather cryptic. He claims that 'if idealism in the subjective sense said that the I is everything, Idealism in the objective sense would be forced to say the reverse: everything is = I' (Schelling 2012b: 142). Such a move implies a change of emphasis in the nature of the absolute. Whereas for subjective idealism, the world emerges from the subject, here the world is given priority. Thus, for Schelling, it would appear to be the case that here he gives his Spinozistic tendencies primacy in his interpretation of the world. In his *Further Presentation from the System of Philosophy* (1802), Schelling expresses the same point from another angle, arguing that knowledge of the absolute and the absolute itself cannot be distinguished from one another once knowledge is properly conceived: 'it is but a small step to the insight that

---

[20] Cf. Beiser 2002: 552.

this cognition is immediately a cognition of the absolute itself, and is accompanied by the abolition of all differences that contrast the absolute as cognised to the subject who cognises it' (Schelling 2012a: 209). At the heart of this claim is the Hölderlinian insight that in order to be absolute, the absolute must be free from any distinction between subjective and objective. As Schelling puts it, 'Absolute identity *is* only under the form of quantitative indifference of the subjective and objective' (Schelling 2012b: 154). In this sense, Schelling's general approach is well captured by a claim made by Hegel about his own form of absolute idealism:

> Objectivity of thought, in Kant's sense, is again to a certain sense subjective. Thoughts, according to Kant, although universal and necessary categories, are *only our* thoughts – separated by an impassable gulf from the thing, as it exists apart from our knowledge. But the true objectivity of thinking means that the thoughts, far from being merely ours, must at the same time be the real essence of things, and of whatever is an object to us. (Hegel 1991: §41)

Schelling's absolute is not simply free from any distinction between the subjective and the objective. Just as Hölderlin's being was a ground for judgement by being prior to the originary division that made judgement possible, so for Schelling the absolute has to also be prior to all divisions. As he argues, were reason not to be simply self-identical, 'the being of reason would require some additional ground other than reason itself' (Schelling 2012b: 147). For this reason, Schelling takes the proposition A = A to be emblematic of the nature of the absolute. Now, taking the absolute to be a moment of identity without differentiation naturally leads us back to the same problem we found in Hölderlin's original formulation of absolute idealism. If the absolute is undifferentiated, how do we explain the genesis of the differentiated world of judgements, subjects, and objects that emerges from it?

In fact, for Schelling, the nature of the absolute precludes our giving an account of the genesis of the world we find around us on the basis of the absolute. Schelling elucidates this point by claiming that the absolute can also be understood as the 'simple infinite', since if it was not infinite, it would require a ground outside of itself, and hence would not be absolute. We can draw from this claim two different arguments for the impossibility of the deduction of a finite world from the infinite. First, if the infinite were to give rise to the finite, then the infinite would be limited by its creation. As such, the creation of something external to the absolute would destroy the absolute's nature. Second, if the infinite were to give rise to something outside of itself, 'it would have to be related to this outside something as objective item to objective item' (Schelling 2012b: 148). What Schelling means by this claim is that the only conceivable way of understanding the relationship between the infinite and the finite is by understanding them as opposed, which is to understand them according to the categories we use to relate different objects to one another. As we have seen from both Kant and Hölderlin's accounts of the nature of objectivity, the logic of objects is captured by the categories of judgement. For Schelling, therefore, to understand the connection between judgement and being as one of the generation of a field of finite beings from being (or the absolute) itself is to rely on the categories of judgement, and hence to once again apply the categories of judgement to being itself. This is once again to illegitimately apply the categories of judgement prior to their proper domain. Hence, if we are not to treat the absolute as an object, we must give up the kind of account that would see it effectively as one thing causing another. Ironically, therefore, the infinite could only be the ground for the finite by already being understood according to the categories of finitude. The absolute cannot be a ground for the finite, therefore, and since Schelling is certain that the absolute exists, the finite cannot exist. Thus, for the Schelling of the *Presentation*, 'nothing, considered intrinsically, is finite' (Schelling 2012b: 149).

As such, Schelling's position in the philosophy of identity is effectively a form of Parmenideanism, where the world is understood as a simple One. As Beiser notes, Schelling does provide several descriptions over the course of his *Presentation* and the later *Further Presentation of My System* that attempt to account for the existence of the finite world, but none of these are particularly satisfactory (Beiser 2002: 567–73). In the *Presentation*, Schelling makes the claim that while the absolute cannot be qualitatively differentiated, it can be quantitatively differentiated, and this quantitative differentiation allows us to explain differences we find in the world without having to import real oppositional differences into the absolute. This solution itself fails as it is not at all clear why quantitative differences should be included in the absolute either. In the end, Schelling himself is forced to admit this point, claiming that 'quantitative difference is possible only *outside of* absolute identity' (Schelling 2012b: 152). In the *Further Presentations*, Schelling attempts to resolve this difficulty by arguing that under one aspect at least, finite things are contained within the infinite. In this text, he argues that insofar as objects in the world share a moment of unity with one another, they can be seen as contained within the absolute. Once again, however, Schelling is forced to place the individuating differences of finite things into the sphere of appearances, however:

It is also evident, on the other hand, how every particular *as such* is immediately and necessarily an *individual*. For by its essence, each thing is like every other and in this capacity expresses the whole; so when its form becomes *particular* form, it becomes inadequate to essence and is in contradiction with it, and the contradiction of form and essence makes the thing be individual and finite. (Schelling 2012a: 215)

Clearly, placing those aspects of a thing that make it a finite particular object outside of the absolute does not allow us to say in anything more than a formal sense that the finite is contained within the absolute.

We can see in Schelling's work of the periods leading up to his philosophy of identity that he maintains an implicit belief in the Kantian claim that all determination requires judgement. For Hölderlin, this implied that the grounds for judgement, on pain of infinite regress, would have to lack all determination. Schelling's position radicalises this Hölderlinian insight. If all determination relies on judgement, then we cannot even understand the distinction between infinite and finite, ground and grounded, without falling into the categories of judgement. As such, thinking the absolute involves making the original separation of judgement itself illusory. The world becomes one undifferentiated whole. This result is the origin of Hegel's claim that the absolute of identity philosophy is 'the night in which, as the saying goes, all cows are black' (Hegel 1977: §16).[21] For Hegel, identity philosophy lacks the ability to explain the existence of the finite world. As we shall see in the next section, Hegel's approach to overcoming these limitations is to place the finite firmly within the absolute by making mediation a key part of it. Hegel's strategy for achieving this aim is to begin with the finite, and to show how it immanently develops into the absolute. As such, he inverts the direction of Schelling's approach in the *Presentation* and *Further Presentation*. Placing the finite within the infinite involves developing a more complex conception of how one thinks in a philosophical manner in order to overcome the objections developed by Schelling. In particular, it will involve thinking opposing determinations within a unity, which, on a traditional understanding of

---

[21] Hegel himself often claims that his target is not Schelling himself, but those philosophers who have taken up Schelling's work without fully understanding it. Thus, in the *History of Philosophy*, he writes that it is 'of the greatest importance to distinguish Schelling's philosophy, on the one hand, from that imitation of it which throws itself into an unspiritual farrago of words regarding the Absolute; and on the other, from the philosophy of those imitators, who, owing to a failure to understand intellectual intuition, give up comprehension, and with it the leading moment of knowledge, and speak from so called intuition' (III, 543). Such a reading is difficult to sustain in the light of his direct criticisms of Schelling's formulations of claims about the Absolute that he makes in, for instance, Hegel 1991: §12.

logic, would mean thinking a contradiction. Nonetheless, this new conception of philosophical thought is an augmentation of the model of thinking as judgement, rather than a replacement of it.

1.12 Hegel and Infinite Thought

Hegel develops two main criticisms of Schelling. The first of these is that Schelling does not provide a proper derivation of his concept of the absolute. Rather, he begins with the assumption that those with a natural ability to philosophise will be able to relate directly to it. Second, Hegel claims that Schelling's conception of the absolute is abstract. As we shall see, these two claims are in fact directly related to one another, since it is through showing the dialectical development of the absolute that Hegel argues that it becomes concrete. Having examined Hegel's account of the limitations of Schelling's identity philosophy, I want to look at the problems Hegel finds with the classical account of judgement, before turning to Hegel's own positive solution. Hegel's systematic philosophy is vast, and so here I will focus on the dialectic of the finite and infinite, drawing on Hegel's early *Jena Logic* to show the connections between these concepts and several others that we have encountered already in this chapter. I want to conclude by looking at Hegel's account of the speculative proposition, and its relation to the structure of judgement.

In Schelling's *Further Presentation from the System of Philosophy*, he begins by briefly exploring the methodological presuppositions for thinking the absolute. Schelling's claim, essentially, is that our ability to think (or not) the absolute is something simply given that cannot bear further explanation:

> The absolute mode of cognition, like the truth that subsists within it, has no opposite outside itself, and it cannot be demonstrated [to one who lacks it] just as light cannot be demonstrated to those born blind, or space to someone who lacked spatial intuition (were it possible that an intelligent being lacked it), on the other hand, it cannot be contradicted by anything. It is the dawning light that is itself the day and knows no darkness. (Schelling 2012a: 209)

The first difficulty with this approach is immediately apparent. As Hegel puts it, on Schelling's reading, 'Science lacks universal intelligibility, and gives the impression of being the esoteric possession of a few individuals' (Hegel 1977: §13). If philosophy is seen simply as the innate possession of a select few individuals, then it becomes impossible to justify the view of the world presented by philosophy. Schelling's approach is therefore open to scepticism about the possibility of philosophical thinking on the part of ordinary consciousness. Hegel's solution to this difficulty is his *Phenomenology of Spirit*. In terms of the problems of justification at the heart of Schelling's approach, Hegel suggests that '[t]he individual has the right to demand that Science should at least provide him with a ladder to this standpoint [of Science itself], should show him this standpoint within himself' (Hegel 1977: §26). What the *Phenomenology of Spirit* provides, therefore, is an account of how natural consciousness itself develops into a form adequate to knowing the absolute.

Hegel's other major criticism of Schelling bears upon the manner in which this development is conceived. As he writes, 'it can happen, even in a developed philosophy, that only abstract principles or determinations are apprehended (for instance, "That in the Absolute all is one," "The identity of the subjective and the objective"), and that with regard to what is particular these same principles are simply repeated' (Hegel 1991: §12). To understand why Schelling's approach is abstract for Hegel, we need to turn to the mode of development of consciousness to absolute knowing. We could understand this development as proceeding according to the application of a formal method to the beliefs of consciousness. This approach, with its distinction between method and content, is, according to Hegel, the standard approach of enquiry, and he labels this method of thinking about the world 'finite thinking' (Hegel 1991: §28 Add. 1). Such a procedure would be much like the deduction of theorems in geometry, and can be understood as the classical logic of judgement. There are a number of limitations of such an approach that are relevant to Hegel's project. First, such a deduction is essentially non-ampliative. The results of our analysis are already contained implicitly within the axioms presupposed by our geometry. While this is not a problem for geometry itself, it is a limitation for an account that aims to trace the actual development of consciousness. The second and third consequences stem from the fact that the formal procedures that we find in mathematics are external to the subject matter that we are investigating. First, each one of the steps in a mathematical proof is to a certain extent arbitrary. That is, while it follows according to the formal application of a rule to the content of the proof, there is no reason why *this* rule has to be applied in developing the proof rather than another rule. '[T]he instruction to draw precisely these lines when infinitely many others could be drawn must be blindly obeyed without our knowing anything beyond except that we believe that this will be to the purpose in carrying out the proof' (Hegel 1977: §44).

More important for our present purposes is the fact that the formal procedures remain external to the result that we want to obtain. If we take Pythagoras' Theorem, for instance, it is apparent that we can make clear the meaning of the theorem without knowing its proof. We can make sense of the notion that the square of the hypotenuse of a triangle is equal to the sum of the squares of the other two sides without understanding how this theorem can be derived from the axioms of geometry. The difficulty with this approach is that it does not allow for the possibility that the meaning of our terms may change as we work through a problem. 'Subject and object, God, Nature, Understanding, sensibility and so on, are uncritically taken for granted as familiar, established as valid, and made into fixed points for starting and stopping' (Hegel 1977: §31).

If he rejects the notion that we understand the development of consciousness through the application of a formal calculus to our basic concepts, how does Hegel understand the notion of method? Hegel's claim is that rather than operating externally to the material under consideration, we must simply allow the implications of our initial categories to develop themselves. This is what Hegel calls 'infinite thought' (Hegel 1991: §28 Add. 1). In the case of the *Phenomenology of Spirit*, this involves showing that consciousness' conception of its object shows itself to be inadequate under scrutiny, and hence develops into a more adequate form of categories. Thus, the *Phenomenology* begins with the categories of sense-certainty, the pure recognition that consciousness is confronted with something that is without any further qualifications. Hegel's dialectic aims to show that this mode of consciousness' categories for understanding the object overturn themselves. Thus, what appear to be the most particular categories, 'this', 'here', and 'now', are shown to in fact be the most universal. 'When I say: "a single thing", I am really saying what it is from a wholly universal point of view, for everything is a single thing; and likewise "this thing" is anything you like' (Hegel 1977: §110).[22] Similarly, once we have reached the position where we have shown that thought is adequate to thinking the absolute, our consideration of the absolute itself proceeds by simply allowing the content of the absolute to explicate itself. There is no distinction, therefore, between the content of the dialectic, and its method:

> [N]ot only the account of scientific method, but even the Notion itself of the science as such belongs to its content, and in fact constitutes its final

---

[22] For a more detailed analysis of the dialectic of sense-certainty, see Houlgate 2013: 31–44; Stern 2002: 43–50.

result; what logic is cannot be stated beforehand, rather does this knowledge of what it is first emerge as the final outcome and consummation of the whole exposition. (Hegel 1989: 43)[23]

Insofar as Hegel's approach attempts to track the development of the object itself, it is clear that any transformations in the subject matter that it uncovers are not for him arbitrary choices of the application of rules of a calculus, but necessarily track the development of the object itself. Similarly, in that the transformations of the object or categories under consideration are real changes, such a logic is ampliative – it is not simply a re-examination of content, but a transformation of it. Most important for our purposes here, though, is the result that the object cannot be distinguished from its method, and hence from its development. This means that in contrast to the proofs of geometry, we cannot understand the result of a dialectical proof prior to working through the process of the proof itself. As such, the meaning of our terms is constituted during the dialectical process itself. Finally, the fact that the meaning of our categories is inseparable from the process by which they develop, combined with the fact that new categories emerge through showing the contradictions in prior categories, means that the categories of thought contain within themselves opposing or opposed determinations:

> It is the process which begets and traverses its own moments, and this whole movement constitutes what is positive [in it] and its truth. This truth therefore includes the negative also, what would be called the false, if it could be regarded as something from which one might abstract. (Hegel 1977: §47)

Having set out the principal differences in approach between formal, finite thought and infinite thought, we are now in a position to ask why Schelling's approach is characterised by Hegel as involving a purely formal approach. As we saw, Schelling conceives of the world as a Parmenidean One. The reason for this was that the infinite could not be conceived as being in relation to the finite, as such a relation would involve a limitation of the infinite itself. Hegel's interpretation of such a claim is that Schelling's method of understanding the infinite still operates in terms of finite thinking. In discussing the question of the magnitude of the world, Hegel presents an argument parallel to Schelling's as a paradigm case of formal thinking:

[23] I am here following the reading of Hegel as a philosopher without presuppositions expressed in the work of Stephen Houlgate (particularly 2006) and William Maker (1994). Rosen 1982 provides an extended analysis of the interrelation of method and content in Hegel's work.

Or again, the question of the finitude or infinity of the world was raised. Here infinity is sharply contrasted with finitude, yet it is easy to see that if the two are set against one another, then infinity, which is nevertheless supposed to be the whole, appears as *one* side only, and is limited by the finite. But a limited infinity is itself only something finite. (Hegel 1991: §28)

Thus, Schelling presupposes the meaning of the categories of finite and infinite in his account, and as a consequence discovers that these purely finite determinations cannot be used to determine the infinite. His response to this is to leave the absolute indeterminate. Hence, for Hegel, Schelling's formalism leads him to develop an entirely formless absolute. Schelling's philosophy thus 'denounces and despises' this formalism, 'only to see it reappear in its midst' (Hegel 1977: §16).

Hegel's account of the absolute develops from his alternative conception of infinite thought. As we have just seen, for Hegel, the meaning of our categories develops through the process of their explication. The process of the development of these categories proceeds immanently through uncovering their own internal inadequacies, and tracing how they develop in response to these inadequacies. Given this process is internal to the categories themselves, what we find is that the categories are not inadequate in response to a presupposed conception of the world, but rather show themselves to be internally contradictory, much as sense-certainty aimed to be the most concrete form of knowledge, but, when allowed to develop itself, showed itself to in fact be the most abstract. Thus, the categories develop through an immanent process of making explicit their own inadequacies. As the meaning of a category is determined by its development, such categories therefore contain opposed determinations within themselves. The result of this is that we cannot suppose that 'infinity is different from finitude, that content is other than form, that the inner is other than the outer, also that mediation is not immediacy' (Hegel 1989: 41); rather, we discover that each of these categories contains the other. In developing his own conception of the infinite, Hegel calls the infinite that we find in Schelling (and in classical metaphysics), the 'spurious infinite' (Hegel 1989: 139). Such a conception of the infinite is defined essentially as what the finite is not. The infinite is a beyond of the finite, but, as we have seen, such a beyond relies on a limit that defines the infinite just as much as the finite. Determining the beyond according to the finite thus limits it, and in turn makes it finite. When we extrapolate from this process, we find that we have an infinite progression of alternations between finite and infinite terms.

We can note that these two categories are inherently related to one another. They are united with one another, but can also be distinguished

by placing a different emphasis on each of them. The infinite is determined, in part, by its differentiation from the finite. As such, however, it is
tied to the notion of a limit, and thus finitude. It is a finitised infinite. But
the finite also is defined by its reference to a beyond as limit. As such, it is
an infinitised finite. Each of these terms is no longer defined simply on its
own, but we need to recognise that *as part of its structure*, finitude has
a reference to infinity, and the infinite contains a reference to the finite.
The infinite alternation of terms shows that whichever term we begin with,
we are led to the other. Instead of seeing them as an infinite series (the
spurious infinite), we can now view this as a circle that relates the two
determinations to each other:

> The image of the progress to infinity is the *straight line*, at the two limits of
> which alone the infinite is, and always only is where the line – which is
> determinate being – is not, and which goes *out beyond* to this negation of its
> determinate being, that is, to the indeterminate; the image of true infinity,
> bent back into itself, becomes the *circle*, the line which has reached itself,
> which is closed and wholly present, without *beginning* and *end*. (Hegel
> 1989: 149)

The true infinite emerges when we realise that the circular movement
between the finite and the infinite itself is the infinite. The consequence
of this for our reading of Schelling's absolute is that for Hegel, the fact that
the absolute is infinite does not imply that it excludes the finite. Rather,
finite determinations are seen as a necessary moment within the infinite
itself. Rather than an undifferentiated One, therefore, the absolute is
a mediated substance containing internal differences. In the next section,
I want to explore this conception of Hegel's 'good infinite' further, by
looking at some of the connections Hegel makes between infinity and the
problems of the one and the many, and the nature of contradiction, in an
early work known as the *Jena Logic*. While this logic precedes Hegel's
distinction between phenomenology and logic, it makes explicit a number
of parallels between different categories in Hegel's system. It will also allow
us to draw out the continued reliance of infinite thought on the model of
judgement, even while infinite thought puts the structure of judgement in
motion.

1.13   The *Jena Logic*

We have already encountered the question of how we are to relate the one
to the many several times, and it is intimately connected to the question of

judgement. Kant sees judgement as a way of forming a unity from a diverse set of representations. Similarly, Hölderlin took an account of the genesis of judgement to involve showing how a unity could be divided into a diverse field of objects. In positing a sharp distinction between the nature of the one and the many, Hölderlin develops an implication of Kant's assumption that the basis of the unity of judgements and objects is something transcendental (whether a transcendental subject or a transcendental object). We can see Schelling as drawing the implication from this that if the one and the many must exist on different ontological planes, and if the one is absolute, then there can be no many. In the *Jena Logic*, Hegel interprets the relation of the one and the many in terms of the logic of the infinite. Specifically, the *Jena Logic* takes this assumption that the one and the many must operate on different levels to be related to the structure of the bad infinite. He writes that 'the subsistence of the many qualities as of the many quanta has simply the "beyond" of a unity that has not yet been taken up into them and would sublate the subsistence if it were so taken up' (Hegel 1986: 33). Here, Hegel's claim is that a field of diversity is not united by an external unity, whether this unity is the ground of being or the synthetic unity of a consciousness. Rather, the diverse unifies itself immanently when viewed in terms of its dialectical development, just as the infinite developed out of the finite: 'In order to subsist, the aggregate is not allowed to take up this beyond into itself, but just as little can it free itself from it and cease to go beyond itself' (Hegel 1986: 33). The kind of interpretation of the one and the many taken up by Kant, Hölderlin, and Schelling, therefore, is one that results from artificially suspending the development of the diverse, such that its immanent moment of unity is not allowed to develop. The implication of this reading is that unity is a necessary, inherent, and non-arbitrary result of a field of diversity. 'Only the infinitely simple, or that unity-and-multiplicity, is one' (Hegel 1986: 33). A subject, as a centre of unification, is thus a necessary moment of a philosophical enquiry.

How does this relate to the question of judgement in Hegel's thought? The issue with judgement mirrors that which we found with geometrical proofs. A judgement is a process whereby we subsume an individual under a universal. As Rosen (1982: 102) notes, however, the relation between the universal and the diverse individuals that fall under it is abstract on our standard reading of judgement, as the relationship between the two is arbitrary: 'abstract universality is deficient because, although the particular may be subsumed under the universal, there is no intrinsic relation between the two'. Furthermore, judgement relies on the structure of opposition to function. As we saw in relation to Hölderlin and Schelling, judgement operates by sorting objects according to opposed predicates. Objects are subsumed under predicates such as the one or the many, or the finite or the infinite. What the dialectic of the finite and the infinite shows us, however, is that when viewed from the perspective of infinite thought, such determinations are in fact contained within one another, rather than opposed to one another. Judgement is therefore one-sided to the extent that it operates according to a logic of exclusion. In the *Jena Logic*, when Hegel sets out the logic of the good infinite, he relates it directly to a different logical structure – that of contradiction: 'Genuine infinity ... is not a series that always has its completion in some other yet always has this other outside itself. Rather, the other is in the determinate itself; it is a contradiction' (Hegel 1986: 35). In contradiction, as in the structure of the good infinite, opposed determinations are unified with one another. This process is what Hegel calls 'the absolute contradiction of the infinite' (Hegel 1986: 38). For finite thought, it is impossible to think a contradiction, just as it is impossible for it to think the unity of the finite and the infinite:

> The contradiction that bad infinity expresses, both that of infinite aggregate and that of infinite expansion, stays within the acknowledgement of itself; there is indeed a contradiction, but not *the* contradiction, that is, infinity itself. Both get as far as the requirement that the two alternating members [positing and surpassing the limit] be sublated, but the requirement is as far as they go. (Hegel 1986: 33)

Just as there are two forms of contradiction, there are also two forms of relation between subject and predicate, which Hegel outlines in the *Phenomenology of Spirit*. For Hegel, the way that we normally understand a judgement relies on an 'objective, fixed self' (Hegel 1977: 37) to which we attach predicates. Such a model of judgement sees the subject of judgement as essentially a 'passive subject inertly supporting accidents' (Hegel 1977: 37), which therefore has no necessary relation to its predicates. Hegel's speculative proposition does not relate subjects to predicates, but instead relates categories of thought to other categories. Whereas in a non-speculative proposition we have a structure such as 'the rose is red', Hegel gives us as an example of the speculative proposition 'God is being' (Hegel 1977: 38). The fact that we have two subjects to the proposition prevents finite thought from understanding it. As Rosen (1982: 140) notes, the structure of the speculative proposition relies on two meanings of the copula 'is'. In that it has two subjects, it appears as if the copula is being interpreted as asserting an identity between the two terms. In that these two terms differ from one another, however, it appears that the copula is being used to assert the second term as a predicate of the first. The second term cannot straightforwardly be attached to the first, and instead appears to determine its essential nature. 'The passive subject itself perishes' (Hegel 1977: 37) through this movement whereby we are 'thrown back' (Hegel 1977: 39) onto the original term as a subject, but as one which has been altered in the movement back and forth between the two terms. The speculative proposition allows terms to be identified which remain different from one another. 'In the philosophical proposition the identification of subject and predicate is not meant to destroy the difference between them, which the form of the proposition expresses; their unity, rather, is meant to emerge as a harmony' (Hegel 1977: 38). In this sense, the speculative proposition mirrors the structure of the infinite, which asserted an identity of opposed categories. What unified the infinite was the recognition that the infinite was itself the motion of the finite and the infinite, and similarly, what Hegel attempts to achieve with his notion of the speculative proposition is to model a thought that is inherently in motion. Hence, the speculative proposition 'is merely dialectical movement, this course that generates itself, going forth from, and returning to, itself' (Hegel 1977: 40).

In embodying the structure of the infinite, the speculative proposition is thus a contradiction, and cannot be grasped by finite thinking, which 'is checked in its progress, since that which has the form of a predicate in a proposition is a substance itself' (Hegel 1977: 37). In elaborating the limitations of finite thought, Hegel notes that this limitation is not that it operates according to finite categories, but that it fails to push these categories to the point at which they become speculative. Thus, Hegel writes that 'it is usually said also that the understanding should not go too far. This contains the valid point that the understanding cannot have the last word. On the contrary, it is finite, and, more precisely, it is such that when it is pushed to an extreme it overturns into its opposite' (Hegel 1991: §80). Hegel's ultimate complaint against the structure of judgement, therefore, is not against understanding the world in terms of subjects and predicates, but that such an understanding normally involves positing fixed forms, and arbitrary connections. What is needed is to understand the structure of judgement as composed of terms whose meanings are composed organically through their interactions. This structure, which is the identity of identity and difference, can be understood as the structure of judgement put into motion, just as the categories of finite thought are simply frozen moments of the dialectic of infinite thought. In describing the relationship between the absolute and its particular forms, Hegel explicitly brings in the notion of judgement:

> The Absolute is the universal and One Idea, which particularizes itself in the act of *judging* into the *system* of determinate ideas – whose whole being consists, nonetheless, in their returning into the One Idea, i.e., into their truth. It is because of this judgement that the Idea is *at first* just the One and universal *substance*, but its developed, authentic actuality is to be as subject and so as spirit. (Hegel 1991: §213)

1.14   Conclusion

Both transcendental and absolute idealism, therefore, take judgement to be the central structure of thinking. In all of the figures that we have looked at, determination operates through the attribution of predicates to subjects. Where the structure of judgement is not in play, we discover a lack of any determination, whether this is Kant's thing-in-itself, Hölderlin's being, or Schelling's absolute. While Hegel's account of the speculative proposition represents a break with the kind of logic of judgement found in the work of prior idealists, his approach operates as a development, rather than a rejection, of the logic of judgement. What is at issue in Hegel's approach is that traditional accounts of judgement are too static. Hegel's solution, therefore, is to put judgement into motion. Such an approach involves the development of a model of thinking that takes contradiction as its primary category. Nonetheless, such a logic still operates in terms of the general structures of subject and predicate, universal and particular, and represents a revaluation of traditional logical categories such as opposition and contradiction. As we shall see, modern French philosophy addresses many of the same questions of determination and the relation of the one to the many that we encountered in the traditions of German idealism. The thesis of this book will be that modern French philosophy operates by attempting to develop accounts of thinking that avoid seeing it primarily as judgement. Whereas Hegel combines the singular and the universal, the alternative approach will be to seek out something that is outside of these categories. In the next chapter, we will see the beginnings of this approach in the work of Henri Bergson. As we shall see, rather than developing a philosophy of synthesis, what will be central to Bergson's account of thinking is a process of dissociation, whereby a dynamic world of processes is configured as a world of objects by the intellect.

CHAPTER 2

Bergson and Thinking as Dissociation

2.1 Introduction

In this second chapter, I want to begin to explore the questions of the legacy of German idealism within the French tradition, and the rejection of judgement as a model of thinking, by turning to the work of Henri Bergson. Bergson's thought was highly influential on the development of the French tradition. Jean-Paul Sartre claims, for instance, that it was the discovery of Bergson that led him to become a philosopher.[1] Nonetheless, Bergson was on the surface pushed into the background by the emergence of phenomenology in France, only to re-emerge in the work of Gilles Deleuze, precisely as a counterpoint to those earlier phenomenological tendencies. German idealism developed along a trajectory from a transcendental idealism which was concerned with the categories that structured any possible experience for us to an absolute idealism, where the distinction between categories of thought and ontological categories is elided. Bergson's own work charts a similar trajectory, which we will follow in this chapter. His first book, *Time and Free Will*, argues that our internal states cannot be analysed according to the same categories that we apply to the external world without falsifying them. What the categories that we apply to the external world ultimately lack is any reference to the lived time of experience. In attempting to recognise the difference of our inner states from the nature of the material world, Bergson's first project, then, is essentially psychological. Beginning with *Matter and Memory*, however, Bergson begins to argue that the characteristics that make duration a central aspect of our psychological lives are in fact features of the objective world. In

---

[1] As Sartre notes, it was his reading of Bergson that convinced him to consider the vocation of philosopher. 'At sixteen, you see, I wanted to be a novelist. But I had to study philosophy in order to enrol in the *École Normale Supérieure*. My ambition was to become a professor of literature. Then I came across a book by Henri Bergson in which he describes in a concrete way how time is experienced in one's mind. I recognized the truth of this in myself (Sartre 1965: 70).

Creative Evolution, duration becomes a characteristic feature of life, and inert matter becomes itself an abstraction from a living world.

In this chapter, I want to explore how this development affects Bergson's account of thinking. I will begin by outlining what Deleuze calls Bergson's 'logic of multiplicities'[2] – his account of how parts and wholes are organised. This is developed in *Time and Free Will* as a way of contrasting the structure of mental and physical states, but develops into an account of the relationship between time and spatiality. Bergson's philosophy revolves around two multiplicities. The first, the continuous or confused multiplicity, characterises temporal phenomena and our mental states. The second, the discrete multiplicity, is the organisation we find in space, and which Bergson also explicitly associates with judgement. As we shall see, Bergson's claim will be that the discrete multiplicity presupposes the continuous. In the second half of the chapter, I want to explore Bergson's critique of judgement by revisiting Kant's transcendental deduction. As we shall see, Bergson argues that Kant's account of judgement as unifying a manifold of representations presupposes an account of the constitution of the elements that make up this manifold itself that Kant himself cannot give because of his reliance on judgement. I want to conclude by looking at how Bergson's logic of dissociation differs from the synthetic dialectic developed by Hegel.

2.2 Counting

In order to start to lay out Bergson's account of the two kinds of multiplicities, I want to begin by returning to Kant's account of time. While Bergson holds there to be a difference in kind between space and time, for Kant, time is implicitly understood in the same terms as space. In his early lectures on Kant's *Critique of Pure Reason*, Bergson claims that:

> Kant consistently reunites time and space; he establishes between these two forms a constant parallelism. There is here an identification, or at least a reconciliation, whose legitimacy is far from obvious. What Kant says about time would hardly apply, we believe, to anything but time translated into space – which is how we ordinarily perceive time. But his critique would not have much value for time seen from within, such as it is presented to consciousness, time represented as a prolongation of states of consciousness into one another, time envisaged as quality, rather than quantity. (Bergson 1990: 151)

---

[2] Deleuze takes up this insight that one of the central threads running through Bergson's work is the attempt to develop a logic of multiplicities. See Deleuze 1988a: 115–18 for a programmatic statement of the importance of this logic.

Bergson's claim here, therefore, is that Kant's account of time is essentially a spatialised form of time. Bergson in fact extends this claim to the post-Kantian tradition in general. Whereas Feuerbach, for instance, criticises Hegel for privileging time over space, Bergson claims that while 'ideas of becoming, or progress, of evolution, seem to occupy a large place in their philosophy' (Bergson 1998: 362), the post-Kantians in fact ignored the proper role of real duration, substituting for experience 'a method of construction' (Bergson 1998: 362). We will return to this idea of construction at the end of the chapter, but we can note that in this case too, therefore, time is only understood as a translation or abstraction of its proper form.

Bergson's observation of a 'constant parallelism' in the *First Critique* between space and time is apparent in the transcendental aesthetic, where Kant develops analogous arguments for the a priori and non-conceptual natures of space and time.[3] Similarly, in his analysis of synthetic a priori judgements, Kant gives two fields of mathematics which are paradigm cases of synthetic a priori knowledge: geometry and arithmetic. What makes geometry a priori is the fact that it relies on our *representation* of space (Kant 1929: B40), which in turn derives from our intuition of space. Thus, Kant claims, our intuition of space is the basis for the synthetic a priori judgements we find in geometry. When we analyse a proposition such as 'the straight line between two points is the shortest' (Kant 1929: B16), we can see that it is not analytic since we cannot derive the fact of the line being the shortest from its being straight. To do so requires the introduction of our intuition of space. Arithmetic contains similar synthetic a priori judgements, this time dependent on our intuition of time. Kant claims that a proposition such as '7 + 5 = 12' is synthetic. While we can combine the concepts of 7 and 5 analytically, this does not give us the sum of the elements, as neither 7 nor 5 contain within their concepts the number 12. In order to combine them under the specific form of a summation, we require the representation of time, since it is through time that we can represent the successive addition of elements needed to add the second number to the first. Later in the *First Critique*, Kant makes this connection with time explicit by defining number as 'a representation which requires the successive addition of homogeneous units' (Kant 1929: A142–3). While there are a number of problems with this account,[4] for our purposes it is

---

[3] Cf. Gardner 1999: 74. Kant sets out these arguments in Kant:1929 A19–A36/B32–B53.

[4] Guyer 1987: 173 notes that Kant doesn't eliminate the possibility that the synthesis of number could rely on a spatial manifold, for instance.

enough to note that the activity of counting which Kant takes to be central to our understanding of number relies on a successive synthesis, and as reliant on succession it is grounded in our representation of time. Geometry and arithmetic are related to one another, therefore, in that for both, their central propositions can only be formulated through the application of concepts of the understanding to the manifold of intuition. Bergson's claim is that this parallelism between time and space in fact obscures the possibility of an authentic understanding of time itself. As Kant notes, in order to represent time, we need to translate it into spatial terms.[5] For Bergson, the error Kant makes in the *First Critique* is in attributing characteristics of this necessarily spatial representation of time to time itself. To see why this error might arise, we can turn to Bergson's own analysis of counting.

2.3   Spatial Multiplicities

At the heart of Bergson's early account of consciousness is the claim that we suffer from a natural illusion whereby we assimilate what are essentially temporal phenomena to a spatial mode of understanding. In doing so, we misapprehend both the nature of the elements that make up our experience and the connections between those elements. In order to explain this process of abstraction and translation, Bergson presents counting as a paradigmatic case of this spatialisation of experience. Counting involves bringing together a collection of entities, but also bringing them together in a particular way. As Bergson notes, given a collection of entities, we could enumerate the members of this group by taking a register rather than counting them directly, just as for Kant it would be possible to think the numbers 5 and 7 together without thinking them as a summation. Doing this would allow us to list every person in a room, but it would not give us a total. To arrive at a total, we need to leave to one side the fact that each individual is different from the others and treat each element as identical to one another. To use Bergson's example, 'we can count sheep in a flock and

---

[5] 'Now how it is possible that from a given state of a thing an opposite state should follow, not only cannot be conceived by reason without an example, but is actually incomprehensible to reason without intuition. The intuition required is the intuition of the movement of a point in space. The presence of the point in different locations (as a sequence of opposite determinations) is what alone first yields to us an intuition of alteration. For in order that we may afterwards make inner alterations likewise thinkable, we must represent time (the form of inner sense) figuratively as a line, and the inner alteration through the drawing of this line (motion), and so in this manner by means of outer intuition make comprehensible the successive existence of ourselves in different states' (Kant 1929: B292).

say there are fifty, although they are all different from one another and are easily recognised by the shepherd: but the reason is that we agree in that case to neglect their individual differences and to take into account only what they have in common' (Bergson 2008: 76). To turn to the question of how we actually move from the collection of individuals to a summation, Bergson suggests two possibilities. First, we can represent the individuals 'side by side in an ideal space' (Bergson 2008: 77), in which case the operation of counting will be based on our representation of space, or we can instead see the act of counting as grounded in time. In order for us to reach a summation in this way, the previous presentations of individuals need to be retained. We do so by representing time as a line upon which each of the different objects (the sheep we count in Bergson's example) are placed at regular intervals. By viewing time as a line, we effectively are able to juxtapose the elements that make up the number, and thus come to a total.

What makes counting possible in this case is a representation of time that is borrowed from space. Seeing time as a line allows us to conceive of time as a container in which the various elements are discrete units, much as we see objects in space as juxtaposed, and separated from one another by being in different positions in a homogeneous medium. What therefore allows us to count is not the succession of moments in time, as, for instance, Kant thought was the case, but rather the representation of that succession in a spatial milieu. As Bergson puts it, 'when we are adding up units, we are not dealing with these moments themselves, but with the lasting traces which they seem to have left in space on their passage through it' (Bergson 2008: 79). At this point, there is not, strictly speaking, a disagreement between Kant and Bergson, both of whom view counting as operating with represen-tations. As we shall see, however, a difficulty arises when we take the characteristics of this representation of time to inhere within time itself.

Bergson draws a number of consequences about our notion of number (and time) from this account of spatialised time. The first point is that counting involves two different sets of categories – the one and the many, and the continuous and the discontinuous. When we count, we take up a number of units to make up a total. Counting proceeds by discontinuous jumps as we add a new unit to our total. This is much like what happens when we add elements in space to one another. What allows us to take these different entities as forming a collection isn't some natural unity we find within them. If we are counting sheep, what allows us to say that they add up to a certain number, and to treat them as a group, is the fact that we synthesise our different perceptions of them into a unity. With counting, therefore, we are dealing with a division between the natural many and the unity (oneness) that we give to them in forming them into a group. In this sense, counting is a form of synthesis which meets Kant's definition of judging, and Bergson sees space as the origin of both counting and judgement. The other feature of bodies we find in space is that it is possible to divide them. We can cut a body into different pieces in a variety of different ways. The way in which we choose to divide up bodies we find in space is relatively arbitrary, and to an extent the divisions are already present within the matter itself. These two points together essentially add up to the fact that, because counting involves a synthesis which is subjective, we can divide numbers into different groups without changing their nature. Number is essentially an imposition on the world, and so we can choose how to carve it up. As Bergson puts it:

> There is no change in the general appearance of a body, however it is analysed by thought, because these different analyses, and an infinity of others, are already visible in the mental image which we form of the body, though they are not realised: this actual and not merely virtual perception of subdivision in what is undivided is just what we call objectivity. (Bergson 2008: 84)

What Bergson is describing in relating our concepts of space and time is a question of method as well as a question of the nature of time itself. In *Time and Free Will*, Bergson does not dispute the adequacy of understanding the external world in spatial terms, but argues that the extension of a spatial understanding of the world to the mind is illegitimate.

What are the implications of this spatialisation of time? First, time is here seen as a container for events, just as homogeneous space is a container for objects. Time is that within which moments are juxtaposed. Second, understanding the mind in spatial terms allows us to see mental states as quantifiable – that is, to make sense of concepts such as feeling an increasing sense of joy, for instance. Bergson argues that the key feature of talking about the more and the less is that we understand objects in essentially geometrical terms. Essentially, if we see a space, a distance, or an area as greater than another space, distance, or area, we are effectively assuming that the smaller space could be contained within the larger space. The notion of a homogeneous space is key here, as the essentially passive nature of space entails that an object in such a space can change position without altering its nature. This ability to change location without deforming an object is a key assumption of Newtonian physics. Thus, understanding the world in terms of a multiplicity of elements within a homogeneous space allows us to either ideally or physically bring these bodies into relation with one another to compare their magnitude. When we understand time in terms of space, then we can use our spatialised conception of time to allow us to measure time as well. If we want to determine a length of time, we do so in terms of distances travelled and simultaneities. So we define two periods of time as being equal to one another by saying that 'two intervals of time are equal when two identical bodies, in identical conditions at the beginning of each of these intervals and subject to the same actions and influences of every kind, have traversed the same space at the end of these intervals' (Bergson 2008: 115). In defining time in this way, it is implicitly defined purely in terms of space (the distance traversed), as this is the only variable which is actually measurable. Third, understanding the world in spatial terms allows us to separate it into clearly defined elements. These elements are both related to one another and distinguished from one another by being placed within a homogeneous medium. Such an ability to conceive of elements distinctly is the foundation of the kind of analysis we find in the work of Descartes, and in the *Regulae*, for instance, he claims that 'problem[s] should be re-expressed in terms of the real extension of bodies and should be pictured in our imagination entirely by means of bare figures. Thus [they] will be perceived much more distinctly by our intellect' (Descartes 1985b: *Rule 14*). Once we are able to distinguish parts from one another, we are able to solve problems by breaking them up into distinct components without needing to worry that such a process will change the nature of what is being analysed. Fourth, an analysis in terms of homogeneous material precludes the possibility of genuine novelty. As Bergson notes, insofar as we see a system defined in terms of a collection of discrete elements within a homogeneous milieu, then what appear to be novel states are simply different relations between parts that are in theory perfectly reversible.[6] This explains the non-ampliative nature of judgement.

The importance of this analysis of number is that it presents a way in which philosophers have often thought about time and mental states. Time is often treated as a continuity that can be divided up into an arbitrary number of subdivisions in a manner that is analogous to number. Similarly, it is common

---

[6] Bergson develops this point in *Creative Evolution*, where he notes that the reversibility of mechanical motions means there is no genuine novelty: 'Now, we say that a composite object changes by the displacement of its parts. But when a part has left its position, there is nothing to prevent its return to it. A group of elements which has gone through a state can therefore always find its way back to that state, if not by itself, at least by means of an external cause able to restore everything to its place. This amounts to saying that any state of the group may be repeated as often as desired, and consequently that the group does not grow old. It has no history. Thus nothing is created therein, neither form nor matter. What the group will be is already present in what it is, provided "what it is" includes all the points of the universe with which it is related' (Bergson 1998: 11).

to treat emotional states as essentially distinct, or at least distinguishable from one another. This is the case for Descartes, for instance. For Descartes, God guarantees that when we conceive of something clearly and distinctly, the idea we have in our mind resembles its cause, and hence if the cause is capable of being understood in discrete quantifiable terms, then so will our representation of it. Thus, God guarantees the correlation of internal structure of the mind to that of the world, and with it the possibility of our application of analytical tools to it. While Hume's model of the psyche on the surface differs substantially from that of Descartes, the same assumption that mental states must be understood in spatial terms is very much in play. Hume's associationism argues that it is the imagination rather than reason that is primarily responsible for the connections we find between ideas. Hume argues that there is what he calls a 'kind of attraction' by which an idea 'upon its appearance, naturally introduces its correlative'. As he writes, 'a picture naturally leads our thoughts to the original: the mention of one apartment building naturally introduces an enquiry or discourse concerning the others: and if we think of a wound, we can scarcely forebear reflection on the pain which follows it' (Hume 2007: III.3). The discussion of a 'kind of attraction' by Hume is not arbitrary. Hume was heavily influenced by Samuel Clarke, one of Newton's disciples, and Hume's model here takes Newton's theory of gravitation as a paradigmatic model of explanation. Hume conceives of impressions in the mind effectively as atoms that are brought into relations with one another by the forces of association, much as Newton saw the world as composed of physical atoms brought into relations with one another by the force of gravity. Bergson will claim that when we look at our mental life, we find that it operates according to a different logic of organisation than that of spatial juxtaposition. Rather than a complex mental state containing elements that are separable and awaiting division, we often find that, although a mental state contains different elements, these elements can become clarified only at the cost of altering the nature of the mental state itself that we are examining. As such, the kind of analysis Descartes believes is possible can only be accomplished at the price of a translation of the phenomenon in question that changes its nature. The elements that make up our mental life don't follow the logic of mathematical units, therefore, and so mental life cannot be understood in the spatial sense that we attribute to counting.

2.4 Melody and Confused Multiplicities

If we accept Bergson's claim that we typically represent our mental states in spatial terms, borrowing from the structure of the external world, the question naturally arises: what is conscious experience itself? This question is somewhat problematic to answer, since the same tendency to represent the world in spatial terms is also present within language itself. Nonetheless, Bergson does provide a number of examples of conscious experience. Here, for instance, he provides a clear counterpoint to the representation of counting:

> Whilst I am writing these lines, the hour strikes on a neighbouring clock, but my inattentive ear does not perceive it until several strokes have made themselves heard. Hence I have not counted them; and yet I only have to turn my attention backwards to count up the four strokes which have already sounded and add them to those which I hear. If, then, I question myself on what has just taken place, I perceive that the first four sounds had struck my ear and even affected my consciousness, but that the sensations produced by each one of them, instead of being set side by side, had melted into one another in such a way as to give the whole a peculiar quality, to make a kind of musical phrase out of it. In order, then, to estimate retrospectively the number of strokes sounded, I tried to reconstruct this phrase in thought: my imagination made one stroke, then two, then three, and as long as it did not reach the exact number four, my feeling, when consulted, answered that the total effect was qualitatively different. (Bergson 2008: 127)

We can see in this account of the reconstruction of the time of the striking clock in imagination that the mode of organisation Bergson is presenting here is radically different from that of the representation of time we find in Kant. Whereas counting involves the juxtaposition of entities within a homogeneous space, the elements we find in our conscious life instead interpenetrate one another. When Bergson starts attending to the sound of the clock, the previous strokes are still present within the sensation of the fourth. Rather than the sensations being distinct entities in a homogeneous space, the first stroke is contained in the perception of the final stroke, and changes its nature. As Bergson notes, this shows that our mental life cannot be mapped out in the same way that physical objects are mapped out. One of our central assumptions about a spatial mode of organisation is that two bodies cannot occupy the same place at the same instant.[7] Here, however,

---

[7] As Bergson notes, the impermeability of bodies is understood by us as a logical truth: 'We sometimes set up impenetrability as a fundamental property of bodies, known in the same way and put on the same level as e.g. weight or resistance. But a purely negative property of this kind cannot be revealed by our senses; indeed, certain experiments in mixing and combining things might lead us to call it in question if our minds were not already made up on the point. Try to picture one body penetrating another: you will at once assume that there are empty spaces in the one which will be occupied by the particles of the other; these particles in their turn cannot penetrate one another unless one of them divides in order to fill up the interstices of the other; and our thought will prolong this operation

we have an example of just such an interpenetrative structure, where mental states are simply incompatible with the kind of geometrical analysis favoured by Descartes. In order to give a proper account of mental phenomena, therefore, we need to move away from a geometrical conception of the mental.

For a spatial multiplicity, all of the possible divisions we could make in them are already present in them. Dividing numbers doesn't change their fundamental nature. In the case of the sensation of the clock striking, the quality of the multiplicity, and not just its extension, is governed by the number of elements. Changing the number of elements changes the nature of the multiplicity, as well as the nature of the elements themselves, since each sound retains the impression of the previous striking. An implication of this is that rather than the elements simply being outside of one another as spatial objects are, the elements in a confused multiplicity define one another through their interrelations. As such, the unity of the elements isn't something we simply impose from the outside on such multiplicities, as we might choose a sample at will, but rather is something intrinsic to them. What this tells us is that here we are dealing with a manifold that is constituted in a different manner from the discrete multiplicity we find in the representation of space. Given its interpenetrative nature, Bergson dubs such a manifold a confused multiplicity. While counting might be the best example of a discrete multiplicity, the best example of a confused multiplicity is a melody. Here, each of the elements in the melody form an organic unity, rather than simply being juxtaposed with one another. Rather than counting, where previous states are set alongside present ones, when we listen to a melody, the notes cannot be understood as distinct from one another, and instead retain the past while opening out onto future notes. As Bergson notes, this lack of distinctness comes to the fore in the fact that it is the melody as a whole that is affected by a mistake in performance, rather than an individual note: 'if we interrupt the rhythm by dwelling longer than is right on one note of the tune, it is not its exaggerated length, as length, which will warn us of our mistake, but the qualitative change thereby caused in the whole of the musical phrase' (Bergson 2008: 100–1). Bergson's claim therefore is that our mental life operates more like a melody than like a spatial multiplicity. Different states

indefinitely in preference to picturing two bodies in the same place. Now, if impenetrability were really a quality of matter which was known by the senses, it is not at all clear why we should experience more difficulty in conceiving two bodies merging into one another than a surface devoid of resistance or a weightless fluid. In reality, it is not a physical but a logical necessity which attaches to the proposition: "Two bodies cannot occupy the same place at the same time"' (Bergson 2008: 88).

meld into one another and form their own unity. They are not unified by simply being in the same abstract space, or differentiated in the same manner.

Bergson's key concerns in *Time and Free Will* are expressed clearly by its English title, and his aim in this text is to show that our belief that our mental life is determined originates from our belief that our spatial representation of it adequately captures its nature. When the question of free will or determinism is posed in spatial terms, it becomes impossible to answer. That is because the dynamic nature of consciousness is set aside, and we no longer deal with the *process* of deliberation. As we saw, spatial representation deals with already constituted entities. It is concerned with the trajectory of an already completed movement, and not with the movement itself, and so the process of creation itself remains outside of its remit. In representing our thought processes in spatial terms, we falsify our conception of deliberation. We represent our thought process as a line where decisions are points where the line branches in different directions. We therefore either fall into the kind of mechanistic account of the psyche represented by associationism, or argue that the fact that another path appears possible shows that we are free. 'All the difficulty arises from the fact that both parties picture the deliberation under the form of an oscillation in space, while it really consists in a dynamic progress in which the self and its motives, like real living beings, are in a constant state of becoming' (Bergson 2008: 183). Freedom for Bergson has a somewhat Spinozistic edge, as the rejection of external determination in order to reach a state where we act from our own nature:

> The greater part of the time we live outside ourselves, hardly perceiving anything of ourselves but our own ghost, a colourless shadow which pure duration projects into homogeneous space. Hence our life unfolds in space rather than in time; we live for the external world rather than for ourselves; we speak rather than think; we 'are acted' rather than act ourselves. To act freely is to recover possession of oneself, and to get back into pure duration. (Bergson 2008: 231)[8]

Time and Free Will contains a similar limitation to the *First Critique*, in that just as Kant is not concerned with the origin of the faculties, Bergson is not concerned with the origin of the two multiplicities. In arguing for the purely temporal nature of our mental lives, and the purely spatial nature of

---

[8] Here Bergson's analysis reverses the direction of Plato, seeing the atemporal realm as an illusion that prevents our engagement with duration. For an extended analysis of this theme in Bergson, centred on his *Introduction to Metaphysics*, see Lawlor 2011: 15–37.

the external world, Bergson remains within the remit of the narrow problem of freedom. He leaves un(or under-)explored several central questions. First, he does not explain the origin of a durational consciousness in a world of extensity. Second, he provides a very limited explanation for why we translate our inner experience into spatial terms.[9] And third, he fails to account for the interrelation between the spatial and the durational. As such, we appear to have a split in our account of thinking that is unreconcilable. It is in order to resolve these difficulties that Bergson's later works develop this project along two interrelated lines. First, Bergson develops an account of the genesis of our understanding of spatiality, and of consciousness itself. Second, he moves from an understanding of duration that is essentially subjective to one where duration characterises the fundamental nature of the world. We can therefore see in the development of Bergson's thought a parallel to the move from formal to absolute idealism we looked at in the previous chapter. In the following sections, we will explore these developments, while simultaneously extracting an account of the logic of multiplicities from Bergson's work.

2.5   The Logic of Multiplicities

In *Time and Free Will*, Bergson claims that 'within our ego, there is succession without mutual externality; outside the ego, in pure space, mutual externality without succession' (Bergson 2008: 108). Such a sharp distinction between duration and extension leaves us with something analogous to Descartes' mind–body problem. How are we to understand the interaction of these two kinds of multiplicity?[10] By the time Bergson is writing *Creative Evolution*, however, he sees duration as the central characteristic of the external world. As he writes:

> Yet succession is an undeniable fact, even in the material world. Though our reasoning on isolated systems may imply that their history, past, present and future, might be instantaneously unfurled like a fan, this history, in point of fact, unfolds itself gradually, as if it occupied a duration like our own. If

---

[9] Bergson provides a limited account of our use of our spatialised understanding of conscious experience in *Time and Free Will* in terms of a pragmatic need to communicate with others. See Bergson 1998: 138. As we shall see, this claim that spatial representation is essentially practical will become more prominent in his later writings.

[10] As Lawlor 2003: 18 and Moulard-Leonard 2008: 11–32 note, another way of viewing this move beyond *Time and Free Will* is to read it as an effort to give an account of the genesis of consciousness. This only becomes possible once one shows that the multiplicities of space and time can be brought into relation with one another, as otherwise consciousness must emerge through a leap between disparate ontological domains.

I want to mix a glass of sugar and water, I must, willy nilly, wait until the sugar melts. This little fact is big with meaning. For here the time I have to wait is not that mathematical time which would apply equally well to the entire history of the material world, even if that history were spread out instantaneously in space. It coincides with my impatience, that is to say, with a certain portion of my own duration, which I cannot protract or contract as I like. It is no longer something *thought*, it is something *lived*. (Bergson 1998: 9–10)

Such a re-conception clearly alters the relationship between the two kinds of multiplicity that we looked at in relation to *Time and Free Will*, as spatiality appears to no longer be a characteristic of either the inner or the outer world. The key to understanding this alteration comes from an inversion in the priority of our categories for understanding the world that is already familiar from the German idealist tradition. In *Creative Evolution*, rather than see life as a form of organised matter, Bergson takes life itself as primary, and sees brute matter as a tendency of duration which is never fully actualised. Thus, the kind of juxtaposition of elements that Bergson attributed to the external world is now seen as the limit case of a relaxation of duration. The conception of life that Bergson develops is radically different from that of the German idealists, however. We can begin to see this difference between life and spatiality by returning to the characteristics of conscious states. As we saw, a continuous multiplicity of the kind found in consciousness had a number of characteristics. Most importantly, it formed a successive, interpenetrative structure. We saw this in the case of Bergson's example of the striking clock, where the qualitative perception of each strike was affected by the retention of the prior sounds. Even in cases where we have a perception of a single unchanging object or a pure unchanging note, our perception alters as past moments are retained within the present.[11] A consequence of this is that novelty is an inherent characteristic of our mental life, to the extent that as each moment contains the past within it, it is in excess of that past. In *Creative Evolution*, Bergson claims that these characteristics of consciousness are characteristics of life more generally. Rather than being formed as a juxtaposition of elements, life exhibits structure in a manner that simply cannot be explained within

---

[11] 'Let us take the most stable of internal states, the visual perception of a motionless external object. The object may remain the same, I may look at it from the same side, at the same angle, in the same light; nevertheless the vision I now have of it differs from that which I have just had, even if only because the one is an instant older than the other. My memory is there, which conveys something of the past into the present. My mental state, as it advances on the road of time, is continually swelling with the duration which it accumulates: it goes on increasing – rolling upon itself, as a snow ball on the snow' (Bergson 1998: 4).

the mechanistic paradigm of a spatial multiplicity. Whereas matter tends towards a reduction in complexity, life instead increases in complexity and interpenetration of elements.

As we saw, a spatial multiplicity operates by understanding a system as a set of discrete elements brought into unity with one another. As such, the tendency of thinking in terms of space is to isolate systems from one another to render them open to analysis. Bergson notes, however, that such an approach is problematic when it comes to analysing living systems. If we take the example of the structure of the eye, for instance, we can see that an analysis in terms of a process of bringing into alignment a multitude of parts fails to explain how the variety of complex elements could be brought into the kind of precise reciprocal determinations needed to make a simple act like vision possible. Similarly, finalism goes too far in holding that 'nature has worked like a human being by bringing parts together' (Bergson 1998: 89). Bergson's diagnosis of these difficulties is that understanding life in terms of mechanism involves decomposing what is a continuous process into an infinite number of discrete moments. Once we have done this, the process becomes susceptible to analysis and quantification, but is also no longer able to throw any light on the relationship and constitution of the parts. Rather than attempting to reconstruct the structure of the eye through the integration of passive matter, Bergson instead suggests that at some level, matter, as life, has the capacity to self-organise. Bergson claimed that in counting we do not represent the process itself, but rather the traces of this process left behind in space. Similarly here, Bergson claims that the real unity of the evolution of the organism cannot be understood in terms of analysis, but is instead like the movement of our own body, which when viewed from the inside is simple and continuous, but when decomposed into a trajectory, it may be divided into an infinity of elements:

> [M]echanism and finalism both go too far, for they attribute to Nature the most formidable of the labors of Hercules in holding that she has exalted to the simple act of vision an infinity of infinitely complex elements, whereas Nature had no more trouble in making an eye than I have in lifting my hand. Nature's simple act has divided itself automatically into an infinity of elements which are then found to be coordinated to one idea, just as the movement of my hand has dropped an infinity of points which are then found to satisfy one equation. (Bergson 1998: 91)

This claim that the evolution of the organism cannot be understood in spatial terms is mirrored by a claim that even the organism at the lowest point of the animal spectrum, the amoeba, can only be partially under-stood in terms of the categories of chemistry and mechanism. As Ansell Pearson notes (1999a: 148–9), even the simplest of organisms needs to be understood in terms of an active engagement with an environment which brings into play the notion of a history of the organism, and with it the notion of a psychology (Bergson 1998: 36).

If the complexity of the organism cannot be analysed into parts, neither, according to Bergson, can organisms themselves be clearly isolated from one another into perfectly individuated structures. As Bergson notes:

> For the individuality to be perfect, it would be necessary that no detached part of the organism could live separately. But then reproduction would be impossible. For what is reproduction, but the building up of a new organism with a detached fragment of the old. Individuality therefore harbors its enemy at home. (Bergson 1998: 13)

As well as relating to its future, the organism maintains this openness in its relation back through its progenitors to the origin of life. Similarly, as we know from the fundamental role symbiosis plays in the functioning of even integrated organisms such as the human being,[12] we are not simply a closed unity of parts – 'an element or group of elements suddenly reveals that, however limited its normal space and function, it can transcend them occasionally; it may even in certain cases, be regarded as the equivalent of the whole' (Bergson 1998: 42). The organism, therefore, operates as a confused multiplicity of elements that cannot be isolated in the manner which is a precondition for spatialised thought.

If we accept Bergson's claim that the unity and creativity of life can only be understood in terms of duration, then the question naturally arises: how does Bergson characterise non-living matter? It would seem that when discussing the interaction of simple mechanical systems, we *could* talk about the world in terms of spatial multiplicities. In fact, however, even in these cases, such systems cannot be completely isolated from the rest of the universe, nor can they be understood as operating without duration. Let us take Bergson's example of the instantaneous perception of a body of a particular colour, for instance red. While we appear to be perceiving a state in this situation, Bergson notes that in fact what appears to take place in an instant involves the presentation of a vast number of physical events. In what Bergson takes to be the smallest interval of empty time we can detect, 0.002 seconds (Bergson

---

[12] This recognition of the openness of the organism to the outside is taken up by Deleuze and Guattari in their model of the rhizome (see Deleuze and Guattari 1987: 3–25). See Somers-Hall 2013c for an analysis of the relationship between this model of the organism and the account we find in Kant.

1991: 206), we find 400 billion vibrations in the composition of the wave of red light we receive. 'Thus the sensation of red light, experienced by us in the course of a second, corresponds in itself to a succession of phenomena which, separately distinguished in our duration with the greatest possible economy of time, would occupy more than 250 centuries of our history' (Bergson 1991: 206). As Čapek (1971: 198) notes, within quantum mechanics this vibratory character is attributed not simply to light, but to all matter, a claim that Bergson is prescient in making. The implication of this is that there is no pure state of the juxtaposition of matter, and no purely divisible time. Rather, even the most elementary of physical phenomena operate within duration, in that their pulsational nature means that the past is to some degree condensed into the present.

Even when we move to the level of purely physical phenomena, therefore, we find that existence has to be understood in durational terms. Throughout *Creative Evolution*, Bergson uses the metaphor of life as a mathematical curve. By combining shorter and shorter straight lines, we can form a closer approximation of the form of the curve itself, but ultimately the juxtaposition of straight lines can never coincide with the curve. 'In reality, life is no more made of physico-chemical elements than a curve is composed of straight lines' (Bergson 1998: 31). Nonetheless, it still appears to be the case that there are different degrees to which the past is retained in the present. The elementary vibrations of light tend to instantaneity in a way that appears radically different from the complex interpenetration of the past and present found in many of our conscious states. In perhaps one of the most radical aspects of his logic of multiplicities, Bergson claims that corresponding to these degrees of duration are degrees of spatiality. That is, phenomena can tend towards a more juxtaposed or a more interpenetrative form of organisation. Together with this tendency towards juxtaposition is a tendency towards the appearance of a homogeneous space. Insofar as systems we discover in the world tend to retain the past to a lesser degree, the elements that make them up become less connected to one another, to the extent that they tend towards a state of mere juxtaposition with one another, where relation is represented by position in a homogeneous space. Bergson's account of this process of the relaxation of the past is posed in psychological terms, but it is clear that he sees the account as having both ontological and logical significance. Here, for instance, is one formulation of the relation of continuous and confused multiplicities, which is worth quoting at length:

> The more we succeed in making ourselves conscious of our progress in pure duration, the more we feel the different parts of our being enter into each

other, and our whole personality concentrate itself in a point, or rather
a sharp edge, pressed against the future and cutting into it unceasingly. It is
in this that life and action are free. But suppose we let ourselves go and,
instead of acting, dream. At once the self is scattered; our past, which till
then was gathered together into the indivisible impulsion it communicated
to us, is broken up into a thousand recollections made external to one
another. They give up interpenetrating in the degree that they become fixed.
Our personality thus descends in the direction of space. It coasts around it
continually in sensation. We will not dwell here on a point we have studied
elsewhere. Let us merely recall that extension admits of degrees, that all
sensation is extensive in a certain measure, and that the idea of unextended
sensations, artificially localized in space, is a mere view of the mind,
suggested by an unconscious metaphysic much more than by psychological
observation. No doubt we make only the first steps in the direction of the
extended, even when we let ourselves go as much as we can. But suppose for
a moment that matter consists in this very movement pushed further, and
that physics is simply psychics inverted. (Bergson 1998: 201–2)

We can now answer the question of the relationship between the two
multiplicities that Bergson had introduced in *Time and Free Will*. While
Bergson initially conceives of both duration and homogeneous space as
actual modes of organisation within their respective domains, by *Creative
Evolution* he instead conceives of homogeneous space as a tendency of
certain phenomena within duration. As Deleuze puts it, 'Space, in effect, is
not matter or extension, but the "schema" of matter, that is, the representation of the limit where the movement of expansion would come to an
end as the external envelope of all possible extensions' (Deleuze 1988a: 87).
In this sense, there is no longer any question of the interaction of the two
multiplicities. Pure homogeneity as a state is indeed incompatible with
duration, but the tendency towards homogeneity is a fundamental feature
of our experience of a temporal world. Thus, while there is a difference
in kind between the two multiplicities, what we discover in duration
itself is merely a series of differences in degree of tension and relaxation
of duration.

Bergson's characterisation of pure spatiality as the limit of a movement
within duration itself opens the way to an explanation of why we conceive of
durational phenomena in spatial terms. Here we can return to the Kantian
question of the correspondence of our thought to its object. Kant posits three
possible accounts of the relation of thought to its objects: 'either the mind is
determined by things, or things are determined by the mind, or between the
mind and things we must suppose a mysterious agreement' (Bergson 1998:
205). Bergson instead develops a fourth possibility, which is that the thought

and the fact to which it relates form by a process of reciprocal determination over the course of the development of a species. In this, Bergson takes up an idea of the evolutionary theorist Herbert Spencer.[13] Spencer argued that our categories of thought have a pragmatic origin, whereby organisms survive on the basis of the correspondence of their internal processes to the physical structure of the milieu that exists outside of the organism. As organisms gain in complexity, so the number of structures and relations in the world that they are able to relate to increases, leading to an increase in the complexity of their milieu. Those creatures whose internal state corresponds to the world survive, and those who misrepresent the world die out. For Spencer, when we reach the most complex species, humans, what was originally a pragmatic correspondence between our categories and the world becomes objective. This is because our categories no longer represent a mere part of existence, but instead are co-extensive with the whole of it. Spencer took the success of modern physics in mapping the universe as evidence that the categories of thought employed by the human being had reached this point of correspondence. Thus, there is a gradual attunement of the organism to its environment. In effect, Spencer ends with a position similar to Kant's, in that for the individual, our categories of thought are guaranteed a priori, even if at the level of the evolution of the species our categories are of an a posteriori nature. The difficulty with such an approach is that it presupposes that the facts our categories of thought are supposed to correspond to are essentially inert, and are not themselves subject to a process of genesis. One of the main characteristics of a spatial multiplicity was that we were able to divide phenomena presented in such a multiplicity in an arbitrary manner. Similarly, once we understand the world in terms of the categories of homogeneous space, we naturally develop an understanding of the world that accords with those categories. '[O]nce we posit this particular mode of cutting up such as we perceive it to-day, we posit the intellect such as it is to-day, for it is by relation to it, and to it alone, that reality is cut up in this manner' (Bergson 1998: 367). In this, the intellect follows, but extends a natural tendency within matter itself:

> The mind finds space in things, but could have got it without them if it had had imagination strong enough to push the inversion of its own natural movement to the end. On the other hand, we are able to explain how matter accentuates still more its materiality, when viewed by the mind. Matter, at first, aided mind to run down its own incline; it gave the impulsion. But, the impulsion once received, mind continues its course. (Bergson 1998: 202)

---

[13] For Bergson's early reading of Spencer, see Čapek 1971: 3–14.

In the next section, I want to look at Bergson's account of these categories of intellectual thought themselves, before looking at their limitations and relationship with duration. I want to conclude by looking at why Bergson's own account of the need to move beyond judgement differs radically from that of the German idealists. We will see how this move from the relations of the two multiplicities in *Time and Free Will* to the privileging of duration in his later ontology relates to Bergson's account of thinking.

2.6   Judgement and Multiplicity

For Bergson, judgement is the paradigm form of representation: 'intelligence has as its essence to judge, and judgement operates by the attribution of a subject to a predicate' (Bergson 1946: 69). As with Kant, judgement precedes experience for Bergson, who gives the metaphor of

> [t]he schoolboy, who knows that the master is going to dictate a fraction to him, draws a line before he knows what numerator and what denominator are to come; he therefore has present to his mind the general relation between the two terms although he does not know either of them; he knows the form without the matter. So is it, prior to experience, with the categories into which our experience comes to be inserted. (Bergson 1998: 148–9)

For Bergson, we can draw a clear analogy between the nature of judgement and the way in which we tend to represent movement. When we represent a change through a series of judgements, for instance, what we represent is not the change itself, but a series of waypoints that the object moves through. Each of the elements of a judgement, the subject and the predicate, are defined as atemporal: 'we put on one side the absolutely definitive stability of the subject and on the other side the stabilities of the qualities and the states' (Bergson 1946: 69). By doing so, we are able to represent change by the substitution of one stable state for another, or by the replacement of one qualification with another. If Bergson's analysis of the nature of matter is correct, then in actuality the universe as a whole forms an interpenetrative multiplicity, such that all distinction is merely partial. Judgement allows us to instead understand the world by relating together essentially distinct elements into an artificial unity. It has two pragmatic benefits. First, it allows us to communicate with others about mental states and structures in terms that the other will understand. Second, understanding the world itself in terms of judgement allows us to isolate systems from the world more generally. In this section, I want to explore Bergson's analysis of the limitations of judgement. With reference in particular to Kant's transcendental deduction, I want to show why Bergson believes that our understanding of the world in terms of judgement in fact presupposes an awareness of duration, through which the properties dealt with by the intellect are first constituted.

Bergson notes that seeing the world in terms of distinct entities and properties is the cornerstone of science. The basis of an inductive inference is a recognition that the same cause has led to the same effect in a number of previous instances of an event. An immediate presupposition of such a method is that the world is decomposable into moments that are identical with one another, in order that we can identify the same causes across multiple occasions.

> If I boil water in a kettle on a stove, the operation and the objects that support it are, in reality, bound up with a multitude of other objects and a multitude of other operations; in the end, I should find that our entire solar system is concerned in what is being done at this particular point of space. But, in a certain measure, and for the special end I am pursuing, I may admit that things happen as if the group *water-kettle-stove* were an independent microcosm. (Bergson 1998: 214)

As we saw with magnitudes, what the spatialisation of time let us do was to superimpose two different temporal segments onto one another. In the case of the system of the boiling kettle, we do something similar, superimposing the system of today on the system of yesterday, 'kettle on kettle, water on water, duration on duration' (Bergson 1998: 215). As we saw in the previous chapter, Kant also argues that experience involves understanding the world in terms of a system of stable properties and objects. In the transcendental deduction, Kant argued that it was a condition of the possibility of experience that experience be ordered. Kant claimed that if an object's various properties constantly altered ('if a man changed sometimes into this and sometimes into that animal form, if the country on the longest day were sometimes covered with fruit, sometimes with ice and snow' [Kant 1929: A101–2]), it would be impossible to re-identify it on seeing it again. Given that there is order in the world, Kant argues that what makes this order possible is that our associated representations must have an 'affinity' (Kant 1929: A122) with each other. As well as being brought together, as the first synthesis of the transcendental deduction shows, they must be related to one another in such a way that they have some coherence to each other. Drawing a line in thought requires the reproduction of the prior moments in order for the thought to be complete. What makes the relation of ideas possible, therefore, is that we are able to reproduce past moments such that they can be brought into the kinds of relations of identity required by cognition. This role of reproduction is played by the imagination, which mediates between intuition and the categories of the understanding. It is these associations between events that make possible the kind of stable representations across different objects that make judgements possible.

Bergson takes Kant's assumptions that memory operates in terms of discrete moments, and that these moments can be represented alongside the present moment, as evidence that his account rests on the spatialisation of the past. In order for a present moment to be related to the reproduction of a past moment, 'the latter must have waited for the former, time must have halted, and everything become simultaneous: that happens in geometry, but in geometry alone' (Bergson 1998: 216). Once we have understood the relationship of the past to the present on the model of geometry, understanding the affinity between moments becomes problematic, however. As Bergson notes, 'we should seek in vain for two ideas which have not some point of resemblance or which do not touch each other somewhere' (Bergson 1991: 163). The question naturally emerges: what is the condition for the possibility of the kind of affinity that is a prerequisite for judgement?

We can begin to answer this by returning to Bergson's claim that a property can only be an approximation to the actual nature of an object. Kant presupposes the existence of the kinds of properties we use to determine resemblance. Just as extensity emerges from duration, Bergson argues that we need an account of the genesis of these properties themselves. Once we recognise that a system has to be understood in context, then each object will be singular, as it will differ in its relations to the rest of the world. As Bergson puts it, '[t]he concept can symbolise a particular property only by making it common to an infinity of things. Therefore it always more or less distorts this property by the extension it gives to it' (Bergson 1946: 140). As such, in order to recognise a resemblance, we do not simply need to compare the properties of two objects, but also to constitute the properties upon which the resemblance will be founded:

> But the question before us is whether individual qualities, even isolated by an effort of abstraction, do not remain individual, and whether, to make them into genera, a new effort of the mind is not required, by which it first bestows on each quality a name, and then collects under this name a multitude of individual objects. The whiteness of a lily is not the whiteness of a snowfield; they remain, even as isolated from the snow and the lily, snow-white or lily-white. They only forego their individuality if we consider

their likeness in order to give them a common name; then, applying this name to an unlimited number of similar objects, we throw back upon the quality, by a sort of ricochet, the generality which the word went out to seek in its application to things. (Bergson 1991: 157)

Properties therefore involve a twofold process: first, there is an extraction of a singular property from a process, then there is an abstraction according to which a general property is constituted. In effect, therefore, Bergson's claim is that the synthesis of reproduction, whereby we find resemblances between objects based on shared properties, is in fact dependent on a prior effort whereby properties themselves are constituted in things. This moment cannot be understood within the framework of judgement, as judgement merely allows us to relate together different properties into unities. The point Bergson is making is that once we have separated memories into a series of passive givens, in a manner such as Kant's, the principle whereby they are related to one another appears to be arbitrary: 'why should an image which is, by hypothesis, self sufficient, seek to accrue itself to others either similar or given in contiguity with it?' (Bergson 1991: 165). Kant is seeking to explain how we can determine the laws of nature. The difficulty is that if we begin our analysis in terms of discretely determined entities, then it is impossible to explain the process whereby those entities themselves become determined. Similarly, once we have reached the level of discretely determined sensations, it is impossible to determine the principles by which they are related to one another, primarily because their self-sufficiency means that they are not internally related to other memories. Because of this, we need something external to the elements, such as the active synthesis of consciousness, to unify them into a set of relations. If this process of unification is external to the elements, however, we cannot explain how this takes place in terms of an affinity internal to them. Bergson provides an alternative which for now will remain cryptic: 'In fact, we perceive the resemblance before we perceive the individuals which resemble one another; and in an aggregate of contiguous parts, we perceive the whole before the parts' (Bergson 1991: 165). Bergson's point is that there is a self-relation of the moments prior to their constitution as individuals that can be given to the synthesis of a subject. This in effect is the claim that prior to the kind of synthesis Kant takes to be responsible for the affinity we find between entities, there must be a prior synthesis whereby those entities themselves are constituted.

In his lectures on Kant's *First Critique*, Bergson declares that 'the imagination, in that it unites intuition and concepts, is in effect Kant's category of memory – it allows concepts to apply themselves to experience' (Bergson 1990: 162). Bergson's own account of memory relates three terms: recollection-memory, habit-memory, and perception. For Kant, these three terms are run together. Whether the imagination is forming habits or reproducing particular events, it does so through the re-representation of actual past experiences, which are represented in the same terms as perceptions. As we know, however, there is a clear difference between a habit which involves orientating ourselves towards a world of things and the experience, for instance, of day-dreaming, which involves a detachment from concerns. If we want to understand how these two notions are related, we need to begin by recognising that consciousness is, for Bergson, fundamentally orientated towards action. That means that the present moment of time is to be understood in terms of the connection between perception and action. Action implies that our orientation will be towards the future rather than the past, though this will be informed by the past experience, insofar as it can provide a guide for future action. This was the basis of Kant's claim that forming habits requires an affinity of perceptions, in order that relations of similarity and contiguity can be established between the past and present. Bergson argues that it is only through memory that the past as duration can be brought into a form such that it can be used by the practical concerns of the intellect. As such, he is right to note a parallel between his own conception of memory and Kant's imagination.

We can note that the recollection of the past often bears on the pragmatic concerns of the present moment. Bergson notes that children often have far greater facility of recall than adults, which is inversely proportional to their ability to actualise the experiences appropriate to the present context. If detail of one's recollections is inversely proportional to action in this way, then 'a human being who should dream his life instead of living it . . . would no doubt keep before his eyes at each moment the infinite multitude of the details of his past history' (Bergson 1991: 155). So memory that functions by recollection contains a greater and greater part of the past, until we reach a point at which it is completely detached from action and hence, in the state of pure memory, contains a complete record of the past.

Once we recognise that accounts of memory such as Kant's see it as disconnected and successive (Bergson characterises such an account as composing memories as 'self-sufficient atoms'), then the rejection of this model is going to mean that we no longer see memory composed of separate parts. This in turn means that we will no longer be able to separate a discrete set of memories from others. This implies that memory stores the whole of the past as a confused multiplicity rather than moments of particular interest to the subject. Given that the past cannot be divided up into elements, then it must be the case that the whole of the past is also present in our practical relations to the world. Selection on the basis of similarity will not explain how only a small part of the past is related to the present, as selection implies detachable elements and, as we saw, similarity is presupposed rather than explained by Kant's model. What allows us to form the correct affinities between past events and the present is not a simple affinity between properties of the past and present, but rather a process of translation of a durational past into a present represented by the intellect. This process of translation is one that represents the processes of the past as states, and hence constitutes the kinds of properties between which affinities could be found:

> [M]emory, laden with the whole of the past, responds to the appeal of the present state by two simultaneous movements, one of translation, by which it moves in its entirety to meet experience, thus contracting more or less, though without dividing, with a view to action; and the other of rotation upon itself, by which it turns towards the situation of the moment, presenting to it the side which may prove to be the most useful. (Bergson 1991: 168–9)

Pure memory is far removed from action, and so the field of memory is at its most expansive, making apparent the particularity of memories. As we contract memory towards a point, we move from particularity to generality, until we arrive at the point of the present itself, where, while the whole is still present, it is manifested in the form of habit where all particularity of experience has been lost. Thus:

> A foreign word, from a foreign language, uttered in my hearing, may make me think of that language in general or of a voice which once pronounced it in a certain way . . . [these two associations] answer to two different mental *dispositions*, to two distinct degrees of tension in memory; in the latter case they are nearer to the pure image, in the former, they are more disposed toward immediate response, that is to say, to action. (Bergson 1991: 169)

By noting that judgement is dependent on intuition, Bergson is not claiming that science is without validity within its domain. In fact, science and judgement map the structure of one kind of multiplicity, a spatial multiplicity, and as such it does relate to the 'essence of the real' (Bergson 1946: 30), even if it can only embrace 'no more than a part of that reality'. As Bergson's comments on the need for a moment whereby the qualities, and also the magnitudes, that we find in a spatialised world are constituted show, we cannot think of the world purely in terms of judgement, but need an originary experience of duration through which the structures that judgement manipulates are instantiated in the first place. Against the logic of association that we find presupposed by judgement, Bergson talks of a thinking in terms of dissociation, whereby duration is separated into a multiplicity of juxtaposed and generalised terms.[14] As Pete Gunter notes, Bergson considers this process of dissociation to be at the origin of all advances in science, and that paradigm shifts in scientific enquiry involve a return to duration on the part of a thinker, and with it a reconceptualisation of the very objects of scientific enquiry (Gunter 1987). What is needed is a return to duration itself to allow for more than simply a haphazard connection between science and metaphysics. In effect, therefore, we could read Bergson's enquiry as an investigation into the conditions for the possibility for the kinds of stable identities that Kant presupposes for his theory of judgement:

> To every true affirmation we attribute thus a retroactive effect; or rather, we impart to it a retrograde movement. As though a judgment could have pre-existed the terms which make it up! As though these terms did not date from the appearance of the objects they represent! As though the thing and the idea of the thing, its reality and its possibility, were not created at one stroke when a truly new form, invented by art or nature is concerned! (Bergson 1946: 22)

In the final section of this chapter, I want to explore further the connection between duration and judgement by drawing some comparisons with Hegel's account of dialectic. As we saw in the first chapter, Hegel too sees judgement as incomplete, and as part of a larger moment. I want to show how these surface similarities in fact mask some substantial differences in approach.

2.7   Duration and Infinite Thought

In moving to privilege life over mechanism, Bergson appears to be repeating a characteristic development of German idealism.[15] In Hegel's earliest

---

[14] Cf., for instance, *Matter and Memory*: 'It would seem, then, that we start neither from the perception of the individual nor from the conception of the genus, but from an intermediate knowledge, from a confused sense of the striking quality or of resemblance: this sense, equally remote from generality fully conceived and from individuality clearly perceived, begets both of them by a process of dissociation' (Bergson 1991: 158). Similarly, in 'The Perception of Change', Bergson writes that 'our knowledge, far from being made up of a gradual association of simple elements, is the effect of a sudden dissociation: from the immensely vast field of our virtual knowledge, we have selected, in order to make it into actual knowledge, everything which concerns our action upon things; we have neglected the rest' (Bergson 1946: 137).

[15] While I will be focusing on Hegel in this chapter, we noted in the last chapter that Schelling also develops an organicist conception of the world.

writings, he calls the structure that combines unity and multiplicity 'life',[16] and while life is displaced in his systematic writings by spirit, it is still the case that the structure of life provides a model for the movement beyond thinking as judgement.[17] For Hegel, organic life exemplifies the Notion through its combination of a diversity of individual organs, each of which fulfils a separate purpose, and the unity of the organism itself. Hegel notes that the nature of each organ can only be understood in terms of the organism as a whole, since they are defined by their function, and that function of the whole is determined by the interrelation of all of the organs:

> In so far as the animal's members are simply moments of its form, and are perpetually negating their independence, and withdrawing into a unity which is the reality of the Notion, and is for the Notion, the animal is the existent Idea. If a finger is cut off, a process of chemical decomposition sets in, and it is no longer a finger. The unity which is produced has being for the implicit unity of the animal. This implicit unity is the soul or Notion. (Hegel 2002: §350)

We therefore have something that on the surface is a parallel for Bergson's rejection of judgement, with life incomprehensible to any categorisation as the combination of self-subsistent atoms:

> The thinking that clings to the determinations of the relationships of reflection and of the formal Notion, when it comes to consider life, this unity of the Notion in the externality of objectivity, in the absolute multiplicity of atomistic matter, finds all thoughts without exception are of no avail; the omnipresence of the simple in manifold externality is for reflection an absolute contradiction, and as reflection must at the same time apprehend this omnipresence for its perception of life and therefore admit the actuality of this Idea, it is an incomprehensible mystery for it, because it does not grasp the Notion, and the Notion as the substance of life. (Hegel 1989: 763)

How does such an account differ from Bergson's?

---

[16] For instance, in the 1800 'Fragment of a System', Hegel writes, 'Life is the union of union and nonunion. In other words, every expression whatsoever is a product of reflection, and therefore it is possible to demonstrate in the case of every expression that, when reflection propounds it, another expression, not propounded, is excluded. Reflection is thus driven on and on without rest; but this process must be checked once and for all by keeping in mind that, for example, what has been called a union of synthesis and antithesis is not something propounded by the understanding or by reflection but has a character of its own, namely, that of being a reality beyond all reflection. Within the living whole there are posited at the same time death, opposition, and understanding, because there is posited a manifold that is alive itself and that, as alive, can posit itself as a whole' (Hegel 1971: 312).

[17] For more on Hegel's concept of life, see Stern 1990: 77–106; Stone 2005; Houlgate 2005: 106–9.

The key difference is that whereas for Hegel, finite thinking is an *abstraction*, in that it is unable to adequately think the unity of opposing determinations in the object, for Bergson, the limitation of thinking that operates according to judgement is that it begins from a *translation* from duration into stable states. In *Time and Free Will*, Bergson notes that 'in reality there are neither identical sensations nor multiple tastes: for sensations and tastes seem to be *objects* as soon as I isolate and name them, and in the human soul there are only *processes*' (Bergson 2008: 131). What we have here is not the movement of things to which categories such as unity and multiplicity could be attached, but rather a different kind of organisation that is entirely prior to the structure of the object. Rather than bringing unity and multiplicity into a proper relationship with one another, as Hegel wishes to do, Bergson instead attempts to show how these categories themselves emerge. When we looked at memory, for instance, it did not operate in terms of individuals or generalities, but in terms of resemblances that were prior to these kinds of determinations. While we normally conceive of a process as something that an object undergoes, Bergson holds this to be an illusion. Rather, the fundamental element of reality is change without a container:

> What is the 'mobile' to which our eye attaches movement as to a vehicle? Simply a coloured spot which we know perfectly well amounts, in itself, to a series of extremely rapid vibrations. This alleged movement of a thing is in reality only a movement of movements. (Bergson 1946: 148)

The idea that motion requires something that moves is, for Bergson, the result of understanding the world in terms of homogeneous space. Within such a space, motion needs to be attributed to a position, and as the space is itself homogeneous, the assignment to a position involves the assignment of movement to a body at that position. Similarly, the concepts of the one and the many are intimately bound up with homogeneous space. In both *Creative Mind* (Bergson 1946: 71) and *Creative Evolution* (Bergson 1998: 3–4), Bergson uses the analogy of conscious processes being naturally connected through forming an interpenetrative multiplicity, which, as we draw them out to the point where they become discrete elements, must be connected with a thread analogous to that which connects beads on a necklace which is 'neither this nor that, nothing that resembles beads, nothing that resembles anything whatsoever – an empty entity, a single word' (Bergson 1946: 71). We employ the categories of the one and the many once we have translated our experiences into spatial terms. We cannot reconstitute the original moment of duration with them, not because they are too abstract, but rather because they differ in kind from the phenomena they are attributed to. The one and the many apply to manifolds of states, not to processes. Thus, while 'nothing is easier than to say that the ego is multiplicity, or that it is unity, or that it is both, or that it is a synthesis of both', to do so is to resort to 'ready-made garments which will suit Peter as well as Paul because they do not show off the figure of either of them' (Bergson 1946: 175).

As Deleuze (1988a: 45) notes, Bergson's analysis of the one and the many is here profoundly anti-dialectical. Bergson's claim is that it is impossible to recompose an understanding of duration through abstract categories, and that the combination of opposed determinations is a symptom of this failure. 'This multiplicity that is duration is not at all the same thing as the multiple, any more than its simplicity is the same as the One' (Deleuze 1988a: 46). As a consequence of this, Bergson agrees with Hegel that our use of finite categories generates contradictions,[18] but these contradictions cannot be resolved by a more sophisticated understanding of the unity of opposites. They result from the abstract nature of our categories, but are an inevitable consequence of inappropriately reconstituting duration through the categories of judgement: 'According to whether we start, for example, from unity or from multiplicity, we shall form a different conception of the multiple unity of duration' (Bergson 1946: 167). These differences in emphasis lead to systematic differences between philosophies that in turn lead to contradictions. Bergson illustrates the failure of philosophies of the one and the many by giving the analogy of attempting to reconstruct the city of Paris from a series of paintings of it. It is impossible to reproduce Paris from a series of paintings because the paintings we produce of Paris are not actually parts of Paris, but merely what he calls 'partial expressions'. Each painting is a fragment of a symbol of Paris, rather than a fragment of Paris itself. As such, at best we can form a more complete representation. We need to have had an originary experience of Paris to which we relate the representations if we are to make sense of them. Similarly, the sense we attribute to a dialectical vision of the world is parasitic on a non-dialectical view of duration. It is in this sense that Bergson criticises the reliance on a 'method of construction' in post-Kantian thought. If we return to the question of the role of life in *Creative Evolution*, we can similarly see that what Bergson is concerned with is not organic life, as the organisation of

---

[18] In his *Introduction to Metaphysics*, Bergson presents a number of images of duration for the intellect, each of which on its own is inadequate, but which cannot be coherently thought together. Bergson argues that the contradictory nature of these images opens the way to a genuine intuition of duration. See Lawlor 2012: 19–22.

a multiplicity of parts into a unity. Rather, life is the original creative force of duration which, 'traversing the bodies it has organised one after another, passing from generation to generation, has become divided amongst species and distributed amongst individuals without losing anything of its force, rather intensifying in proportion to its advance' (Bergson 1998: 26). Just as within our own experience, the past is translated into the representational language of the intellect, so the organism as a unity of unity and multiplicity is a translation of the purely processual character of life itself. What for Hegel is an emblem of spirit is for Bergson a purely secondary phenomenon.

While Hegel presses us to move forward beyond the finite categories of the understanding by embracing the unity of opposites through the higher faculty of reason, therefore, Bergson instead believes that philosophy must instead 'do itself violence, reverse the direction of the operation by which it normally thinks, continually upsetting its categories or rather, recasting them' (Bergson 1946: 190). Rather than proceeding by synthesis of determinations, Bergson instead asks us to return to the moment before those determinations were constituted by the process of the dissociation of duration. In his early lectures on Kant's *First Critique*, Bergson sets out Kant's model of judgement clearly in terms of the unification of a juxtaposed manifold of elements by the transcendental unity of apperception: 'This unity, descending on this [manifold of intuition] to embrace it, covers it over with a network of pure concepts, schemata, principles, all of which are formulae of that impersonal unity' (Bergson 1990: 167). To reverse the course of thought is therefore to return to the conditions that make an account such as Kant's possible, and hence to return to a moment prior to the dissociative translation that makes possible our practical application of the categories of judgement to the world. It is to rediscover the natural articulations of matter prior to the imposition of the categories of the intellect.

2.8 Conclusion

Bergson gives little clear indication of what such an approach would look like, which follows quite naturally from his belief that philosophy must depart from many of the categories and characteristics that make practical engagement with the world possible, such as the distinction of elements and the imposition of external structures.[19] In an essay on Ravaisson, he

---

[19] In his *Introduction to Metaphysics*, he makes the extreme claim that 'metaphysics is therefore the science that claims to dispense with symbols' (Bergson 1946: 162).

gives some idea of what such a method might involve. In talking about how we might develop a concept of colour, Bergson first suggests that the approach of the intellect would be to take a series of different colours and remove each of them from them all of those characteristics in which they differ from each other. In doing so, we create 'an affirmation made up of negations, a form circumscribing a vacuum' (Bergson 1946: 225). We can see in this procedure the flattening out of variations that leads to the 'extinction of the light' rather than a proper illumination of the concept of colour. To reverse the direction of thought, and hence to travel against the current of dissociation, involves returning to the point before which the various colours became juxtaposed with respect to one another:

> In this case it consists in taking the thousand and one different shades of blue, violet, green, yellow and red, and, by having them pass through a convergent lens, bringing them to a single point. Then appears in all its radiance the pure white light which, perceived here below in the shades which disperse it, enclosed above, in its undivided unity, the indefinite variety of multi-coloured rays. Then would also be revealed, even to each shade taken individually, what the eye did not notice at first, the white light in which it participates, the common illumination from which it draws its colouring. (Bergson 1946: 266)

In the next chapter, we will see how Bergson's critique of judgement is affected by the introduction into French thought of phenomenology. As we shall see, in taking up intentionality, Jean-Paul Sartre struggles to relate the intuitive insights into consciousness present in Bergson's immanent philosophy of duration and Husserl's transcendent notion of intentionality.

CHAPTER 3

Sartre and Thinking as Imaging

3.1 Introduction

In the last chapter, we saw that Sartre claimed his decision to become a philosopher was premised on his belief in the acuity in Bergson's analysis of the nature of consciousness. It was his discovery of phenomenology, however, that led to the development of his own existential philosophy. Central in this regard is Sartre's whole-hearted adoption of Husserl's doctrine of intentionality: the claim that consciousness is to be understood as a relation to a world of objects. Intentionality is opposed to what Sartre calls the 'illusion of immanence' (Sartre 2004: 5) or 'digestive philosophy' (Sartre 1970: 4), which understands consciousness as a container within which the objects of thought are brought together and examined. Once the mind is understood as a container, there is a natural, though not inevitable, tendency to understand thinking as the kind of categorial synthesis we found in Kant's philosophy.

The move to phenomenology represents a radical break with Bergson's philosophy of multiplicities, since Sartre interprets Bergson's account of consciousness as essentially viewing it as a thing, albeit one in process, and hence also falling under the illusion of immanence. Rather than thinking being in possession of its objects, it is instead a 'veering out there beyond oneself' (Sartre 1970: 4) and into the world. In light of Sartre's move to phenomenology, much of the analysis, both favourable and critical, has taken as its frame of reference the work of Husserl and Heidegger.[1] This

---

[1] The relation to the phenomenological tradition is almost exclusively taken as the basis for both positive and negative assessments of Sartre. Hubert Dreyfus, for instance, writes of Sartre that he 'started out as a Husserlian ... then he read Heidegger and was converted to what he thought was Heideggerian existentialism. But as a Husserlian and a Frenchman he felt he had to fix up Heidegger and make him more Cartesian .... When I visited Heidegger he had *Being and Nothingness* on his desk, in German translation, and I said, "So you're reading Sartre?", and he responded, "how can I even begin to read this muck?" (His word was "*Dreck*".) That's pretty strong, but I think accurate' (Dreyfus interviewed in Magee 2000: 275). Catalano 1974: 100–1, by contrast, presents a more

approach has its strengths, particularly in the light of *Being and Nothingness*, which borrows heavily from the terminology of the German tradition. Nonetheless, Sartre takes up the concept of intentionality within the context of his prior Bergsonism, and just as Sartre rejects many of Bergson's conclusions on the basis of Husserlian considerations, he also rejects key aspects of Husserl's thought on the basis of distinctly Bergsonian arguments. Thus, for instance, Sartre's rejection of Husserl's transcendental ego can be traced back to arguments we looked at in the previous chapter. In fact, in Sartre's works of the 1930s, which anticipate the arguments of *Being and Nothingness*, we find Sartre often citing Bergson approvingly, reinterpreting the implications of his arguments, radically altering the significance and application of his distinctions, and attempting to maintain the validity of Bergson's descriptions of experience while rejecting the inferences he draws from them. Thus, phenomenology becomes a new tool to avoid seeing the paradigm case of thinking as judging. In the first part of this chapter, therefore, I will explore the way Sartre navigates the relationships between intentionality and Bergsonism in these early works as Sartre explores the role of the imagination in the constitution of our world of experience. As we shall see, for Sartre, '[the] imagination is not an empirical power added to consciousness, but is the whole of consciousness as it realises its freedom' (Sartre 2004: 186). As such, any analysis of the imagination in Sartre's work must also develop an account of intentional consciousness. While Sartre holds that all consciousness is self-consciousness, this self-consciousness is not a structure of reflective knowledge. In exploring this characterisation of consciousness, we shall see that it represents a radical break with the transcendental structures Kant believed necessary to explain our relations to a world of objects. As we shall see, Sartre's characterisation of the imaginary as a mode of relating to absent objects develops naturally into his later account of consciousness as constituting a world in terms of a central lack. In the later part of this chapter, we will explore Sartre's development of this account in the

positive account of Sartre, arguing that Sartre deals more authentically with the contingency of existence, which is covered over by Heidegger in *Being and Time*. In both cases, however, it is in relation to the phenomenologists, and primarily Heidegger, that Sartre is judged. Bergson receives no mention in recent commentaries such as Catalano 2010, Hatzimoysis: 2010, or Webber 2009, and is only mentioned in general terms in passing in Catalano 1974 and Gardner 2009. Similarly, Descombes 1980 recognises the importance of Bergson for the development of French thought in general, but only includes one brief, tangential reference to Bergson in his account of Sartre. While there are some articles that address Sartre's relationship to Bergson, such as Gioli 2007 and Richmond 2007, these emphasise the differences between Bergson and Sartre.

more overtly Heideggerian text of *Being and Nothingness* in more detail. Specifically, we will look at the implications for Sartre's philosophy of his recognition of the importance of the other in the constitution of the world and of the self. In one regard, Sartre's recognition of the place of the other begins to overturn many of the more solipsistic tendencies of his earlier work. The introduction of the other illuminates the centrality of a pre-judicative moment of world constitution in Sartre's thought, however, where the fundamental categories of thought are constituted within the context of our differing fundamental projects.

In order to explore Sartre's response to the question of judgement, I want to explicate Sartre's thought in the following order. First, we will look at Sartre's arguments and diagnosis of what he calls the illusion of immanence. As we shall see, Sartre's claim is that models of thought that see thinking as the manipulation of mental objects tend to reduce thinking to a synthesis of self-sufficient elements according to either laws of judgement or of cause and effect. Such models prove unable to account for basic aspects of our experience of the external world, either by implicitly assuming all ideas are innate, or by being unable to distinguish perceptions from ideas. We will then move on to explore Sartre's own positive account of consciousness, which is essentially a radicalisation of Husserl's model of intentionality. As we shall see, here, Sartre introduces a novel model of self-consciousness that implies that thinking's relationship with itself falls outside of the categories of judgement. Sartre's claim is that we cover over the nature of the self by understanding it in terms of categories inappropriate to it. As such, there is a parallel here with Kant's paralogisms, but whereas Kant argues that transcendental illusions emerge through reason's attempts to systematise judgements of the understanding, for Sartre it emerges through reason's desire to understand the subject as an object of judgement in order to avoid anxiety in the face of freedom. We will then move on to consider Sartre's account of our relationship with the world. In particular, we will look at Sartre's account of the imagination in his early work, and its relation to his later thought in *Being and Nothingness*. Sartre here sees the imagination as playing the kind of dissociative role which was at the heart of Bergson's account, with what Sartre calls an 'irreal' providing the ground for the kinds of distinctions presupposed by judgement. We will conclude by looking at Sartre's account of our relations with others. Here, Sartre maintains a proximity to Hegel, but we shall see that while for Hegel recognition of the rational nature of the other provides the structure of reason, for Sartre this moment shows the impossibility of understanding the world in terms of judgement.

3.2 **Immanent Thought**

Sartre published two early works on the imagination, translated into English as *The Imagination* and *The Imaginary*. The first of these develops a sustained critical engagement with historical approaches to understanding the imagination, while the second concentrates on developing Sartre's own positive account of imagination. These two works were originally conceived of as forming two parts of a single work, entitled *The Image*,[2] though the original publisher chose to publish only the first part. As we shall see, Sartre's claim will be that thinking as judging is only possible on the basis of a prior operation of the imagination that operates in a manner that is different in kind from judgement. I want to begin by looking at the reasons why Sartre believes that traditional models have failed to give a proper place to the role of the image in our mental lives. In the previous chapter, we saw that Bergson began from the claim that we suffer from a certain natural illusion in understanding our mental lives in the same terms as extensive physical objects. This claim is also at the heart of Sartre's account of the imagination. As he writes, 'existence-as-imaged [*l'existence en image*] is a mode of being quite difficult to grasp. Grasping it requires some straining of the mind, but above all it requires us to get rid of our almost unbreakable habit of construing all modes of existence on the model of physical existence' (Sartre 2012: 5).[3] The result of this habit is that we tend to understand the image in the same terms as the perceived object. When I close my eyes and bring to mind the image of this piece of white paper that I have just been inspecting, then I am guided by a natural illusion to claim that the image has the same properties as the object itself, and exists like the object itself, albeit possibly in an inferior manner. Sartre sums up this account as follows:

> Pure *a priori* theory made a thing out of the image, but internal intuition teaches us that the image is not *the* thing. The data of intuition are thus going to be incorporated in the theoretical construction under a new form: the image is a thing, just as much as the thing it is an image of, but by the very fact that it is an image, it receives a sort of metaphysical inferiority in

---

[2] Translator's introduction, Sartre 2012: xiv.

[3] Sartre keeps the traditional idea that the imagination deals with images, but reconceives images as ways in which we relate to objects. As such, Sartre uses the word image as a verb, rather than a noun: 'As the word "image" is long-standing, we cannot reject it completely. But, to avoid all ambiguity, I repeat here that an image is nothing other than a relation. The imaging consciousness that I have of Pierre is not a consciousness of an image of Pierre: Pierre is directly reached, my attention is not directed at an image, but at an object' (2004: 7).

comparison with the thing it represents. In a word, the image is a lesser thing. (Sartre 2012: 7)[4]

Understanding the imagination as operating on objects within consciousness brings with it a number of problems, several of which we have already looked at in the last chapter. Before moving on to look at those problems, it is worth considering how Sartre develops his account of the imagination's relation to thinking at this point. For Sartre, once imagining has been taken to be the production of images, then there are only three basic ways in which we can understand the relationship between thinking and images, archetypally expressed by Descartes, Hume, and Leibniz. In essence, we either see the image and thought as separated from one another, or we see thought as simply the movement of images, or images as a confused presentation of thought. In each of these cases, thinking will be the synthesis of discrete representations, either according to the structure of judgement or of association.

For Descartes, the division between thought and the imagination is bound up with his radical ontological distinction between the mind and the body. Images are essentially bodily:

> [T]he difference between this mode of thinking [of the imagination] and pure understanding may simply be this: when the mind understands, it in some way turns towards itself and inspects one of the ideas which are within it; but when it imagines, it turns towards the body and looks at something in the body which conforms to an idea understood by the mind or perceived by the senses. (Descartes 1984: 73)

This claim has a number of important consequences for our understanding of the relationship between the imagination and thinking. First, if images have their origin in the body, and are then translated into the mind, then for the mind there is no straightforward way of distinguishing products of the imagination from products of the senses that also must reach the mind through the body. This leads to Descartes' claim that there are no 'certain marks' (Descartes 1984: 9) that can distinguish between, for instance, the sense-data we receive in sleep and the sense-data we receive when awake. Second, there is a radical break between thinking and imagining. As Sartre notes, for Descartes, in order for thinking to be possible, the material images must be translated into the immaterial realm of thought. 'The motions of the brain, caused by external objects, although they do not

---

[4] Deleuze 1988a: 17–21 argues for the centrality of recognising false problems where differences in kind are replaced by differences of degree, and traces the recognition of these kinds of false problems back to Bergson.

resemble the latter, awaken ideas in the soul. The ideas do not come from the motions; they are innate in man . . . . The motions are like signs that provoke certain feelings in the soul' (Sartre 2012: 10). As Sartre suggests, therefore, we have in effect two processes in the mind for Descartes. There is the normative process of reason, governed by judgement, and the causal process of the generation of images by the nerves and the body. 'Descartes posits both image and thought without image' (Sartre 2012: 19). On Sartre's reading, therefore, there is a veritable leap between the imagination and thinking. Even when we do use images or diagrams to work through a problem, 'the only function of these images is to prepare the mind to make the conversion [to imageless thought]' (Sartre 2012: 17).

If the body simply produces signs that move the soul, we have an effective Platonism of thought, where the ideas which form the basis for thinking itself pre-exist its encounter with the world. For Descartes, then, there is no account of the genesis of ideas, and no real encounter with the world itself. As such, the categorial nature of our understanding of the world is established prior to any engagement with it.[5] One way to overcome the sharp distinction between thinking and images is to follow Hume in reducing all thought to the plane of the association of images, thus excising Descartes' category of imageless thought. For Hume, ideas are simply copies of impressions, giving a simple account of the genesis of ideas. They are related together according to the laws of association, which in turn are modelled on the success of Newton in explaining the relations of bodies to one another according to the laws of universal gravitation. Thus, ideas are related to one another through the principles of association – their contiguity, resemblance, and proximity in time. This model, in turn, brings with it a number of specific problems, however. First, as Sartre notes, Hume has difficulty explaining the kind of abstract thought which is central to Descartes' account, as here all thinking occurs through images (Sartre 2012: 16), and because thinking lacks the normative component that judgement contains: there is no sense to an idea being false if it is simply a moment in a causal sequence. Second, if ideas and impressions simply differ in degree, it becomes impossible to distinguish impressions and ideas. Finally, as Sartre notes, Hume effectively reduces the mind to a realm of objects that can be brought to consciousness through the laws of association. In doing so, he is unable to explain why any of these objects in

---

[5] This claim that philosophy must begin with an encounter that draws us away from the self-contained structures of thinking as judgement will be central to Gilles Deleuze's account of the beginning of philosophy. See Somers-Hall 2015 for an extended analysis of the encounter in Deleuze's work.

particular has the characteristic of the focus of our conscious attention over any other. 'They are always present in the mind; however, they are not always perceived? Why? And how does the fact of their being pulled by a given force to a conscious idea confer upon them a conscious character?' (Sartre 2012: 15). Here, Sartre takes up Bergson's critique of mechanistic models of the mind, declaring that at best consciousness for Hume is 'a sort of phosphorescence' (Sartre 2012: 15) with no active power of its own.[6]

The final way of reconciling thought and images is that of Leibniz. Rather than positing a sharp divide between thought and images, or equating them directly, Leibniz argues that images are simply a confused presentation of thinking as judging. Thus, it is a result of our being finite beings that we are forced to represent what are essentially analytic conceptual relations as manifested in extensive space. Hence, when elucidating his views on the nature of space, Leibniz writes:

> As for my own opinion, I have said more than once that I hold space to be something purely relative, as time is – that I hold it to be an order of coexistences, as time is an order of successions. For space denotes, in terms of possibility, an order of things that exist at the same time, considered as existing together, without entering into their particular manners of existing. And when many things are seen together, one consciously perceives this order of things among themselves. (Leibniz and Clarke 2000: 15)

By seeing images as confused thoughts, Leibniz in effect introduces a panlogicism that Sartre argues can never explain the brute a-rational experience of a world of qualities (Sartre 2012: 14).

These three solutions, according to Sartre, capture the whole range of possible ways that we can understand the relationship between thought and the imagination once we have accepted the notion that an image is a thing – either we see it as separated from thought, or we see thinking as essentially the manipulation of images, or we reduce the image to a confused thought. In *The Imagination*, Sartre presents two contradictions which emerge from treating thought as the manipulation of images within consciousness. First,

---

[6] While Sartre applies this analogy of phosphorescence to Hume's mechanistic model of the mind, for Bergson the analogy is applied to models that directly attempt to reduce the mind to a physical mechanism. In *Creative Evolution*, for instance, he writes, 'let us merely recall that a theory such as that according to which consciousness is attached to certain neurons, and is thrown off from their work like a phosphorescence, may be accepted by the scientist for the detail of analysis; it is a convenient mode of expression. But it is nothing else. In reality, a living being is a center of action. It represents a certain sum of contingency entering into the world, that is to say, a certain quantity of possible action a quantity variable with individuals and especially with species' (Bergson 1998: 285).

repeating Bergson's criticism of Hume,[7] Sartre notes that once images are understood as passive objects within consciousness, we cannot understand their characteristic distinctness from perception. While we intuitively believe that there is a difference in kind between images and perceptions, an immanent understanding of consciousness can only leave as *probable* the difference between them. Hume's criterion for the distinction between impressions and ideas is the relative liveliness of each (Hume 1978: 1.1.1). Clearly, such a criterion does not provide a definitive way of distinguishing impressions and ideas. 'Why doesn't the image of the noise of a cannon blast appear like a weak but real creaking?'[8] (Sartre 2012: 84). We might follow Descartes in giving a more explicit role to judgement in distinguishing perceptions and ideas. Sartre quotes Albert Spaier as an example of this approach:

> It is in judging the agreement or disagreement of a sensible datum either with the system of my current external universe or with that of my imagination (which long, incessant trials have taught me to distinguish from the former), it is in making judgements of comparison, adequacy, inadequacy, belonging, etc., that I class an impression among real perceptions or among images. (Sartre 2012: 92)

As Sartre notes, such an account is once again phenomenologically false, not only because it can only give us probable knowledge of the difference between perceptions and ideas, but also because it misrepresents the immediate nature of our recognition of this difference:

> [A]t each instant there arises around us a multitude of little strange incidents, objects that move by themselves (in appearance), that creak and groan, appear or disappear, etc. All these fantastic events are explained upon reflection in the simplest way in the world, but at first pass they should surprise us. We should be, at least for an instant, tempted to rank them amongst images. (Sartre 2012: 96)

Second, Sartre points to a difficulty in explaining the relationship of thinking to images. We can only explain our own body's relationship to

---

[7] Bergson formulates the criticism that Sartre takes up as follows: '[The psychologists] will have it that these mixed states, compounded, in unequal proportions, of pure perception and pure memory, are simple . . . . The first effect of this error, as we shall see in detail, is to vitiate profoundly the theory of memory; for, if we make recollection merely a weakened perception, we misunderstand the essential difference between the past and the present, we abandon all hope of understanding the phenomena of recognition, and, more generally, the mechanism of the unconscious' (Bergson 1991: 67–8).

[8] As Sartre notes, there are instances when we appear to take images for perceptions, such as when we mistake a tree trunk for a man. As he notes, in these kinds of cases, what we have is a false interpretation of a real perception, rather than a confusion between a perception and an image.

a world of objects by treating the body itself as an object. 'If I can lift this book or this cup, it is insofar as I am an organism, that is to say, a body subject to the same laws of inertia' (Sartre 2012: 112). Similarly, when we view the mind as analogous to a mechanical system, we likewise leave no place for a spontaneous subject that would differ from the objects of thought that it manipulates. In rejecting the notion of a self, therefore, 'Hume is perfectly logical. His system must be accepted or rejected *en bloc*' (Sartre 2012: 109).

Finally, in his positive account, *The Imaginary*, Sartre reiterates Bergson's critique of the associationist logic of resemblance. Sartre poses this problem by asking how it is that we are able to see a music hall performer, Franconay, give an impersonation of Maurice Chevalier. The question is how this 'small, stout brunette' woman can imitate a man. Following Bergson, Sartre notes that supposing it is resemblance that operates in this case to allow us to see in Franconay the figure of Chevalier is problematic, since so few details are shared between the figure of Franconay and that of Chevalier:

> This intuitive matter [within which the image of Chevalier is to be realised] is very poor; the imitation reproduces only a few elements that are, more-over, the least intuitive in intuition: they are relations, such as the angle of the boater on the ears, the angle formed by the neck and the chin . . . . An imitation is already a studied model, reduced to recipes, to schemas. It is with these technical recipes that consciousness slips into an imaged intu-ition. Let us add that these schemas – so dry, so abstract that a few moments ago they could be read like signs – are engulfed in a mass of details that seem to oppose this intuition. (Sartre 2004: 27)

In describing how one is able to see Chevalier in the performance of Franconay, Sartre cites with approval Bergson's claim from *Matter and Memory* that resemblance has to be seen as operating prior to the constitution of the entities it brings into relation.[9] As such, once again, the notion that

---

[9] Bergson's claim in *Matter and Memory* is that once we have separated elements into a series of passive givens, the principle whereby they are related to one another appears to be arbitrary: 'why should an image which is, by hypothesis, self sufficient, seek to accrue itself to others either similar or given in contiguity with it?' (Bergson 1991: 165). The difficulty is that once we have reached the level of discretely determined impressions, it is impossible to determine the principles by which they are related to one another, primarily because their self-sufficiency means that they are not internally related to other impressions. For this reason, we require an external force, such as the active synthesis of consciousness, to impose a set of relations on them. If this act of relation is external to the elements, and comes after them, then we cannot explain how it is able to operate according to an affinity we find within them. Bergson's solution is to claim that 'in fact, we perceive the resemblance before we perceive the individuals which resemble one another; and in an aggregate of contiguous parts, we perceive the whole before the parts' (Bergson 1991: 165). The elements of the discrete multiplicity are therefore an expression of a prior confused multiplicity.

synthesis *operates on* the objects of the mind, as is fundamental to the model of thinking as judging, is shown to be inadequate. Instead, Sartre follows Bergson in arguing that the image itself is a synthesis. In clearing the ground for his own account of the imagination, therefore, Sartre takes up Bergson's criticism of seeing consciousness as an essentially spatial container for inert ideas. As we shall see, however, Sartre rejects Bergson's account of what such a synthesis consists in. As such, at the heart of Sartre's account of thinking is a rejection of the model of thinking as judging that we explored in the first chapter, but this rejection of judging sends us in a different direction to the one proposed by Bergson.

3.3 Critique of Bergson

In what way does Sartre's analysis differ from Bergson's own analysis? If we return to *Time and Free Will*, we can note that the original French title is *An Essay on the Immediate Data of Consciousness*.[10] That is, Bergson is concerned with the structures within consciousness. As such, while Bergson may develop a more sophisticated account of the image, this image is nonetheless understood within an immanentist context. This has a number of consequences. While Bergson believes that he has given an account of images that distinguishes them from perception by attributing to them a different form of multiplicity, as Sartre notes, this distinction is not one that is ever present to consciousness, since in order for a memory to be brought to consciousness, it must be actualised in a present image. Thus, while there is a distinction between memory and perception, it is not one that is present to consciousness itself. This difference in kind is only one of tendency, and is actualised only in differences of degree. Thus, Bergson fails to avoid his own criticism of Hume.[11]

Similarly, Sartre contends that while Bergson is correct to understand images as syntheses, his adherence to an immanent conception of thought leads him to conflate the process and result of synthesis. At points, Bergson considers consciousness as a process of synthesis, the rule whereby images are generated, whereas at other points, he considers consciousness as the

---

[10] See Lawlor 2010: 25 on the relationship between intentionality and Bergsonism.
[11] We can see here already the radicality of Sartre's commitment to the descriptive methodology of phenomenology in this criticism, which largely rests on the impossibility of making the discrimination *within* consciousness. This rejection of metaphysical explanations will ultimately lead to the development of a fundamentally perspectival ontology. Sartre is somewhat vague on the differences between metaphysics and ontology, but see Catalano 1974: 228 and Gardner 2009: 200–4 for interpretations of this distinction.

result of this process of synthesis. Consciousness is both what relates to the world and, given Bergson's continuation of the illusion of immanence, what is related to itself:

> [H]aving constantly confounded the noema and noesis, he was led to endow the syncretic reality he names *image* now with the value of a noema, now with a noetic value, depending on the needs of his construction. (Sartre 2012: 48)

In discussing Bergson's criticism of traditional accounts of resemblance, as we saw earlier, Sartre is sympathetic to Bergson's approach. He notes, however, that while Bergson provides a synthetic model of images that sees them as posterior to the resemblances that relate them, this synthetic model fails to give an account of the agent responsible for this synthesis:

> No doubt, it is already a synthetic organisation, and this is better than a simple association of images. But one seeks in vain, in Bergson, a positive description of the intentionality that constitutes it. Such is indeed the constant ambiguity of Bergsonian dynamism: melodic syntheses – but without a synthetic act; organisations without an organising power. (Sartre 2004: 60)

Despite criticising Bergson for failing to recognise the synthetic role of consciousness in the emergence of images, Sartre's relationship to Bergson here is nuanced. While rejecting Bergson's analyses of the implications of experience, Sartre at many points maintains the accounts of experience themselves, holding Bergson to have succumbed to a transcendental illusion. As Sartre notes in the *Transcendence of the Ego*, we do have an awareness of the self, much as Bergson described. 'The *me* is given as an object' (Sartre 1960: 86). The source of this object, however, is the reflection of consciousness on itself. We will return to this point later, but for Sartre, since consciousness relates to objects, when it relates to itself, it constitutes itself as an object for itself. While we take consciousness to be an emanation of our ego, Sartre claims that this is an illusion, and in fact the ego is constituted from our intentional acts. Thus, when we attempt to introspect, we discover an interpenetrative multiplicity, but this is an object transcendent to consciousness, rather than the source of consciousness. Nonetheless, Sartre claims that when we do reflect on our ego structure, it has precisely the structure that Bergson attributed to it:

> Everything happens as though the ego were *of* consciousness, with only this particular and essential difference: that the ego is opaque to consciousness. And this opaqueness is apprehended as *indistinctness*. Indistinctness, which under different forms is frequently utilized in philosophy, is interiority seen

from the outside; or, if one prefers, indistinctness is the degraded projection of interiority. This is the indistinctness, for example, that one may find in the famous 'interpenetrative multiplicity' of Bergson. (Sartre 1960: 85)

Sartre's ultimate complaint, therefore, is that while Bergson attempted to escape from the logic of things, even an interpenetrative multiplicity is still too thing-like. Bergsonian consciousness 'is clearly in no way an act; it is a thing' (Sartre 2004: 60).

'All or almost all have made the confusion indicated above between identity of essence and identity of existence' (Sartre 2012: 7). What is this confusion? Ultimately, it results from seeing images and the objects as contents of consciousness. While we see images as things that conscious-ness relates to, in the same way that it relates to its sense-data, then there is a natural tendency to move to the claim that images have the same ontological status as perceptions. The mistake arises from the failure to recognise that the imagination is not a faculty of thing-like images contained within a consciousness; rather, imaging is a way that con-sciousness is able to relate to an object that is absent. As Sartre puts it in *The Imaginary*, to be able to imagine an object is not to have an image of that object, but to have a rule by which we can intend towards that object. In effect, therefore, perceiving and imagining an object are not two different objects of the same nature, but rather two acts of different natures that take the same object. To use Sartre's example, when I turn my head away from this sheet of white paper in front of me, and fix my eyes on the grey wallpaper of my office, I can still relate to this piece of paper through my imagination. In doing so, it is the *same* piece of paper that I relate to. 'The sheet that appears to me at this moment has an identity of essence with that sheet that I was looking at earlier. And by "essence" I intend not only the structure but also the very individuality' (Sartre 2012: 4). At the heart of this claim is a radical transformation in our understanding of the nature of consciousness. Rather than seeing it as manipulating representations, we now view consciousness as relating to objects in the world. In making this move, Sartre takes up one of the central insights of Husserl.

3.4 Intentionality

It is by understanding of consciousness as a relation to an object that Sartre is able to overcome the illusion of immanence. Sartre's account of inten-tionality has an ambivalent relationship both to that of Husserl and to

Kant's transcendental philosophy. As we saw in the first chapter, Kant argues in the transcendental deduction that one of the key characteristics of our experience of a world of objects is that 'it must be possible for the "I think" to accompany all of our representations' (Kant 1929: B132). If this were not the case, then experience would become fragmentary. The 'I think' signifies that we are able to hold together a number of perspectives in a unified vision of a single subject, and thus to recognise in turn that those unified perspectives are of the same world. As Sartre notes, however, the 'I think' of Kant's transcendental deduction is not a subject responsible for synthesising experience. Rather, the fact that we are able to accompany any of our representations with an 'I think' is a clue to a transcendental synthesis that gives rise to the unity we find in experience. Kant therefore claims that what makes possible the analytic 'I think' is a synthetic transcendental unity of apperception that unifies our experience by relating our perceptions in a rule-governed manner to a transcendental object. Thus, the analytic 'I' of empirical experience presupposes a synthetic 'I' that makes our unified conception of experience possible. As we have seen, this model of synthesis is fundamentally related to the idea that thinking is judging. The claim that a subject is necessary to constitute experience is also held to by Husserl, for whom the transcendental ego holds together different intentional acts.[12] If consciousness is purely an awareness of objects in the world, then it would seem to be the case that different intentional acts would lack any personality. If intentional acts are pure, then we can show how we have access to an object only at the price of rendering different intentional acts essentially interchangeable. As such, for Husserl, phenomenology loses any sense that intentional acts are tied to particular individuals without the transcendental ego. Similarly, it is the transcendental ego that allows the same subject to tie together the variety of different intentional acts that it experiences into a unified experience by one individual. For Husserl, the transcendental ego provides unity and personality for the subject. Introducing a transcendental ego into consciousness comes at a cost, however, since once we have introduced the notion of a transcendental ego, we are left with the difficulty of explaining how it is able to relate to an object that is supposed to be transcendent to it.

---

[12] See, for instance, Husserl 1960: §45: 'The transcendental ego emerged by virtue of my "parenthesizing" of the entire Objective world and all other (including all ideal) Objectivities. In consequence of this parenthesizing, I have become aware of myself as the transcendental ego, who constitutes in his constitutive life everything that is ever Objective for me – the ego of all constitutions, who exists in his actual and potential life-processes and Ego-habitualities and who constitutes in them not only everything Objective but also himself as identical ego.'

Husserl's solution is to posit a medium that shares the properties of both the transcendental ego and the object, and hence is able to mediate between the two. As Sartre notes, however, this curtails the radicality of phenomenology in a fundamental manner. This medium, or *hyle*, prevents consciousness from relating directly to the object, as its relationship is now mediated. Furthermore, insofar as *hyle* is a structure of the subject, it effectively returns us to the illusion of immanence: consciousness now effectively becomes a container for an immanent intentional relationship to the *hyletic* object.[13]

Sartre's response to the question of the transcendental ego is to reverse the direction of explanation taken by Kant and Husserl. Rather than see the subject as the source of the unity we find within consciousness, he instead argues that it is a *product* of the unity inherent to consciousness: 'the *I Think* can accompany our representations because it appears on a foundation of unity which it did not help to create; rather, this prior unity makes the *I Think* possible' (Sartre 1960: 36). Before turning to the account Sartre gives of the 'I', I want to briefly present the three arguments against Kant and Husserl's positions that Sartre puts forward. The first two show why the transcendental ego is not necessary for the 'I think' to be able to accompany our experience of the world, and the third shows that the presence of a transcendental ego behind consciousness would actually prevent consciousness from relating to a world. First, Sartre notes that if the object that consciousness relates to is transcendent to consciousness, then the unity of this object can serve to unify our representations. Second, if we accept the kind of durational analysis of consciousness that Bergson puts forward, then there is no need to posit a moment of unity for the various acts of consciousness since these moments interpenetrate. In this respect, as Sartre notes, 'it is consciousness that unifies itself, concretely, by a play of "transversal" intentionalities which are concrete and real retentions of past consciousnesses' (Sartre 1960: 39). If Sartre's arguments here are correct, then there is no need to posit the transcendental ego. Sartre's final claim is that 'if [the transcendental ego] existed, it would tear consciousness from itself; it would divide consciousness; it would slide into every consciousness like an opaque blade' (Sartre 1960: 40). Sartre's point is that if we were to claim that the transcendental ego is a moment within consciousness, then consciousness itself would no longer simply be a relation to an object, but would contain a moment of opacity within it. As soon as this were the case, we would once again need to explain how

---

[13] See Sartre 1978: lix for Sartre's own formulation of these criticisms.

consciousness was able to relate to an object transcendent to it. So long as consciousness is entirely without content, and is simply a relation to an object, then there is no need to explain how it is able to relate to an object transcendent to it – consciousness is pure transcendence.

Given this account of the nature of consciousness as a pure intending towards an object, the question of where our notion of *self*-consciousness arises from naturally emerges. As Sartre notes, when we relate to the world, there is a necessary distance between us and the object, even if consciousness is a pure relation. Were this not the case, consciousness would collapse into its object. Even in situations where we do not appear to be aware of our conscious activity, it becomes clear on further examination that there is a moment self-consciousness. Sartre gives the following example:

> If I count the cigarettes which are in that case, I have the impression of disclosing an objective property of this collection of cigarettes: they are a dozen. This property appears to my consciousness as a property existing in the world. It is very possible that I have no positional consciousness of counting them. Then I do not know myself as counting . . . . Yet at the moment when these cigarettes are revealed to me as a dozen, I have a non-thetic consciousness of my adding activity. If anyone questioned me, indeed, if anyone should ask, 'What are you doing there?' I should reply at once, 'I am counting.' This reply aims not only at the instantaneous consciousness which I can achieve by reflection but at those fleeting con-sciousnesses which have passed without being reflected-on, those which are forever not-reflected-on in my immediate past. (Sartre 1978: liii)

What is the structure of awareness here? As we have just seen, consciousness is not an object, and so self-consciousness cannot involve consciousness of a particular kind of thing. Nonetheless, consciousness of counting here must relate across different moments of relations to the object, as counting takes time. Sartre's claim, therefore, is that consciousness of counting is a mode of consciousness. Given consciousness is a pure relation, then the consciousness of counting cannot be something like a quality added to consciousness. Rather, it is simply the manner of relating to the object. In this respect, Sartre's account of pleasure provides an illuminating addition to this account. As Sartre notes, pleasure is a mood that can only be considered as something that one is conscious of. It makes no sense to talk of a pleasure that one is not conscious of, though, of course, we can experience different degrees of pleasure. Similarly, pleasure cannot exist as anything prior to consciousness of pleasure. 'A potential pleasure can exist only as consciousness (of) being potential' (Sartre 1978: xliv). As such, our relation to ourselves as experiencing pleasure is unmediated. For Sartre, then, pre-reflexive consciousness involves an awareness that is not an awareness of an object, but rather of the manner of presentation of an object: 'nonthetic consciousness is not a consciousness one has, somewhat abridged or underdeveloped, of a reality like pleasure, anger, sadness, etc. Nonthetic consciousness is rigorously the mode of being that certain forms of being which one calls pleasure, anger, sadness, etc. take on' (Sartre 1967: 125).

Central to this account of consciousness is that it draws a distinction between questions of being and questions of knowledge. Traditionally, the question of self-consciousness has been understood in terms of knowledge of the self. That is, the self has been understood as falling under the same categorial schema that we use for judging objects that we find in the external world, as, for instance, in Descartes' characterisation of the self as a thinking thing. As Sartre notes, the kind of self-consciousness Sartre introduces cannot be a knowledge relation. If we did understand consciousness as operating in terms of knowledge, then we would have to see it as relating to itself as an object to which it can apply its categories. In this case, I would be conscious of both knowing and the known. In this situation, either it seems impossible to reunite the two moments into a unity, or we require a third moment to ground the relation of the first two (I require a knowledge of the knowledge that I know), and so we fall into an infinite regress. The only solution, therefore, is that there is a difference in kind between self-knowledge and the being of consciousness, Thus, 'it is advisable to conceive that the consciousness which I have of knowing, is not of the same type as that which is called knowing. What this means is that consciousness and knowing are two radially different phenomena' (Sartre 1967: 122). As such, whereas for Kant counting is a paradigm case of thinking operating as judging, for Sartre in counting there is a tacit awareness of the self that escapes from categorial determinations.

In separating self-consciousness from knowledge of the self, Sartre needs to provide an explanation of why, given this difference, the two structures have been conflated throughout the history of philosophy. In *The Imagination* and *The Imaginary*, Sartre relies on something like a Bergsonian account of illusion, arguing that the failure to understand consciousness properly rests on the presupposition of a priori principles at the beginning of our enquiry, namely our tendency to spatialise inner experience and hence to understand the self according to the categories of judgement. This claim is not rejected in *Being and Nothingness*, but Sartre goes further in seeking to explain why we choose to apply these categories in the first place. In this regard, Sartre reiterates Kant's challenge to Descartes in the paralogism that we can apply the categories of judgement beyond their natural domain. In the *Critique of Pure Reason*, Kant claims that Descartes makes an error of reasoning (a paralogism) in moving from the claim that 'I think, therefore, I am' to the claim that I am a thinking substance. This mistake essentially results from the application of categories that we can use legitimately within a circumscribed domain to know the world beyond that domain. Descartes makes this mistake because he fails to see that substance is merely a category that makes thinking of something as an object possible (this was the outcome of the transcendental deduction). Rather than seeing it as a way of organising intuition, he believes that it can be applied to all objects, regardless of how, and whether, they are given to subjects. Descartes' mistake is therefore to take this category that is used to organise something given in time and apply it to the *cogito*, which is not an object given in intuition. He is guilty of attempting to apply a determination outside of its proper sphere of application, by not using it as a form of synthesising intuitions, which leads him into error. As we shall see in more detail when we look at Derrida's account of transcendental ideas, Kant claims that the paralogism Descartes falls into is a natural result of reason's attempt to totalise knowledge. In order to operate, reason assumes that the totality of conditions of knowledge can be given as a *focus imaginarius* by which to focus the task of science. Descartes falls into error in taking this task of assuming that the totality can actually be given, and hence applying the categories to it.

For Kant, the analytic unity of apperception presupposes a pre-categorial synthetic unity of apperception. Descartes' error therefore emerges because he conflates two different levels: 'the unity of apperception, which is subjective, is taken for the unity of the subject as a thing' (Kant 2005: 240). In effect, therefore, Descartes applies the categories necessary for something to be an object for consciousness to consciousness itself. In reality, what makes knowledge possible – for Kant, the transcendental unity of apperception – is prior to the categories, and so cannot legitimately be understood as an object of knowledge. While Kant's claim is that Descartes failed to recognise that substance was a determination that could only be applied to something given in time, Sartre's claim is that a certain analysis of consciousness fails to realise that certain determinations only apply to it insofar as it is already understood within the framework of knowledge. As such, the same basic structure of the paralogism appears in Sartre's work. There are two pertinent differences between Kant's account and Sartre's at this point, however. First, Kant conceives the transcendental unity of apperception to be a posit that must be inferred from the nature of experience, whereas Sartre follows Husserl in developing a descriptive phenomenology of the world. Second, as we saw in

Chapter 1, Kant saw all forms of determination to be essentially categorial – that which lacked the structure of judgement was considered to be indeterminate. The implication of these differences for Sartre's model of consciousness is that unlike for Kant, consciousness as the existential ground of knowledge is present to itself. This allows Sartre to concretely develop a non-categorial account of the relation of self-consciousness to itself without having to see consciousness as indeterminate. It is only indeterminate from the point of view of knowledge.

At the heart of Sartre's paralogism is the ambiguous structure of consciousness. As Sartre notes, 'a table is a table, and that is all. This means that it is a table totally, without there being a presence of the table to itself, in a total indistinguishability, in an indestructible unity' (Sartre 1967: 128). Non-conscious objects simply are what they are. Consciousness, on the contrary, is an intending towards the world. While consciousness is self-consciousness, it cannot become a knowledge of self without a transformation in its structure. As a result, rather than a self-identity, 'presence to self presupposes a slight distance from self, a slight absence from self' (Sartre 1967: 127). We are thus in a position where at the heart of thought is a moment that escapes our discursive categories: 'Here is a phenomenon of being which we can no longer describe with our ordinary categories, which are the categories applied to being in itself' (Sartre 1967: 127). It is as a result of this non-categorial mode of being outside of judgement that we encounter what we might call the moral paralogism at the heart of Sartre's thought. As we shall see when we look at Sartre's account of our relationship with the world, in consciousness' engagement with the world, while consciousness cannot coincide with itself, it is still 'haunted by a totality which it is without being able to be it' (Sartre 1978: 90). Consciousness emerges contingently from within the world of what Sartre calls being-in-itself, and so is not its own foundation; nonetheless, consciousness *is* responsible for the way it takes up its position in the world and holds it together as a situation. This mix of contingency and responsibility is at the origin of our projects. Consciousness wishes to ground itself by coinciding with the being it emerges from, but precisely because it transforms this being by relating to it, such coincidence is impossible. As such, much as reason posits the totality of conditions as a *focus imaginarius* to make the project of striving for scientific knowledge possible for Kant, consciousness for Sartre is driven by the attempt to realise an unrealisable totality. Consciousness attempts to become one with the totality of factical conditions that it emerges from, but fails to do so precisely because it is aware of these conditions and thus transcends them. Consciousness in effect wishes to be governed by the same categorial conditions we would apply to objects, since if this were possible, it would escape from the responsibility for giving meaning to its situation, but precisely insofar as it is able to constitute its world as a world with a sense, it transcends the categorial determinations of objects. This explains Sartre's assertion that 'man is a useless passion' (Sartre 1978: 615). We are driven by a project of constituting our existence as a totality that is contradictory, since consciousness' mode of constitution is founded on lack. If consciousness were able to coincide with being, then being would become its own foundation. The impossible aim of consciousness, therefore, for Sartre, could be re-thought as the desire to become a self-grounding unity, or, in other words, God.[14] By conceiving of the being of consciousness in terms of the knowledge of consciousness, therefore, we posit the illusion of escaping the interplay of contingency and responsibility that defines the human. It is for this reason, for Sartre, that Descartes falls prey to the paralogism of conceiving of consciousness as a substance:

> In other words, if we use animistic terms to explain this, it is as if one were to say that consciousness wanted to be absolute being, like the absolute and substantial being of all things, all the while being consciousness. Basically, this is what Descartes is criticised for having done: for having conceived that thought as *cogito*, grasping itself, is at the same time substance, which is to say, a being-in-itself endowed with opacity and total adequacy to itself. If this was seen in Descartes, it is not so much because Descartes himself does it and says it, but more because, precisely, the whole tendency of morality, the whole tendency of human reality, consists in looking for a being at the same time on the level of consciousness and of being, so that it realises this synthesis of a for-itself – which makes itself to the extent that it is conscious of itself, which, as a matter of fact, is not the in-itself, and, consequently, has nothing absolute about it – and of an in-itself which is a being-in-itself in the mode of for-itself. (Sartre 1967: 128)

Ultimately, for Sartre, the difficulties one finds within the illusion of immanence stem from the basic structure of judgement. There is the recognition of the need for synthesis, but because of the illusion of immanence, this account of synthesis is understood as the manipulation of essentially inert mental images within the structure of consciousness itself. Such a synthesis is analogous to the Kantian conception of judgement as a '[function] of unity amongst our representations' (Kant 1929: A69/B93–4). When we reflect on

---

[14] As we saw in the first chapter, transcendental realism was also driven by the claim that one's relationship to knowledge was essentially only different in degree from God's knowledge of the world. This was essentially what Henry Allison (2004) called the theocentric conception of the world. At the heart of Kant's account of transcendental illusion is thus a similar claim to Sartre's existential paralogism: that one assumes no difference between a God's-eye view of the world and a human view of the world.

our conscious life, we suffer from an illusion similar to the paralogism that Kant accuses Descartes of falling into. We take the conditions under which something may be an object for consciousness for characteristics of the matter itself. In doing so, we transform what is essentially an intending relation to the world into a thing. As Sartre puts it, 'this affirmation [of the synthetic nature of consciousness] is in a relation of full compliance with the data of reflection. Unfortunately, it draws its origin from *a priori* ideas. It *complies* with the data of inner sense but does not *arise* from it' (Sartre 2012: 143). Echoing Bergson's claim once more – that the unity of life cannot be reconstructed if one begins with a field of discrete, passive elements – Sartre claims that 'it follows that the effort of psychologists has been similar to that of mathematicians who want to *recover* the continuum by means of discontinuous elements. They have wanted to *recover* psychic synthesis starting from elements provided by the *a priori* analysis of certain metaphysicological concepts' (Sartre 2012: 143).

3.5 Sartre's Account of the Imagination

Now we have a sense of Sartre's understanding of consciousness, we can begin to explore how consciousness relates to the world itself. As we have already noted in passing, Sartre's account of our relationship to the world centres on the ambiguity that where we are thrown into the world is a matter of contingency, but we are nonetheless responsible for the manner in which we give sense to our situation. For Sartre, the values we find in the world are not secondary judgements on a state of affairs, however, but are inherent to the structure of our situation. As such, what constitutes this structure is a pre-categorial synthesis that actually determines what we consider to be an object and a property, and organises these objects and properties in terms of our projects. As we shall see, this account of the world emerges from the rejection of the illusion of immanence, and the conception of the imagination as now a mode of intending towards the world. How does the recognition of the intentional nature of consciousness allow us to provide a more adequate account of the imagination? Sartre defines four characteristics of the image that form the basis of its distinction from perception.

The first characteristic of the image, as we have already seen, is that the image is not an inert element to be brought into synthesis, but is itself a mode of synthesis. The object of the image is not something within consciousness, but is rather that which is made present to consciousness by the imaging process. In this regard, perception and imaging, as well as conceiving of an object, can all share the same object, even though the manner of synthesis will vary in all of those cases.

The second characteristic is called by Sartre quasi-observation. While perception and the imagination both relate to objects, the imagination relates to an object as absent. This mode of relation is fundamentally different from perception, and Sartre notes, for instance, that we cannot know anything new about an imagined object by observing it, while perception constantly overflows our cognition of the object. Kearney nicely summarises the characteristics of the three different forms of intending towards objects that Sartre discusses as follows:

(1) the percept is a progressive complex of different real presentation: to perceive a cube is to present it 'gradually' and 'exactly' from all its sides

(2) the concept is a single and simultaneous knowledge of the conceived: to conceive a whole cube is to know all of its determinations (length, breadth, height, weight, etc.)

(3) the image, though 'simultaneous' like the concept and 'presentative' like the percept, differs from both in that it fails to provide an 'exact' apprehension of the object intended. (Kearney 1998: 60)

In setting out the difference between perception and imaging, Sartre once again draws on Bergson, conceiving the two kinds of synthesis at play as operating in terms of the two multiplicities of *Time and Free Will*. When we intend towards an object of perception, we can note that 'the object of perception constantly overflows consciousness' (Sartre 2004: 10). Its essence is given by the infinity of relations it holds to the world around it. A consequence of this is that in perception, 'one must learn objects' (Sartre 2004: 8) as they unfold. Sartre notes that, as with Bergson, the distinguishing feature of perception is that it must be lived, and Sartre explicitly repeats Bergson's example of lived experience of needing to wait for the sugar to dissolve in order to make sugar water.[15] In contrast, the imagination operates purely in terms of the knowledge I have when I construct the image. If I imagine the Pantheon, and attempt to count the number of pillars, I can only do so if I already know the number in

---

[15] Compare Bergson 1998: 12: 'If I want to mix a glass of sugar and water, I must, willy-nilly, wait until the sugar melts. This little fact is big with meaning. For here the time I have to wait is not that mathematical time which would apply equally well to the entire history of the material world, even if that history were spread out instantaneously in space' and Sartre 2004: 8: 'The perception of an object is therefore a phenomenon of an infinity of aspects. What does this signify for us? The necessity of *making a tour* of objects, of waiting, as Bergson says, until the "sugar dissolves".'

advance. No amount of scrutinising the mental image will add to my knowledge. In a similar contrast to perception, mental images do not require spatial or temporal context. 'The smile of Pierre that I represent to myself at this moment is neither the smile of yesterday evening nor his smile of this morning. It is no longer a case of a concept but of an irreal object that gathers in an invariable synthesis the diverse smiles that endured and disappeared' (Sartre 2004: 130). Finally, whereas perception relates consciousness to the full duration of its object, when we image an object, the time of the object 'is similar to the spatialised time that [Bergson] describes in *Time and Free Will: An Essay on the Immediate Data of Consciousness*' (Sartre 2004: 131). The reason for this is that the imaged object is complete. 'I know where I am going and what I want to produce' (Sartre 2004: 132). To this extent, even when the image I produce is one of a movement, it is always viewed in retrospect from the point of view of its completion. Thus, imaging is a procedure that, like Bergson's account of our representation of our mental processes, happens in retrospect, and replaces succession with something more like extension. Here, there is a sharp difference from Bergson. Whereas for Bergson, the two multiplicities were tendencies within duration, for Sartre the same two multiplicities are two actual modes of consciousness' relationship to its object, and it is this actual difference in kind that allows us to explain why we feel an immediate sense of certainty in discriminating images from perceptions. The reduction of time to measurable quantity made possible our practical relationship to the world for Bergson, and as we shall see, the same is true for Sartre, albeit in a rather different manner.

The third characteristic of the imagination is that it 'posits its object as a nothingness' (Sartre 2004: 11). Whereas perception relates to an object which is present to us, imagining takes one of four forms. 'It can posit the object as non-existent, or as absent, or as existing elsewhere; it can also "neutralise" itself, which is to say not posit its object as existent' (Sartre 2004: 12). In taking nothingness to be a characteristic of imaging, and being to be a characteristic of perception, Sartre sets up a radical dichotomy between the two relations to its object – in a sense, each opens out onto a different world. As such, Sartre notes that when I say that I have an image of Pierre, I do not simply mean that I do not see Pierre, but also that I do not see anything at all. As we shall see once again when we look at Sartre's account of our relationship to the world, at the heart of Sartre's account of how nothingness functions is Bergson's own understanding of nothingness. The final characteristic of imagining consciousness is that whereas perception is felt to be something that is passively undertaken, we feel that imaging consciousness carries with it a certain spontaneity. When I imagine a cube, I am free to manipulate it, to change its position instantaneously in a manner of my choosing. When I actually perceive a cube, I must wait upon perception itself to see a different perspective on it.

3.6   Consciousness and the World

In the postscript to *The Imaginary*, Sartre sets out a broader role for the imagination within his philosophy, and shows the centrality of it for his later work in *Being and Nothingness*. Concluding *The Imaginary*, Sartre asks of the relationship of the imagination to consciousness, 'what must consciousness in general be if it is true that the constitution of images is always possible?' (Sartre 2004: 179). Answering this question in turn entails asking whether the imagination is a 'contingent enrichment' (Sartre 2004: 179) of consciousness, or rather whether it is integral to consciousness' functioning. As Sartre notes, there is no special problem about the imagination within the illusion of immanence. Images and perceptions differ merely in degree within the psyche for these models, and the problem here is how we determine the relation of psychic objects to objects in the external world. For Sartre, arguing that 'the type of existence of the imaged object *in so far as it is imaged* differs in nature from the type of the existence of the object grasped as real' (Sartre 2004: 180) means that we have the same problem we found in *Time and Free Will*, namely how to explain the interaction of discrete and continuous multiplicities.

When we looked at the various characteristics of imagining, we saw that in various ways, to imagine an object is to posit it as absent, and to do so is to create a rupture in the real world. When I look at a portrait *as a portrait* (rather than as a material object), for instance, then, Sartre argues, the figure portrayed in the portrait is portrayed as beyond the world. If I change the illumination in the room in which the portrait is situated, for instance, I do not change the illumination of the figure in the portrait. The illumination of the figure is something set by the artist. 'Similarly, if the picture burns, it is not Charles VIII as imaged that burns but simply the material object that serves as an analogon for the imaged object' (Sartre 2004: 183). Now, Sartre's claim is that in order to be able to posit something that is outside of the real world, consciousness must be able to step back from the world itself. Without the ability to withdraw from the real, 'this consciousness could therefore contain only real modifications provoked by real actions and all imagination would be prohibited to it, precisely to the extent which it was bogged down in the real' (Sartre 2004:

184). We can gloss Sartre's claim here by noting that consciousness does not coincide with its objects, but is rather a relationship towards them. It is the imagination that allows consciousness to posit a distance between itself and its object through this ability to introduce what he calls the irreal into the world.

In fact, Sartre notes that there are several consequences to this view of the nihilating nature of consciousness. First, in stepping back from the world, we constitute the world as a totality against consciousness. 'If we can use a comparison, it is precisely in putting themselves at a convenient distance from their paintings that impressionist painters bring out the whole "forest" or "white water lilies" from the multitude of little strokes they have placed on the canvas' (Sartre 2004: 184). As we shall see, Sartre's claim is essentially that in taking up the real, we constitute it as more than a simple set of objects, and rather as a world of sense. To this extent, the nihilating power of consciousness requires us not simply to step back from the world, but in stepping back, we give significance to the relations between objects. There is thus a double movement attributed to the move to the irreal. First, the real is constituted as a totality through a process of stepping back from it, and then the irreal object is posited in relation to this totality. In *The Imaginary*, this process of constitution is rather schematic, and leaves many questions unanswered, but Sartre develops the theory in more depth in *Being and Nothingness*.

3.7 The Constitution of a Situation in *Being and Nothingness*

How does the introduction of a moment of absence lead to the constitution of a situation for Sartre? In *The Imaginary*, Sartre introduces the idea that the irreal object that is intended towards by the imagination plays an essential role in constituting our experience of the world. *Being and Nothingness* takes up this notion that it is the introduction of a moment of absence into the world that constitutes experience, but extends it with a more robust account of what this determination looks like. In *Being and Nothingness*, it is the introduction of nothingness into being that transforms indeterminate matter into the structured and meaningful situation of human existence. I want to explore this by looking at one of Sartre's central examples: Pierre's absence from the café.

In his example, Sartre describes entering a café where he is intending to meet his friend, Pierre. Pierre is normally on time, but today, as he looks around the café, Sartre realises that Pierre is not there. The question Sartre asks us to consider is whether this non-being of Pierre in the café is a real thing, or just a figure of speech. As Sartre notes, when we look around the café, the café at first appears as a 'fullness of being' (Sartre 1978: 9) – it is filled with numerous sights, sounds, and actions. Now, as Sartre notes, in order to perceive an object, we don't just need the object itself; we also need a background against which we perceive it. The kind of notion of a sense-datum that we find in Hume, a spot of colour, for instance, is incoherent – for a spot of colour to show up, it needs to distinguish itself from a background that differs from it. When we look around the café for Pierre, then similarly, as our gaze moves from object to object, people and things raise themselves from the ground of the café to become the object of attention, before falling back into the background of another perception. Eventually, we realise that Pierre is not in the café. Sartre's claim is that we perceive this absence of Pierre concretely against the background of the fullness of the café. When we say 'Pierre is not in the café', this absence is manifested to us prior to our actually making the claim that he is not there. This concrete absence is very different from what would happen if we said that 'Wellington is not in the café' or that 'Andy Warhol is not in the café'. In these cases, we would really just be playing with language.

There are several implications of this theory of negation. First, the example of meeting Pierre in the café shows that it is on the basis of our expectations that negation enters the world (Sartre 1978: 7). For Sartre, following Bergson, therefore, there can be no question of how being emerges from nothingness because the notion of nothingness always emerges within a context of beings. The fact that nothingness is tied to our expectations implies that to interpret the world in terms of nothingness is to fall prey to an illusion. For Sartre, on the contrary, while it is human beings who introduce non-being into the world, non-being is not, there-fore, abstract, subjective, or purely a matter of the limits of our language:

> It is necessary then to recognize that destruction is an essentially human thing and that it is man who destroys his cities through the agency of earthquakes or directly, who destroys his ships through the agency of cyclones or directly. But at the same time it is necessary to acknowledge that destruction supposes a pre-judicative comprehension of nothingness as such and a conduct in the face of nothingness. In addition destruction although coming into being through man, is an *objective* fact and not a thought. Fragility has been impressed upon the very being of this vase, and its destruction would be an irreversible absolute event which I could only verify. (Sartre 1978: 9)

Second, we should note that what Sartre is providing here is a theory of the constitution of a meaningful world, which he calls a situation. In the metaphor of the impressionist painting, marks lacking in all significance are brought together into a meaningful whole. Similarly, the elements and people within the café take on their significance in terms of the absence of Pierre. It is the fact that they are the background for his lack of presence that forms the café into a unity. In this example, what is constituted is a set of relations between objects. In *Being and Nothingness*, the account of constitution Sartre offers becomes more radical. Not only are the relations between objects constituted by our introduction of negation into the world, but the world of objects itself that we relate to is constituted in this manner.

In order to make this point, Sartre provides an analysis of determining the distance between two points. As Sartre notes, the condition for the possibility of there being a distance between the two points is that we introduce a moment of nothingness into the structure of the situation. There are two different ways of doing this, each of which will give rise to a different object. Either we understand the two points as points, in which case we introduce a moment of negation between the two that separates one from the other, or else we understand the two points as the limits of a line segment. In this case, 'there are two forms, and the condition of the appearance of the one is the disintegration of the other, exactly as in perception we constitute a particular object as a *figure* by rejecting another so to make of it a *ground*, and conversely' (Sartre 1978: 20). Sartre argues, however, that while there are several different ways in which we might organise the relation of points, it is a condition of possibility of any relation whatsoever that a moment of negation is introduced into their relationship with one another. 'The two points and the segment which is enclosed between them have the indissoluble unity of what the Germans call a *Gestalt*. Negation is the cement which realises this unity' (Sartre 1978: 21). Thus, in this case, it is negation that is constitutive of the form of the world that we find around us by separating the figure from the background. Without this moment, there would be no possible perception of a world of objects, but there are different ways of constituting the world as figure and background. In this sense, the constitution of a situation is for Sartre a process of decompression of being that allows distinctions to emerge. Here, once again, we find the influence of the imagination, which extracts and separates objects from their contexts, but also Sartre's account of the decompression of being has resonances once again with Bergson's claim that practically orientated perception operates by a process of isolation and extraction of elements rather than by, for instance, the introduction of new moments. Rather than a synthesis that takes place on entities according to the laws of judgement, we have a synthesis of dissociation that generates objects amenable to judgement.

Third, we have noted that what determines how figure/background structures are formed are my expectations, but these in turn are determined by my projects. The example of Pierre in the café provides a very local example of how an irreal can constitute a collection of entities as a situation. Sartre's claim that the sense of the world emerges from the organisation of entities around an irreal object does not simply apply in these local cases, however. Rather, the fundamental significance we give to life is determined by projects that themselves rely on our relation to an irreal object. My project of writing this book, for instance, does not rely on anything that I have already written – each sentence is in itself complete. Rather, my desire to write is founded on the object that at present is not – desire is this process of transcending what is present to what is not. In the process, value emerges as the positive value of what we transcend being towards, and as negative value in terms of what we move away from. Since the basis of our projects is something that is absent from the world, and it is this irreal object that gives meaning to our world, then we have a certain degree of freedom. As our project involves transcending the present, then the meaning of our past and present will be determined by these future projects. 'Who shall decide whether that mystic crisis in my fifteenth year "was" a pure accident of puberty, or, on the contrary, the first sign of a future conversion? I myself, according to whether I decide – at twenty years of age, at thirty years – to be converted' (Sartre 1978: 498). As what determines our actions is the meaning of the past, which is determined by our future projects, we have a degree of freedom. There is, however, a limit to the elasticity of our choice of projects, as the irreal object emerges in the context of the world, and hence is limited by the elasticity of that context.[16]

---

[16] The introduction of the irreal object into the constitution of the world leads to a sharp transformation of a central theme of Bergson's account of constitution. For Bergson, just as we saw for Sartre, the possibility of measurement rests on the introduction of negation into the world. The reason why the organism determines the world as a set of discrete entities is to allow us to engage with it practically. As we saw, by articulating the world as discrete systems, we are able to disregard those aspects of our environment that are indifferent to our form of life. For Bergson, the differences in the way the same object is conceived operate on the level of the species: different forms of life will extract from the world different aspects of interest to it, depending on their practical concerns. Sartre's approach mirrors Bergson's, but rather than seeing our world organised according to the practical concerns of the species, it is instead organised according to the practical necessities of attaining the irreal object of the project. Since this object isn't bound by our situation, but is generative of it, we have here a reversal of Bergson's account of freedom. For Bergson, it is in recognising the value of the deep self that we are truly free. That is, by understanding ourselves as durational entities, we contract our entire past into the present moment. For Sartre, on the contrary, freedom is tied to the power of

Finally, we can further note that the irreal object appears within a context. My project of cycling to the next town is only a concrete possibility if I actually own or have access to a bicycle. Similarly, certain projects are impossible without certain contexts:

> A worker in 1830 is capable of revolting if his salary is lowered, for he easily conceives of a situation in which his wretched standard of living would be not as low as the one which is about to be imposed on him. But he does not represent his sufferings to himself as unbearable; he adapts himself to them not through resignation but because he lacks the education and reflection necessary for him to conceive of a social state in which these sufferings would not exist. (Sartre 1978: 435)

It is only when revolution is conceived of as a possibility that the conditions of work become intolerable. In a stronger sense, however, this contextualism of meaning also implies a perspectivism for Sartre. Our world is not, for Sartre, the totality of objects, as it is, on some readings, for Descartes. Neither is it, however, the shared world of equipment that we find for Heidegger. If what determines the meaning and constitution of my world is its organisation into a unity around a central lack, then the meaning of constitution of different individuals' worlds will vary depending on their projects.

We can therefore see Sartre's initial analysis of the imagination as the first step towards developing what is essentially an account of the constitution of the meaning of the world. As he puts it in his early work, 'the imaginary represents at each moment the implicit sense of the real' (Sartre 2004: 188). The imaginary constitutes the world as a collection of entities whose meanings are related to my fundamental projects (a situation). It is this project of exploring the constitution of the kinds of entities and distinctions that are amenable to judgement that is at the heart of Sartre's account of the imagination.[17] This constitution takes place according to processes that differ in kind from the categorial. Freedom is thus the

the imaginary to institute a radical decompression of being, fragmenting the inherent unity of the world into a field of pragmatic and instrumental relations.

[17] Catalano (2010: 70) puts this point well: '[Sartre's] aim is to describe the metamorphosis of matter into a world of human existence both on the natural and historical levels. The Eskimos distinguished many different kinds of snow in relation to many kinds of needs, and we may wish to claim that these different snows would still exist, even if the Eskimos did not distinguish them. But then each snowflake and drop of rain is different from every other; each current of the air that stirs is different from every other; each hair on our head is different from every other, and each colouring of a sunset or reflection of lights from a leaf or a rock is again different from every other. How many "kinds" of things shall we claim exist in the world before we distinguish them?'

constitution of the articulations of the world through the relation of being-in-itself to a central organising absence within the world.

3.8   Being with Others

I want to conclude by looking at Sartre's account of our relations with others, since this brings together the perspectivism of our relationship with the world with the distinction between questions of knowledge and questions of being that govern consciousness. As we shall see, Sartre's analysis borrows heavily from Hegel, but rather than the introduction of Sartre's perspectivism being the basis for the emergence of Spirit, it is instead the point of fracture of our understanding of an objective, shared world. Sartre claims that traditional accounts of our relationships with others rely on an evidential basis for that relationship. That is, our belief in the existence of the other is based on an inference from, for instance, similarities between the movements of the body of the other and movements that I myself make. As Sartre notes, such an account of the other can at best give us *probable* knowledge of the other's existence. Such an inferential relationship to the other appears to contradict the immediacy of our experience of the other in, for instance, the experience of shame:

> I have just made an awkward or vulgar gesture. This gesture clings to me; I neither judge it nor blame it. I simply live it. I realise it in the mode of for-itself. But now suddenly I raise my head. Somebody was there and has seen me. Suddenly I realise the vulgarity of my gesture and I am ashamed. (Sartre 1978: 221)

Here, the presence of the other is immediately recognised, rather than being inferred. Rather than a probable inference to the other, my sense of the other is existential and immediate. Indeed, it is impossible to make sense of this experience of shame without reference to the other. Also, when we consider what the object of shame is, it isn't the other person that causes us to feel shame. When we feel shame, the object of our feeling of shame is ourselves in relation to the other. This suggests that the presence of other people in the world might not simply affect who we are, but might actually constitute an aspect of ourselves – what Sartre will call our 'being-for-others'.

Fundamental to Sartre's and Hegel's accounts of our relationship with others is the notion that this relationship must be thought of as a relation that is constitutive of consciousness. For Sartre, shame is experienced in front of the other, but it is also the kind of experience that constitutes an aspect of myself, namely my being-for-others. Similarly, for Hegel, my own understanding of myself is mediated through the other. As Sartre notes, '[in making] me depend on the Other in my being' (Sartre 1978: 237), the existence of the other becomes as certain as, for instance, Descartes' claims for the existence of my own cogito. In this section, I want to look at Hegel's account of our relationship with others in *The Phenomenology of Spirit* before turning to Sartre's criticisms of this account, and his own positive account.

Hegel's account of the other occurs in the analysis of self-consciousness in the *Phenomenology*, once consciousness moves to considering the truth of its enquiry to be itself, rather than an object in the world. Self-consciousness' initial understanding of itself, however, is purely abstract. It is the tautology that we dealt with in the first chapter of the 'I am I' (Hegel 1977: §167). At this moment, we can note that consciousness for Hegel has two aspects. As well as this abstract moment of self-identity, consciousness is also presented with a diverse world of objects outside of it.[18] Consciousness understood as pure self-identity is abstract, and it seeks to make itself determinate by opposing itself to the other, thereby introducing a moment of negation into its concept of self. In order to determine itself as self-consciousness, therefore, consciousness must be a movement whereby it returns to itself through a negation of the world outside of itself. Hegel attempts to show that consciousness cannot define itself by negating an object, since in negating the object, the object ceases to exist to oppose consciousness. Here, we have a structure much like the spurious infinite, where consciousness moves from object to object in an endless cycle of desire. 'Thus self-consciousness, by its negative relation to the object, is unable to supersede it' (Hegel 1977: §175). This presents consciousness with a problem. On the one hand, consciousness must relate to an object, but on the other, it still needs to be simply itself. That is, it must now

---

[18] Robert Stern (2002: 71–3) notes that the relation of these two moments is presented clearly in the *Philosophy of Spirit* in Hegel's *Encyclopedia*. Here, we can see that once again, the question of the relation of self-consciousness and consciousness is presented in terms of the problem of the one and the many. Hegel's solution will be to show that these two categories remain abstract if not brought into relation with one another:

> In consciousness, we see the tremendous difference, on the one side, of the 'I', this wholly simple existence, and on the other side, of the infinite variety of the world. It is this opposition of the 'I' and the world which has not yet reached a genuine mediation, that constitutes the finitude of consciousness. Self-consciousness, on the other hand, has its finitude in its still quite abstract self-identity. What is present in the I = I of immediate self-consciousness is a difference that merely ought to be, not yet posited or actual difference. (*Philosophy of Spirit*: §425Z, quoted in Stern 2002: 71–2)

recognise the need for an independent object, but at the same time be conscious of itself alone. In order to meet these two seemingly contradict-ory requirements, consciousness moves to a new dialectical stage: recogni-tion. With this stage, consciousness no longer negates the object, but rather 'can achieve satisfaction only when the object itself effects the negation within itself' (Hegel 1977: §175). Life contains negation within itself, insofar as it is finite, but in negating itself, it dies, and hence no longer exists as an object for consciousness. Self-consciousness, on the other hand, *is* capable of this process of self-negation. It is capable of denying contin-gent aspects of itself and affirming itself as a pure 'I', as the 'genus as such'[19] (Hegel 1977: §176). This process of recognising oneself through the other opens the way to Spirit, for Hegel, as consciousness now sees itself as intrinsically bound up with community. He summarises the situation as follows:

> A self-consciousness, in being an object, is just as much 'I' as 'object'. With this, we already have before us the Notion of Spirit. What still lies ahead for consciousness is the experience of what Spirit is – this absolute substance which is the unity of the different independent self-consciousnesses which, in their opposition, enjoy perfect freedom and independence: the 'I' that is 'We' and the 'We' that is 'I'. It is in self-consciousness, in the Notion of Spirit, that consciousness first finds its turning point, where it leaves behind it the colourful show of the sensuous here-and-now and the nightlike void of the supersensible beyond, and steps out into the spiritual daylight of the present. (Hegel 1977: §177)

In relating to another self-consciousness, self-consciousness finally meets the conditions of the movement of return to self that defines it. It becomes certain of itself through the relation to an object that is genuinely independent of it. In doing so, it no longer desires simply to recognise itself alone as self-consciousness, but now acknowledges the need to recognise the other as also a self-consciousness. While self-consciousness at this stage of the *Phenomenology* is still abstract, the essential structure of mutual recognition has nonetheless been deployed. Self-consciousness only becomes determinate to itself by freely recognising the existence of other self-consciousnesses. This process is mutual. 'Each sees the other do the same as it does; each does itself what it demands of the other, and therefore also does what it does only in so far as the other does the same. Action by one side only would be useless because what is to happen can only be brought about by both' (Hegel 1977: §182). As Hyppolite notes, the movement between the two self-consciousnesses mirrors the structure of the

---

[19] On the genus as such, see Houlgate 2013: 87.

infinite we looked at in Chapter 1. Here, each self-consciousness is determined by its relation to the whole, which in turn is simply the movement of mutual recognition itself. 'The concept of self-consciousness is indeed "the concept of infinity realizing itself in and by consciousness"; that is, it expresses the movement by means of which each term itself becomes infinite, becomes other while remaining self' (Hyppolite 1974: 166).

Sartre makes two related criticisms of Hegel's position, 'a twofold charge of optimism' (Sartre 1978: 240), both of which stem from Hegel's assimilation of the relation to others to the categories of knowledge. I want to turn to these now, before turning to Sartre's more general criticisms of any categorial attempt to think the other. The first criticism stems from Hegel's use of the notions of subject and object in the dialectic of mutual recognition. Sartre notes that the structure of consciousness is such that determinations in terms of subjects and objects only operate on the level of reflection. As we saw, consciousness effects a decompression of being that constitutes a situation, and it is as a centre of this decompression of being – as a creature that constitutes a network of distances and relations – that we first encounter the other:

> Perceiving him as a *man*, on the other hand, is not to apprehend an additive relation between the chair and him; it is to register an organization *without distance* of the things in my universe around that privileged object. To be sure, the lawn remains two yards and twenty inches away from him, but it is also as a lawn bound to him in a relation which at once both transcends distance and contains it. Instead of the two terms of the distance being indifferent, interchangeable, and in a reciprocal relation, the distance is unfolded starting from the man whom I see and extending up to the lawn as the synthetic upsurge of a univocal relation. (Sartre 1978: 254)

Insofar as I recognise the other as a subject, therefore, I am forced to recognise myself as simply a moment within their situation. On the one hand, rather than seeing myself as a subject, I see myself as an object in the other's world. The nature of this object is complicated by the fact that, on the one hand, the 'me' that is known by the other is one that clearly is in some manner who I really am. On the other hand, this 'me' is constituted by the gaze of another who has a different world to me. Thus I cannot be sure what the other takes me to be. As such, the look constitutes an aspect of who I am which is truly a part of me, but at the same time transcends me and is beyond both my control and my knowledge.

Sartre describes this situation as being one of 'transcendence tran-scended' – that is, rather than being a locus for the synthesis of a situation, I myself become an object for another. Similarly, the distances

that I unfold towards the world now become fixed by the other. Before
I felt the presence of the other, the distances I held to the keyhole and the
scene beyond were determined by my projects. It was I who constituted
them. Now that I am subject to the look of the other, these distances
become subject to their projects. This doesn't mean that I cease to unfold
distances in the world. Rather, I and the keyhole and the situation in the
room beyond all become part of a scene for the other's vision. It is possible
in these situations, of course, that I could instead transcend the other's
transcendence in turn, but insofar as the other is then an object for me,
they are unable to provide the basis for the structures of recognition, since
I myself am not an object structure, but rather a pure intending towards the
world. There is thus an epistemological pessimism in Sartre's thought: 'I
cannot know myself *in* the Other if the Other is first an object for me;
neither can I apprehend the other in his true being – that is, in his
subjectivity. No universal knowledge can be derived from the relation of
consciousnesses' (Sartre 1978: 243).

The second criticism is that Hegel is guilty of an ontological optimism.
As we saw in our discussion of the moral paralogism of immanence, we
have a natural tendency to think of consciousness in terms that allow for
the possibility of thinking of it as a totality. For Hegel, this totality is one
that relies on a plurality of consciousness, but it is a plurality nonetheless.
We have just seen that such a plurality is problematic since the relationship
between consciousnesses is not reciprocal. Where does the intuitive appeal
of Hegel's model come from? As Sartre notes, in the discussion of recognition, we have in fact encountered three consciousnesses, rather than two.
'If Hegel has forgotten himself, we have not forgotten Hegel' (Sartre 1978:
243). It is insofar as both consciousnesses are seen against the horizon of the
phenomenologist's own look that the two consciousnesses become objects,
and hence become commensurable with one another. It is only by the
elision of Hegel's gaze that we are able to see the two consciousnesses as
forming a totality. Such an approach operates not by overcoming the
inherent perspectivism of consciousness, but rather by elevating one perspective to an absolute ground of relations, by making Hegel's situation the
situation of all humanity. 'No logical or epistemological optimism can
cover the scandal of the plurality of consciousnesses . . .. The task which an
ontology can lay down for itself is to describe this scandal, and to found it
in the very nature of being, but ontology is powerless to overcome it'
(Sartre 1978: 244).

We can note, therefore, that for Sartre there is no way of reincorporating
consciousness into categorial thought by effecting a higher synthesis, by

opening up thinking in a shared world of distances, or a shared genus. When Sartre presented the main results of *Being and Nothingness* to the *Société français de philosophie*, the Hegelian, Jean Hyppolite, pressed Sartre on whether this moment of pre-reflective consciousness was a moment of immediacy. In response, Sartre alludes to Kierkegaard, claiming that 'I will say readily: there is no innocence; there is neither innocence nor sin' (Sartre 1967: 141). Pre-reflective consciousness is thus outside of the dialectic categories of the mediate and the immediate, as these both presuppose an orientation towards knowledge.[20] In his discussion of Heidegger, he pushes this rejection of an account of the other based on knowledge further, claiming that any kind of categorial understanding of the other is a falsification. If we accept that our category of the other precedes any particular other, we are forced to see the other as a specification of this category, much as Hegel sees myself and the other united in terms of a shared genus. Much as the claim that time is an a priori form of my sensibility prevents any connection with a noumenal time of objects as they might be in themselves, so a categorial understanding of the other insulates me from other people, since, 'as the law precisely *constitutes* its own domain, it excludes *a priori* every real fact which it has not constructed' (Sartre 1978: 249). Positing a fundamental ontological relation to others thus makes impossible any ontical relation. If our relationship to the other is not governed by any juridical categories, then thinking the other involves a radical immediacy or encounter whereby they are not, at least at first, taken up within the kinds of juridical categories by which I understand the world, but instead they open up for me, in a manner that is fully contingent, new ways of engaging with the world.

3.9 Conclusion

We can now see that Sartre's conception of thought is fundamentally at odds with that of the German idealists, even if, perhaps more than any of the other philosophers we will examine in this work, we still find within the philosophical edifice he constructs large structural elements from Kant and Hegel transposed into the setting of an intentional and existential philosophy. With the characterisation of consciousness as a non-categorial condition for the possibility of experience, we find

---

[20] As Sartre puts it elsewhere, 'Two things are established before any interpretation: (1) I encounter non-thetic consciousness in myself, at each moment I can dislodge it by reflection; and (2) it is not to that extent an unconscious if it is not a faculty of knowledge' (Sartre 1967: 141).

a radical revision of the nature of thinking. Sartre discusses many of the implications for thinking of his turn towards phenomenology in a short piece on Husserl's idea of intentionality (Sartre 1970). I want to conclude by just highlighting three of the positive implications Sartre draws out in this text.

First, Sartre notes that intentional consciousness implies that intentionality itself is pure relation that escapes from the categories we use to characterise objects in the world:

> If, impossible though it be, you could enter 'into' a consciousness, you would be seized by a whirlwind and thrown back outside, in the thick of the dust, near the tree, for consciousness has no 'inside'. Precisely this being-beyond-itself, this absolute flight, this refusal to be a substance is what makes it be a consciousness. (Sartre 1970: 4–5)

As we have seen, Sartre argues that we cannot see consciousness as a container for ideas. Rather, consciousness is radically outside of itself and amongst objects. This externality comes about through Sartre's rejection of the structure of the transcendental ego, which means consciousness is simply the decompression of being. As Sartre shows, we normally fail to recognise this radical externality, as we normally operate under the illusion of immanence, which has its ground in a moral paralogism. Consciousness' presence to itself in its externality introduces a radically non-categorial moment into the heart of our thinking about the world.

Second, thinking is no longer understood as the synthesis of elements:

> To know is to 'burst toward,' to tear oneself out of the moist gastric intimacy, veering out there beyond oneself, out there near the tree and yet beyond it, for the tree escapes me and repulses me, and I can no more lose myself in the tree than it can dissolve itself in me. I am beyond it; it is beyond me. (Sartre 1970: 4)

While synthesis does occur for Sartre, since consciousness is the decompression of the in-itself, this synthesis happens within being itself, rather than according to representations of being within the subject. As we saw in relation to the problem of others, the externality of consciousness also introduces the possibility of novelty into consciousness' relationship to the world as consciousness' experience is no longer mediated through its own categories. This implication will become important when we look at Deleuze's philosophy of the encounter.

Finally, and perhaps most importantly, once consciousness is understood as a mood of relation to an object, then we no longer need to understand thinking of an object purely in terms of categorial thought:

> Knowledge, or pure 'representation,' is only one of the possible forms of my consciousness 'of' this tree; I can also love it, fear it, hate it; and this surpassing of consciousness by itself – i.e., intentionality – finds itself again in fear, hatred, and love. Hating another is just a way of bursting forth toward him; it is finding oneself suddenly confronted by a stranger in whom one lives, in whom, from the very first, one lives through the objective quality of 'hatred'. (Sartre 1970: 5)

This affective model of thinking presents a decisive shift from the categorial model.

While Sartre introduces a fracture into thinking with his distinction of being and knowing, his account of the structure of thought is limited by the fact that the radicality of the split between the being of consciousness and knowledge of consciousness means that from the standpoint of knowing, we are often limited to paradoxical formulations in terms of the categories of knowing, rather than a positive account of thinking itself. In the next chapter, we will see how Merleau-Ponty attempts to develop an account of the structure of perception that overcomes this fracture by providing an account of the genesis of categorial thought from perception itself.

CHAPTER 4

Merleau-Ponty and the Indeterminacy of Perception

4.1 Introduction

Just as did Bergson and Sartre, Merleau-Ponty argues that there is a process whereby the true nature of thinking is covered over by understanding it in terms of judgement. For Merleau-Ponty, this process involves a forgetfulness of our perceptual relationship to the lived world of experience and a misunderstanding of the kind of synthesis that holds thinking together. This perceptual relationship to the world is the ground of an illusion that Merleau-Ponty calls 'objective thought', which holds essentially that all determinations can be understood in terms of judgements. Nonetheless, objective thought tends to forget its origins in a non-juridical mode of relation to the world. As we shall see, Merleau-Ponty notes a tendency to read back our reflective analysis of the nature of perception onto perception itself:

> The classical analysis of perception reduces all our experience to the single level of what, for good reasons, is judged to be true. But when, on the contrary, I consider the whole setting of my perception, it reveals another modality which is neither the ideal and necessary being of geometry nor the simple sensory event, the '*percipi*', and is precisely what remains to be studied now. (Merleau-Ponty 1964b: 14)

Merleau-Ponty's claim here is that the nature of perception cannot be reduced either to the synthetic activity of thought or to the inert matter of sensation. As such, prior to reflection, we find a different 'modality' or structure of thought that makes judging possible. In this chapter, we will explore this modality, looking at Merleau-Ponty's account of the structure of perception itself. I will begin by looking at Merleau-Ponty's criticisms of empiricism and intellectualism, and how these lead to his ambivalent relationship with Kant. Merleau-Ponty praises Kant for maintaining the privileged place of experience in his system, but notes that Kant's account of experience itself remains framed in the categories of objective thought.

In particular, Merleau-Ponty notes that Kant's argument that there is a difference in kind between the structure of intuition and the categories prefigures his own argument that perception is organised in terms of a structure irreducible to judgement. I then want to turn to Merleau-Ponty's analysis of the categories of 'up' and 'down' and of depth to see how Merleau-Ponty's account extends one of Kant's key arguments to show that the sense of perception cannot be understood through either judgement or association. I want to conclude by looking in more detail at Merleau-Ponty's differences from Kant, and in particular his use of the idea of a 'transition synthesis' as an alternative to the structures of representation at the heart of judgement. At the centre of Merleau-Ponty's account is the claim that sense, or meaning, cannot be understood within the structures of judgement.

4.2   Empiricism, Intellectualism, and Transcendental Realism

Merleau-Ponty's analysis of the failure of traditional accounts of meaning rests on a distinction between empiricism and intellectualism that has resonances with Kant's philosophy. In this section, I want to draw out these resonances. At the heart of Merleau-Ponty's project is the question of the origin of sense or meaning,[1] and in particular the different acceptations of the French word '*sens*'.[2] Merleau-Ponty takes Hume and Descartes as archetypes of the traditional approaches of empiricism and intellectualism, and argues that they share key assumptions that lead them to fail to explain how the world comes to appear as meaningful.[3] As we have seen in previous

---

[1] See, for instance, Merleau-Ponty's synopsis of his project, *The Primacy of Perception*, where he writes that: 'The point of departure for these remarks is that the perceived world comprises relations and, in a general way, a type of organization which has not been recognized by classical psychology and philosophy' (1964b: 13). 'The meaning which I ultimately discover is not of the conceptual order. If it were a concept, the question would be how I can recognize it in the sense data, and it would be necessary for me to interpose between the concept and the sense data certain intermediaries, and then other intermediaries between these intermediaries, and so on. It is necessary that meaning and signs, the form and matter of perception, be related from the beginning and that, as we say, the matter of perception be "pregnant with its form"' (1964b: 15).

[2] On the various ways Merleau-Ponty uses the term *sens*, see Landes' introduction to Merleau-Ponty 2012: xlviii. See Merleau-Ponty 2012: 452–4 for the connection between *sens* as direction and as meaning. Here, Merleau-Ponty argues that meaning has to be understood as perspectival, and hence directional.

[3] While I focus in this chapter on Descartes and Hume as empiricists and intellectualists, principally because both figures are also central to Kant's development, as we shall see, empiricism and intellectualism are sets of assumptions that Merleau-Ponty takes to govern philosophy and psychology from the seventeenth century to the present – Carmen 2014: 47–8 makes a good case for Daniel Dennett being classified as an intellectualist, for instance.

chapters, Hume claims that the 'first principle ... in the science of human nature' is that '[a]ll our simple ideas in their first appearance are deriv'd from simple impressions, which are correspondent to them, and which they exactly represent' (1978: 1.1.1). Impressions are simple, atomic elements that are immanent to consciousness. All of our ideas derive either directly from impressions or indirectly by being formed as a complex combination of simple impressions. Such simple elements hence provide a foundation for the sense that we attribute to the world: if an idea cannot be traced back to its constituent sensations, then we can take it to be meaningless. The interplay of a small number of principles can together lead to the generation of the complex ideas we find in consciousness through something analogous to physical causal interactions. A meaningful world is therefore built up from the associations between various simple impressions that together form complex unities.

For Descartes, relations of judgement, rather than causal relations of association, hold ideas together. When we encounter complex ideas, we cannot be certain whether the structure of ideas emerges from the structure of the object itself or from the influence of the imagination. Thus, when facing a problem, we begin by reducing it to simple terms meeting the criteria of clarity and distinctness, which we can know with absolute certainty, before determining the necessary connections between these terms (Descartes 1985a: 120). In both empiricism and intellectualism, therefore, we have the claim that meaning is constituted from the combination of simple ideas or impressions into complex structures; in the case of empiricism, through association, and in the case of rationalism, through judgement.

Merleau-Ponty's claim will be that both of these accounts are inadequate. I want to begin by looking at some of his specific criticisms before turning to his more general diagnosis of the problem. Beginning with empiricism, Merleau-Ponty questions its account of resemblance: when one object leads us to recall a second object, it cannot simply be the case that some resemblance has led us to move from one to the other. Humean association cannot be the foundation for sense, since seeing elements as connected according to some aspect is a precondition for applying the laws of association in the first place.[4] Presenting an argument with strong affinities with those of Bergson and Sartre, Merleau-Ponty notes that everything is like everything else in some way, and unlike everything else in another. As such, it cannot be simply the presence of an idea that leads to the emergence of another idea. If this were the case, then it would be impossible for us to explain why *this particular* impression or memory was called to mind by another impression. Rather, what allows us to associate one particular object with another is that we view an object under a particular aspect (or, in Merleau-Ponty's words, as according to a 'synopsis [that] makes possible the resemblance and contiguity among them' [2012: 18]) as *already* having a certain sense or meaning. It is the particular aspect under which we see an object that leads us to associate it with a particular something else. As such, meaning precedes and makes possible association, rather than vice versa (Merleau-Ponty 2012: 16–20). Here is an example that Merleau-Ponty uses to show how resemblance is conditioned:

> If I am walking on a beach toward a boat that has run aground, and if the funnel or the mast merges with the forest that borders the dune, then there will be a moment in which these details suddenly reunite with the boat and become welded to it. As I approached, I did not perceive the resemblances or the proximities that were, in the end, to reunite with the superstructure of the ship in an unbroken picture. I merely felt that the appearance of the object was about to change, that something was immanent in this tension, as the storm is immanent in the clouds. The spectacle was suddenly reorganised, satisfying my vague expectation. Afterward I recognised, as justification for the change, the resemblance and contiguity of what I call 'stimuli', that is, the most determinate phenomena obtained from up close and with which I compose the 'true' world. 'How did I not see that these pieces of wood were part of the boat? They were after all the same colour as the boat, and they match its superstructure perfectly.' But these reasons, drawn from having properly perceived the boat, were not given as reasons prior to correct perception. (Merleau-Ponty 2012: 17–18)

Here, resemblance and contiguity emerge once we see the world as made up of objects, rather than making such a world possible. Ultimately, empiricism takes its model from the natural sciences, and the relations it relies on are causal, rather than meaning-based. As such, empiricism doesn't have the resources to give the kind of account Merleau-Ponty thinks we need of the emergence of sense itself. Impressions relate to

Kant and Merleau-Ponty's theory of the body schema. While this is an important connection, Matherne does not take account of the important difference between the two models: that Kant's account of the imagination remains a constitutive account of synthesis, whereas Merleau-Ponty conceives of perception as organised according to what he calls a transition synthesis. We will return to the question of the imagination later in this chapter.

each other in the space of consciousness, much as atoms relate to each other in a space under the effects of gravity. In neither case is the notion of meaning appropriate. At best, we have the notion that associative connections allow the substitution of one impression for another. Rather than a subject who recognises the affinities of recollections and the present object, we simply have a 'mass of sensations and memories'. There is 'no one who could experience the harmony between the given and the evoked – and, correlatively, no solid object protected by a sense against the swarm of memories' (Merleau-Ponty 2012: 23). Rather than a meaningful world, all we have for the empiricist, therefore, is a simple play of impressions and ideas, with no subject to actually experience the meaning of this play.[5]

Merleau-Ponty argues that intellectualism emerges quite naturally from empiricism as soon as we discover a disparity between what we believe to be affecting our sense-organs and our perceptions (when we note, for instance, that a single vision of the world emerges from two sets of visual impressions). For Descartes, what gives unity to our perceptions is the function of judgement. In this sense, there is some agreement between Descartes and the empiricists, in that both believe that at root perception is built upon sensations. However, for the intellectualist, it is the subject that is responsible for unifying the various properties of the object into a coherent object, since the possibility of error shows that the object is not given to us as such. For this reason, even when we are dealing with objects outside of the subject, we are still in a position whereby we only recognise them as objects insofar as they are brought together by the thinking subject into a unity under the form of an object. The implication of this is that we don't perceive sensations directly, but only as organised by reason. Intellectualism therefore provides one account of how there might be the kinds of structures of meaning inherent to perception that were lacking for Hume. There is a structure to perception because perceiving is a form of judging. What is the problem with the intellectualist account of experience? Here I just want to highlight one difficulty with the model, which is that intellectualism collapses the distinction between perceiving and judging.

It seems to be the case that there is a difference between holding something to be the case and perceiving something: 'Judging [is] a position taking, judgement aims at knowing something valid for me . . . it takes sensing, on

---

[5] We can see here Merleau-Ponty taking up a similar claim to Bergson and Sartre that for the empiricist, consciousness was simply a form of phosphorescence supervening on processes of association.

Figure 4.1 The Zöllner illusion

the contrary, to be the giving of oneself over to appearance without seeking to know it or possess its truth' (Merleau-Ponty 2012: 35–6). This intuition has implications for the intellectualist view that perception itself is judging. Consider the Zöllner illusion, shown in Figure 4.1.

Here, the parallel lines appear to converge and diverge from one another. For the intellectualist, such illusions present a problem, since once we recognise that this *is* an illusion, they have to hold that we have two incompatible beliefs: one from perception that the lines are non-parallel, and one from reflection that they *are* parallel. For the intellectualist, therefore, seeing the illusion involves holding contradictory beliefs, but this is to mischaracterise the dissonance we experience when viewing illusions. Furthermore, the intellectualist cannot explain in the first place why the addition of the auxiliary lines creates the illusion as it is unclear why the addition of qualities would change those already present. Rather, judgement 'break[s] up previous relations and establish[es] new ones' that overwrite 'a perceptual syntax that is articulated according to its own rules' (Merleau-Ponty 2012: 38).

Merleau-Ponty's diagnosis of the problem in both traditions is what he calls the 'experience error': 'we immediately assume that what we know to exist among things is also in our perception of them' (Merleau-Ponty 2012: 5). This leads to the perceptual atomism present in both traditions. The characteristics of unity and determinate quantities they attribute to perceived objects are attributed to the nature of perception itself. At the heart of the empiricist and intellectualist accounts of perception, therefore, is the assumption that the nature of perception is merely different in degree from the nature of objects independent of perception. 'Through optics and geometry we construct a fragment of the world whose image can, at any point, form on our retina'

(Merleau-Ponty 2012: 6). Merleau-Ponty's claim here is not that empiricism and intellectualism necessarily hold that we have access to the world of objects, but that this world provides the norms through which we evaluate and understand the structure of perception. In this regard, Merleau-Ponty echoes Kant's characterisation of empiricism and rationalism as forms of transcendental realism. In the *Critique of Pure Reason*, Kant argues that both confuse appearances with things in themselves (Kant 1929: A490–1/B518–19), and thus combine a (transcendental) realism about the existence of space and time with the possibility of an (empirical) idealism, since it is impossible on this assumption to show that our internal representations correspond with objects within space and time. As Henry Allison convincingly argues, at the heart of transcendental realism is a 'theocentric' conception of cognition where human cognition of objects differs in degree from how objects would be seen from a God's-eye view.[6] Kant argues, conversely, that human cognition is discursive, and takes space and time as intuitions rather than things in themselves, and, since intuition has a different mode of organisation to judgement, involves a difference in kind from the direct cognition God would have, rather than simply being an inadequate form of it. Similarly, Merleau-Ponty notes that in empiricism and intellectualism, phenomena such as depth are understood in terms of a '*pensée de survol*' of the world that takes our perspectival relation to it to be an inessential feature of it. Empiricism and intellectualism are both unable to account for our lived experience of perspective because they attempt and fail to reconstitute it from a similarly objective God's-eye view set of spatial relations where depth and breadth are interchangeable.[7] 'For God, who is everywhere, breadth is immediately

---

[6] Allison 2004: 20–49. Merleau-Ponty makes the same point in several places. For instance: 'We began from a world in itself that acted upon our eyes in order to make itself seen by us; we have arrived now at a consciousness or a thought about the world, but the very nature of this world is unchanged . . .. We pass from an absolute objectivity to an absolute subjectivity, but this second idea is worth only as much as the first, and only finds support in contrast to the first, which is to say, through it' (Merleau-Ponty 2012: 41).

[7] Romdenh-Romluc 2011: 28–30 sees the distinction between empiricism and intellectualism in terms of how they understand the nature of the world, taking them to hold commitments such as assuming we can know the world in itself (empiricism) or not (intellectualism), and seeing consciousness as a part of the world (empiricism) or as separate from and constituting a world (intellectualism). She sees the reliance of empiricism on causal relations and intellectualism on juridical relations to derive from these conceptions of the world. Formulating this distinction in terms of claims such as these is problematic, since empiricists such as Hume deny we can know the world in itself, whereas in different ways, intellectualists such as Descartes and Hegel argue that we can know it. I argue instead that empiricism and intellectualism are distinguished by whether the sense we find in experience is constituted through the interplay of causal (empiricism) or juridical (intellectualism) relations (with both models of relation presupposing a field of determinate entities to be related). Taking the types of relations that constitute sense as primary shows why there is a tendency for empiricism and intellectualism to understand the world in the ways Romdenh-Romluc describes, but also leaves

equivalent to depth. Intellectualism and empiricism do not give us an account of a human experience of the world; they say of human experience what God might think of the world' (Merleau-Ponty 2012: 266–7). As such, we can see a strong structural analogy between Kant and Merleau-Ponty in the ways in which they carve out the space for their own responses to the classical philosophical approaches. Both see traditional philosophical approaches as illicitly presupposing access to the object outside of experience, with Kant arguing that such an object can only be thought rather than known, and Merleau-Ponty denying the coherence of an object outside of the perspectival framework. In this regard, it is worth noting that Merleau-Ponty explicitly adopts something similar to what Kant calls the 'indirect proof of the transcendental ideality of appearances' (Kant 1929: A506/B534), where Kant argues in the transcendental dialectic that the antinomies inherent to empiricism and rationalism can only be resolved by moving to a transcendental idealist understanding of the world.[8] For Merleau-Ponty, this takes the form of showing that neither the empiricist nor intellectualist variants of objective thought, which he describes as 'thesis and antithesis' (Merleau-Ponty 2012: 28, 181), are able to coherently formulate accounts of various aspects of our experience such as our relations to our bodies and to others, and ultimately, as we have seen, to account for the possibility of a meaningful world.[9] In the

space in each category for figures who develop different ontologies on the basis of those relations. Cf. Carmen 2014 for a more sustained analysis of intellectualism and empiricism in terms of sense.

[8] Here, Merleau-Ponty shares with Kant the view that the thesis and antithesis appear to exhaust the field of possible explanations, but that in fact both are false, and rest on the assumption of the independence of the world (in terms of objective thought for Merleau-Ponty, or transcendental realism for Kant). It is only by removing this assumption that we are able to satisfactorily explain the phenomenon in question. Merleau-Ponty's position differs from Kant in that Kant argues that the thesis and antithesis each appear satisfactory in their own terms, but contradict each other; for Merleau-Ponty, the thesis and antithesis are in their own terms contradictory.

[9] In this, I disagree with Gardner's claim that Merleau-Ponty presupposes a transcendental idealist position. Gardner argues that there are three possible interpretations of Merleau-Ponty's analysis of perception: that it 'undertakes an enquiry into the nature of perceptual experience for its own sake' (2015: 300), that it assumes a transcendental position, 'but only provisionally, as a hypothesis to be tested and confirmed by the discussion of perception' (302), or that it assumes, non-provisionally, a transcendental position at the outset. Gardner argues for the third interpretation, claiming that 'the *Phenomenology of Perception* should be regarded as simply not addressed to the naturalist or scientific realist: it is not intended to persuade anyone who is not already of a transcendental persuasion. Though this does mean that in one respect Merleau-Ponty is merely preaching to the converted, it by no means renders his argument pointless' (2015: 306). While Gardner does recognise the importance of the antinomies to Merleau-Ponty's philosophy, he argues that Merleau-Ponty's arguments from antinomies only emerge later in the work in relation to objective thought's accounts of intersubjectivity, temporality, and freedom (308), and so doesn't see these as being used to justify Merleau-Ponty's attempt to give primacy to perception (a thesis Gardner equates with transcendental idealism). I argue instead that Merleau-Ponty holds that objective thought is unable to understand perception as meaningful, since it can only understand the connections between perceptions in causal (thesis) or juridical (antithesis) terms, and each of these interpretations proves incoherent.

next section, I want to look at how this plays out in terms of Merleau-Ponty's analysis of one of Kant's key arguments for the difference in kind between sensibility and the intellect.

4.3 Kant and Merleau-Ponty on Symmetrical Objects

Merleau-Ponty's references to Kant are scattered throughout his work, and show a deep technical knowledge of the *First Critique*. Our initial impression may be that on Merleau-Ponty's distinction, we should categorise Kant as an intellectualist, but there are difficulties with reading Merleau-Ponty as straightforwardly making this move.[10] First, Merleau-Ponty's distinction between empiricism and intellectualism tracks closely the distinction at the heart of Kant's critique of transcendental realism. Second, Merleau-Ponty praises Kant for recognising that experience is at the heart of our relationship to the world. He cites an argument that Kant derives from his paradox of symmetrical objects, a paradox that Kant argues emerges if we attempt to understand the world in purely conceptual terms. Kant's target is Leibniz's transcendental realist claim that while there is a difference between God's thought of the world, and the thought of finite beings, this difference is merely a difference in degree. For Leibniz, all truths are analytic truths for God, in that all properties and events that happen to an object are contained within its concept as an infinite number of predicates. Since finite beings cannot perform the kind of infinite analysis of an object open to God, we cannot distinguish all of these properties, and hence our understanding of the world is confused. We

Merleau-Ponty's solution is therefore to reject the implicit assumption of objective thought and recognise the primacy of perception. As Merleau-Ponty writes:

> One of Kant's discoveries, whose consequences we have not yet fully grasped, is that all our experience of the world is throughout a tissue of concepts which lead to irreducible contradictions if we attempt to take them in an absolute sense or transfer them into pure being, and that they nevertheless found the structure of all our phenomena, of everything which is for us. It would take too long to show (and besides it is well known) that Kantian philosophy itself failed to utilize this principle fully and that both its investigation of experience and its critique of dogmatism remained incomplete. (Merleau-Ponty 1964b: 18–19)

[10] Ultimately, Merleau-Ponty sees Kant as falling into many of the errors of the intellectualist account, and Merleau-Ponty is clear on these limitations (see, for instance, Merleau-Ponty 1963: 201), but the degree to which Kant is seen by Merleau-Ponty as moving beyond the common assumptions of intellectualism and empiricism has not been recognised in the literature. Cf., for instance, Rockmore 2011: 193, who argues that 'Merleau-Ponty's claim about the epistemological importance of phenomenology rests on his critique of idealism and his assertion of the primacy of perception . . . Merleau-Ponty seems not to know much about idealism, which he refutes without adequately characterizing it.'

therefore perceive as spatial relations what an infinite intellect would perceive as conceptual properties. What are analytic a priori truths for God therefore become synthetic a posteriori truths for human beings (Leibniz and Clarke 2000: 15). Leibniz argues, therefore, that perception involves a confused relation to things as they are in themselves and one that only differs in degree from an intellectual relationship to them.

It is against this view that Kant presents the paradox of symmetrical objects. In his critical period, the main formulation of the argument is found in the *Prolegomena to Any Future Metaphysics*:[11]

> What indeed can be more similar to, and in all parts more equal to, my hand or my ear than its image in the mirror? And yet I cannot put such a hand as is seen in the mirror in the place of its original; for if the one was a right hand, then the other in the mirror is a left, and the image of the right ear is a left one, which can never take the place of the former. Now there are no inner differences here that any understanding could merely think; and yet the differences are inner as far as the senses teach, for the left hand cannot, after all, be enclosed within the same boundaries as the right (they cannot be made congruent), despite all reciprocal equality and similarity; one hand's glove cannot be used on the other. What then is the solution? These objects are surely not representations of things as they are in themselves, and as the pure understanding would cognize them, rather, they are sensory intuitions, i.e., appearances, whose possibility rests on the relation of certain things, unknown in themselves, to something else, namely our sensibility. (Kant 1997: 37–8)

Kant's claim, therefore, is that objects encountered in space have properties that cannot be fully captured in conceptual terms. Here we can take up the Leibnizian notion that concepts are relations between terms. If we think about the qualities and relations that make up a hand, we can note that all of the distances and angles between the fingers are the same for the left and the right hand. If an object were purely constituted through conceptual relations, therefore, it would be indeterminate in relation to handedness. There is thus an 'inner difference' (Kant 1997: 37) that exceeds conceptual determination. Kant associates this with the spatial manifold, and uses this argument to justify his claim that there is a difference in kind between intuition and the understanding, and that both are needed for cognition of the world.

---

[11] This argument also appears prior to the *Prolegomena*, where it is deployed against the Leibnizian conception of space, and in favour of Newton's view of space as absolute. He also deploys the argument in the *Metaphysical Foundations of Natural Science* (Kant 2004). See Buroker 1981 for an analysis of the changing uses of the argument, and its importance for the development of transcendental idealism.

Merleau-Ponty cites Kant's paradox of symmetrical objects to make two points about our relationship to the world. First, Merleau-Ponty notes that the paradox shows that 'there is something brute in our experience . . . . We have to install ourselves in an experience' (Merleau-Ponty 2003: 21). That is, the notion that experience is from a given situation or perspective is central to it. Kant himself recognises the importance of this non-conceptual element to experience in *What Is Orientation in Thinking?*, where he argues that it is the 'subjective distinction' (Kant 1991: 239) between left and right that allows me to orientate myself within space. A purely conceptual understanding of the world proves inadequate to explain my experience when 'if for a joke, someone had shifted all the objects [in my darkened room] around in such a way that the relative positions remained the same but what was previously on the right was now on the left' (Kant 1991: 239). It is the non-conceptual 'feeling of difference between my two sides, my right and my left' (Kant 1991: 239), that allows me to navigate the room. Kant goes on to note that not only does my orientation in the world require a non-conceptual installation in experience, but metaphysical speculation itself requires a relationship to our orientation in experience. When thinking of supra-sensible objects, 'we certainly do not turn the object into an object of the senses; but we do at least think something which is itself supra-sensory as capable of being applied by our reason to the world of experience' (Kant 1991: 240). As such, Merleau-Ponty sees in Kant's philosophy an early formulation of the thesis of the primacy of perception.[12]

Second, Kant's paradox of symmetrical objects points to a difference in kind between sensory and intellectual structures. If intuition were simply 'intellectualised appearances' (Kant 1929: A271/B327), as Kant takes Leibniz to believe, then the structure of intuition would be only

---

[12] Merleau-Ponty gives a number of definitions of the primacy of perception that vary in scope. At its broadest, he glosses it as the claim: 'if we reflect on our objects of thought and science, they ultimately refer us to the perceived world, which is the terrain of their final application' (Merleau-Ponty 1964b: 35). This broad claim is one Kant would wholeheartedly affirm, as *What Is Orientation in Thinking?* makes clear. Merleau-Ponty appears to take this statement at points as simply a methodological principle, implying that further claims about the nature of perception follow immediately from it, and at other points sees these claims as aspects of the primacy of perception itself. Kant would also presumably accept some of these richer aspects of the primacy of perception, such as the perspectival nature of experience and the difference in kind between perception (or intuition in Kant's case) and judgement. Other aspects, such as the importance of the body, or the claim that perception contains its own 'nascent logos' or sense, would be difficult to reconcile with his belief in intuition as a passive faculty. One might look to the *Opus Postumum* for a richer conception of the body and a more qualified account of the passivity of intuition (see Beiser 2002: 194–201), but it is beyond the scope of this chapter to determine the degree to which these changes bring Kant closer to Merleau-Ponty.

a confused form of judgement.[13] As Kant points out in the *First Critique*, however, there is instead a difference in the way in which concepts and intuitions are organised. Merleau-Ponty sees in this claim by Kant the seeds of an argument for the difference in kind between the structure of perception and the structure of objective thought:[14]

> The idea must be again taken up and generalised: there is a perceived signification that has no equivalent in the universe of the understanding, a perceptual milieu that is not yet the objective world, a perceptual being that is not yet determinate being. (Merleau-Ponty 2012: 48)[15]

What Merleau-Ponty is suggesting here is that as well as the causal structures of association, and the subsumptive structures of judgement, there may be a third mode of organisation that differs from both of the others. The organisation of perception, which gives sense to the world, would also be generative of our reflective categories of judgement without resembling them.

Merleau-Ponty reads Kant as presenting a philosophy of the situation where the brute necessity of thinking discursively in relation to intuition

---

[13] Compare Merleau-Ponty's analysis of intellectualism, where he writes that 'reflective analysis thus becomes a purely regressive doctrine according to which every perception is a confused intellection and every determination a negation' (2012: 40). This claim points to how uneasily Kant sits within Merleau-Ponty's characterisation of intellectualism.

[14] Merleau-Ponty describes objective thought as 'thought applied to the universe and not to phenomena' (2012: 50), which he takes to be the thought of 'common sense and of science' (74). As such, it presupposes the existence of a field of 'ready-made things' (99) with fully determinate properties. It is therefore the presupposition shared by both empiricism and intellectualism. It provides the basis for traditional scientific and philosophical enquiry by guaranteeing a common objective framework that is 'the same for everyone, valid for all times and for all places' (73–4), independent of the changes in perspective. The determinate model of the world allows for clear and distinct temporally invariant dichotomies in our characterisation of it (50), and hence makes possible traditional models of philosophy or science. The difference in kind between perception and judgement, combined with his contextualism and belief in objective indeterminacy, leads Merleau-Ponty to claim that while we can make judgements about the world, these judgements are always provisional and approximate. For instance, in the *Primacy of Perception*, he claims:

> When I think the Pythagorean theorem and recognize it as true, it is clear that this truth is not for this moment only. Nevertheless, later progress in knowledge will show that it is not yet a final, unconditioned evidence . . .. Thus, here also we do not have a timeless truth but rather the recovery of one time by another, just as, on the level of perception, our certainty about perceiving a given thing does not guarantee that our experience will not be contradicted, or dispense us from a fuller experience of that thing. (Merleau-Ponty 1964b: 20)

[15] Here I differ from Landes, who reads Merleau-Ponty as criticising the distinction between intuition and understanding on the basis that 'sensibility and understanding cannot be divided on pain of destroying the very structures of human experience and precisely because understanding is not a pure activity independent of its particular dialectical embodiment' (Landes 2015: 340). Merleau-Ponty understands clearly that for Kant, 'thoughts without content are empty, intuitions without concepts are blind' (Kant 1929: A51/B75), a claim reiterated in *What Is Orientation in Thinking?*.

signifies the fact that thinking must always be from a particular perspective on the world, and must trace its origin back to perception itself. As such, Merleau-Ponty emphasises something like an element of 'thrownness' in Kant's transcendental idealism. Given the importance of the interrelation of concepts and intuition, the point where Merleau-Ponty recognises an affinity with Kant, the transcendental deduction is obviously of central importance, since it is here that this relationship is worked out. As we shall see, Merleau-Ponty claims that the modes of organisation that each of these models ascribe to our psychic lives, the causal and the inferential, fail to account for the sense we find in perception. Similarly, as Dillon emphasises in his excellent study of Merleau-Ponty, neither of these models can explain our ability to learn, either leaving knowledge ultimately inaccessible (as in empiricism), or already given (intellectualism) (Dillon 1988: 34). Thus we find Meno's paradox played out across the history of philosophy. As we shall see, Merleau-Ponty's approach to thought aims both to institute a new model of sense and to rework the assumptions that lead to the problem of knowledge.

4.4   The Phenomenal Field

Merleau-Ponty's claim is that the inability to determine the origin of the sense of perception emerges from a failure to properly investigate the nature of perception. The key claim shared by empiricism and intellectualism is that perception is composed of simple sensations. Hume, for instance, characterises simple impressions in terms of the limit point where the sensation we receive is on the point of disappearing.[16] If we accept the existence of these givens, then complex ideas can be constructed by their combination, either through causal laws of association or through the synthesis of judgement. In order to develop a critique of this account of perception, Merleau-Ponty draws on the work of *Gestalt* psychology in order to show that this fundamental element of the classical model of perception is in fact never perceived. As Merleau-Ponty notes, experiments show that the basic unit of perception is not the kind of homogeneous unit presupposed by Hume's account. When a subject is placed before a homogeneous field, for instance, the subject quickly begins to perceive distortions in the field, such that patterns emerge on the surface of the wall.

---

[16] 'Put a spot of ink upon paper, fix your eye upon that spot, and retire to such a distance, that, at last you lose sight of it; it is plain, that the moment before it vanished the image or impression was perfectly indivisible' (Hume 1978: I.ii.i).

This points to the fact that perception is necessarily horizonal – that what we perceive is perceived against a background. This background is not a contingent feature of perception.[17] In fact, a 'figure against a background is the most basic sensible given we can have' (Merleau-Ponty 2012: 4). As such, Merleau-Ponty's claim is not that the basic unit of perception is affected by its background, but that the basic unit of perception includes its background. This recognition that the nature of perception is complex leads to a number of important implications that move us away from the classical synthetic model of perception. First, the notion that perception always requires a context makes the kind of foundationalist project taken up by empiricism and intellectualism problematic. We can no longer build up the meaning of our perceptions by a process of analysis and combination. Nonetheless, if sense is given in terms of the constitution of organised wholes, then we can see that the *Gestalt* model of perception provides a model of sense. Rather than sense being imposed on perception through a process of constitution that is external to the elements that make it up, we instead have an autochthonous mode of organisation. As Merleau-Ponty notes, when we look at a patch of colour against a background, we can see that our perception takes on certain formal elements. 'The borders of the white patch "belong" to the patch and, despite being contiguous with it, do not join with the background. The patch seems to be placed upon the background and does not interrupt it' (Merleau-Ponty 2012: 4). Even in the case of this simplest of perceptions, therefore, the parts that make up the perception point beyond themselves, and hence are already organised in terms of sense. *Gestalt* psychology investigates the way in which the elements in the perceptual field organise themselves, and notes that our perception operates in terms of a number of laws that determine the way elements relate. For instance, the law of closure shows that forms such as those in Figure 4.2 have a tendency to be seen as incomplete wholes, rather than simply a collection of elements. We cannot see this law as operating as a synthesis on atomic elements, since the elements themselves can only be presented as figures against a background.

Here, we can see clearly the differences between Merleau-Ponty's account and those that operate under the experience error. If one accepts the claim that there is a direct correlation between the cause of a sensation and the sensation itself, what Merleau-Ponty calls the constancy hypothesis, then as

---

[17]   Dillon 1988: 61 cites a number of studies by Metzger, Koffka, and Corso that show that 'even when, objectively speaking, there is a complete absence of stimulation, the subjects perceived figures against the uniform grounds, figures which either were generated somatically (heart beat, breathing, etc.) or were illusions'.

Figure 4.2 Forms demonstrating the law of closure

an object approaches us, it should appear to become bigger as it takes up more space on the retina. Such an account, based on our understanding of the object, fails to accord with our actual experience of objects. We do not, therefore, set up an exemplary shape for the object through a process of selection. Rather, size is something that emerges within a framework of different phenomena. As such, objects appear with an inherent size, rather than objectivity itself being secondary to appearances. As Merleau-Ponty puts it: 'if I hold my fountain pen close to my eyes such that it conceals almost the entire landscape, its real size remains quite modest, because this fountain pen that masks everything is also a fountain pen *seen up close*, and this condition – always noted in my perception – restores the appearance to its modest proportions' (2012: 313–14).

Similarly, we can note that while we consider objects to have determinate borders and properties, this is not the case with perception. When we examine our own visual field, despite the fact that the edges of the field may correlate with the edge of the sensitive area of the retina, we do not experience our visual field as having a determinate edge to it. 'We ought to thus perceive a sharply delimited segment of the world, surrounded by a black zone, filled with qualities without any lacunae, and subtended by determinate size relations like those existing upon the retina. But experience offers nothing of the sort, and we will never understand what a *visual field* is by beginning from the world' (Merleau-Ponty 2012: 6). This notion of indeterminacy brings us to the heart of Merleau-Ponty's criticisms of traditional models of perception. Similarly, Merleau-Ponty notes that children do not initially perceive a wide range of colours, but until nine months of age appear to only distinguish the coloured and the achromatic. As they develop, they gain a sense of warm and cold tones before developing a whole range of colours. As Merleau-Ponty notes, what we have here is not a failure to properly attend to the nature of colour, but rather a process whereby indeterminate qualities are thematised as consciousness develops. 'To pay attention is not merely to further clarify some preexisting givens; rather, it is to realise in them a new articulation by taking them as *figures*'

(Merleau-Ponty 2012: 32). Even the basic empiricist notion of a patch of colour is something that operates within a context that prevents immediate access to an atomic given: 'When I say I have before me a red patch, the sense of the word, "patch" is provided by previous experiences through which I learned how to employ the word' (Merleau-Ponty 2012: 15).

The space of perception is not simply organised, but it also operates according to normative criteria, though these are not the laws of causal or juridical modes of organisation. The figures that constitute the phenomenal field solicit privileged moments of perception that allow them to present themselves in their fullest determinacy. 'For each object, just as for each painting in an art gallery, there is an optimal distance from which it asks to be seen – an orientation from which it presents more of itself – beneath or beyond which we merely have a confused perception due to excess or lack' (Merleau-Ponty 2012: 315–16). As such, perception provides an alternative account of organisation to that of judgement. I want to bring in two examples here to further clarify the nature of this organisation for Merleau-Ponty: the question of up and down, and the question of depth.

4.5   Up and Down

To explore the orientation of our visual field, Merleau-Ponty turns to an experiment by psychologist George M. Stratton, who wore specially constructed glasses that inverted the image formed on our retinas using mirrors. After an initial period of disorientation, he began to adapt to the situation, and by the second day, the world appeared to re-invert itself. On this day, however, objects around him felt unreal, and his own body felt inverted. Over the next few days, his body appeared to right itself, so that by the seventh day, all perception was relatively normal, though there was still some disruption to his ability to localise sounds. When the glasses were removed, Stratton did not feel his vision once again invert itself, but the feeling of strangeness of objects around him returned temporarily.

Stratton's own interpretation of this experiment rests on a conflict between our visual and tactile sense-data. When we put on the glasses, we now have two different representations of what 'up' and 'down' are that conflict with one another. The resolution comes over time as one of these representations eventually dominates the other. As Stratton notes, the process of adjusting to the experimental conditions is accelerated when we engage with the world practically, which suggests that here the two representations might be most in tension. When one representation comes to dominate the other, the 'upper' part of our old visual field becomes associated with the lower of our new one. At first, this process is deliberate, but over time it becomes automatic.

The difficulty with this empiricist reading is that it assumes that when I put on the glasses, the orientation of objects given in the image I have inverts itself. That is, according to the image itself, what was up becomes down, and what was down becomes up. The assumption made here is that the orientation of the visual field is contained within it. Sensory fields, however, don't seem to have any kind of natural orientation to them. We might try to say, as Stratton does, that there is a nominal sense of up or down given to the visual field by taking as a reference point the tactile field that Stratton opposed it to. This field, too, however, does not seem to contain, in the sense impressions themselves, the kind of directionality that Stratton needs. The experiment shows that the same experiences can represent the world according to either representation. Similarly, we cannot take the image on the retina to be the foundation for our notion of orientation, as the orientation of the world changes even when the stimuli stay the same when the world reorientates itself. Empiricism thus relies on a correspondence between my experience and objective space that simply fails to hold.

What about the intellectualist reading of 'up' and 'down'? For the intellectualist, the notions of up or down are constituted through the subject – the *cogito* in Descartes' case, for instance, or the transcendental unity of apperception in Kant's case. The intellectualist presents an advance over the empiricist, in that they recognise that a subject is needed in order to give directionality to the world. Experience on its own is merely a set of relations between parts for the intellectualist that are orientated by the constituting activity of a subject. The kinds of subjects that the intellectualist proposes are subjects that are prior to any spatial context – the *cogito* is a non-extended substance, and the transcendental unity of apperception is by definition prior to any constituted spatial milieu. As these subjects present a view from nowhere, and simply organise given sense-data, there is no difference between experience before putting on the glasses and afterwards. In both cases, the objective relations, which the *cogito* uses to understand the spatiality of the world, are the same, and so the experience is the same.

In order to understand how orientation in the world really occurs, Merleau-Ponty brings in another study by Wertheimer that, like Stratton's study, involves tilting the visual field of the experimental subject. The experiment is set up in such a way that the subject sees a room in a mirror that is slanted at forty-five degrees. When someone enters this situation for the first time, they see falling objects as falling at an angle, and everything in the room appears to be odd. After a few minutes, however, the room spontaneously reorientates itself, and everything appears normal. What does this experiment tell us about how we understand our orientation in the world? It returns us to the distinction between the traditional conception of the body as an 'I think' or 'I feel' and Merleau-Ponty's conception of it as 'I can'. In terms of the sensations of the body, we can note that it is often the case that our orientation to the world is not reflected by our bodily orientation. When we lie down, for instance, we do not feel that the orientation of the room changes with us, and similarly, when we tilt our heads, although the position of our body changes, we do not feel this as an alteration in the orientation of the world. Our representation of our body position does not, therefore, carry with it any specific orientation. The orientation instead comes from our body's recognition of its possible practical engagement with a situation. Merleau-Ponty describes the situation as follows:

> What counts for the orientation of the spectacle is not my body, such as it in fact exists, as a thing in objective space, but rather my body as a system of possible actions, a virtual body whose phenomenal 'place' is defined by its task and its situation. My body is wherever it has something to do. The moment that Wertheimer's subject takes up a place within the apparatus prepared for him, the area of his possible actions – such as walking, opening an armoire, using the table, or sitting – sketches out in front of him a possible habitat, even if his eyes are closed. (Merleau-Ponty 2012: 260)

The feeling of unnaturalness, therefore, results in these two cases from the fact that my actions in the world do not receive the responses they anticipate from the world. Quickly, however, there is a progressive shift from one system of anchorage in the world to another as my body 'gears in' to its possible actions, and brings my perception and actions into line.

There are two points to take away from this. First, Merleau-Ponty's analysis of the directionality of space does not operate in terms of the constitution of space, but rather on the transition from one relation to our world to another. This move from constitution to transition will be critical to Merleau-Ponty's difference from Kant. Second, we can note that the account of up and down is Merleau-Ponty's own formulation of the argument from symmetrical objects. Just as Kant argues for the difference in kind of intuition and concepts through the inability to formulate left and right through conceptual relations, Merleau-Ponty does the same here for both causal and conceptual relations, in arguing for a difference in kind between perception and representation.

4.6   Depth

Turning to depth, we can see that here, once again, in the approaches of the empiricists and intellectualists our experience of space is derived from a prior objective model of space. Taking Berkeley, his claim is that we do not have a direct impression of depth. Rather, it is extrapolated from our experience of the world:

> It is, I think, agreed by all that distance, of itself and immediately, cannot be seen. For distance being a Line directed end-wise to the eye, it projects only one point in the fund of the eye, which point remains invariably the same, whether the distance be longer or shorter. (Berkeley 2009: §2)

Descartes' intellectualist account operates along similar lines. The Cartesian subject seeing himself in a mirror, according to Merleau-Ponty's interpretation, does not see himself, but rather an image impressed on the retina. In developing his view, Descartes draws an analogy with the art of engravings, where the illusion of perspective is generated through the deliberate deformation of the space of the image:

> Moreover, in accordance with the rules of perspective they often represent circles by ovals better than by other circles, squares by rhombuses better than by other squares, and similarly for other shapes. Thus it often happens that in order to be more perfect as an image and to represent an object better, an engraving ought not to resemble it. (Descartes 1985a: 113)

In order for the painting to represent the object, it is necessary that square shapes take on the form of rectangles, and circles take on the form of ovals. In this case, the operation of seeing a painting is conceived of as an intellectual operation – that of reading the work as if it were a text. The painting provides the cues with which to reconstruct a three-dimensional representation from the lines of projection and relation of forms present within the image. Thus, by recognising that certain forms are both present and obscured by one another within the picture, we are able to 'see a space where there is none' (Merleau-Ponty 1964a: 172). Depth, therefore, for Descartes is a third dimension that is generated from those present.

   What both of these models share is that while they attempt to explain the genesis of depth, they in fact presuppose a conception of space. Depth is derived from an objective realm that pre-exists the subject. An understanding of depth in this way – a depth which is identical to breadth from another point of view – is simply not an accurate account of what it is to experience space from a given perspective. As Merleau-Ponty notes:

By immediately assimilating depth and breadth, both philosophies assume as self-evident the result of a constitutive labour whose phases we must, on the contrary, retrace. In order to treat depth as a breadth considered in profile and to arrive at an isotropic space, the subject must leave his place, his view upon the world, and conceive himself in a sort of ubiquity. For God, who is everywhere, breadth is immediately equivalent to depth. Intellectualism and empiricism do not give us an account of the human experience of the world; they say of human experience what God might think of the world. (Merleau-Ponty 2012: 266–7)

While representation attempts to derive the field of depth from the two given dimensions, thus characterising depth itself as an axis of extended space, Merleau-Ponty reverses this procedure. That is, rather than seeing depth as derived from the given dimensions, he sees it as that by which the given dimensions of extensity are given to us. Depth is not merely breadth seen from another angle, but rather something different in kind that, by making possible a field of autonomous but interrelated objects, also makes possible the system of extensive distances taken as foundational by representation.

Once depth is understood in this way, we can no longer call it a third dimension. In the first place, if it were a dimension, it would be the first one; there are forms and definite planes only if it is stipulated how far from me their different parts are. But a *first* dimension that contains all the others is no longer a dimension, at least in the ordinary sense of a *certain relationship* according to which we make measurements. Depth thus understood is, rather, the experience of the reversibility of dimensions, of a global 'locality' – everything in the same place at the same time, a locality from which height, width, and depth are abstracted, of a voluminosity we express when we say that a thing is *there*. (Merleau-Ponty 1964a: 180)

As Merleau-Ponty notes, this primordial depth is no longer simply a 'container' for objects and qualities which are found within it. Rather, depth is here seen as the horizon against which the axes of homogeneous space are formed. In *Eye and Mind*, he makes the claim that the enigma of depth is one of the primary inspirations of modern painting, and takes the work of Paul Klee and Paul Cézanne as exemplary of the new project of showing 'how the things become things, how the world becomes world' (Merleau-Ponty 1964a: 181). For Descartes, perspective is governed by a rational and intellectual set of rules that allow us to precisely specify the world, and in this regard, the works of art he favours are those that construct their perspectives according to the Renaissance techniques of projective geometry. In focusing on etchings, Descartes chooses an art form where the lines that constitute the space of the scene are fully determinate, and where no ambiguous properties such as colour remain. It is an art form that aligns itself most perfectly to Descartes' account of the substance of the world. Merleau-Ponty takes as his champion Paul Cézanne, for whom,

> In giving up the outline, Cézanne was abandoning himself to the chaos of sensation, which would upset the objects and constantly suggest illusions, as, for example, the illusion we have when we move our heads that objects themselves are moving – if our judgement did not constantly set these appearances straight. (Merleau-Ponty 1993: 63)

Here we can come to one of the key distinctions between what Merleau-Ponty finds in Cézanne and what Descartes found in Renaissance art. Descartes essentially sees perspective as an intellectual puzzle. We use our judgement to determine depth in a painting. A painting is therefore something that allows us to reconstruct an image in our minds, but 'reading' a painting is something that *we* do. Now, if Merleau-Ponty and Cézanne are right that Cézanne lends himself to the chaos of sensation before our reflection on the world, then the organisation we find in his painting is not the consciously imposed organisation of the kind we find in Renaissance work. Rather, what is captured is the way in which sensations organise themselves, much like the next note in a melody appears to follow of its own accord from those that come before. Depth here is the horizonal condition that allows these sensations and objects to present themselves. It is insofar as depth allows objects to obscure one another that it also allows them to communicate.

4.7   Merleau-Ponty's Critique of the Transcendental Deduction

I now want to move on to reconstruct where Merleau-Ponty thinks that Kant's account of experience goes wrong. To begin with a brief summary of the intuitions driving his criticisms, Merleau-Ponty argues that Kant's approach presupposes our perceptual relationship to the world – that 'when Kant justifies each step of his Analytic with the famous refrain "if a world is to be possible," he emphasises that his guideline is furnished him by the unreflected image of the world' (Merleau-Ponty 1968: 34). While Kant recognises this initial moment of unreflective engagement with the world, Kant fails to recognise that there are other modes of possible synthesis than reflection, and hence fails to recognise that our primary engagement with the world has a structure that is different in kind from the structure of reflection. Thus, it operates 'in a style that is not the sole possible one', and 'mixes in presuppositions which we have to examine and which in the end reveal themselves to be contrary to what inspires the reflection' (Merleau-Ponty 1968: 32). Merleau-Ponty's criticism of Kant is therefore that he effectively falls foul of a transcendental illusion when he takes judgement to be the sole possible model for synthesis of representations. Kant begins with the notion of experience as 'mutilated thought' (Merleau-Ponty 1968: 35), and then through the transcendental method attempts to show what this notion of experience would presuppose. 'It thinks it can comprehend our natal bond with the world only by *undoing* it in order to *remake* it, only by constituting it, by fabricating it' (Merleau-Ponty 1968: 32). As we shall see, Merleau-Ponty's criticism, while focused on the question of judgement, moves beyond intellectualism, also showing the limitations of Kant's account of the synthetic role of imagination. Rejecting this assumption leads to a series of revisions of key Kantian claims. Merleau-Ponty's claim will be that in arguing that the 'I think' must be able to accompany all of our representations, Kant implicitly characterises our perceptions of the world as something analogous to propositions which can all be simultaneously held in the mind. A proper analysis of the nature of perception shows this assumption is illegitimate. The nature of perception as involving a horizon leads to a rather different conception of the subject, synthesis, and the nature of the object. In effect, Merleau-Ponty accuses Kant of covering over a non-categorial synthesis of perception with the categorial model of the transcendental deduction, and hence understanding the constitution of experience in terms of a false movement. Merleau-Ponty never develops a sustained criticism of Kant, and so to tie together his scattered comments, I want to structure my account in terms of three questions. First, I want to ask, what is the unreflected image of the world that Merleau-Ponty begins with? The second question follows from this. If experience does not have the character that Kant assumes, then what gives unity to experience? As we shall see, Merleau-Ponty here argues for an alternative to what we might call a juridical model of synthesis, introducing the notion of a 'transition synthesis'. The final question is, given Merleau-Ponty's critique of Kant is based on Kant's misrepresentation of experience, how is it that Kant mischaracterises something so fundamental as the structure of experience?

4.8   The Unreflected Image of the World

In criticising empiricism and intellectualism, Merleau-Ponty's target initially appears to be the atomism at the heart of both accounts. Kant also argues in the third analogy, however, that objects cannot be seen in isolation from each other. 'All substances, so far as they can be perceived in space as coexisting, are in thoroughgoing interaction' (Kant 1929: B256). What is important to note about Merleau-Ponty's criticisms of Kant, therefore, is that they go beyond a criticism purely of atomism: 'Psychological atomism is but a particular case of a more general prejudice: the unquestioned belief in determinate being and in the world' (Merleau-Ponty 2012: 510). This generalisation of the claim is important, and we have already seen the notion of indeterminacy at play in Merleau-Ponty's accounts of the edges of our perceptual fields, and the nature of attention in children.

The reference to the wider problem of determinate being makes clear that there is a sharp divide between Merleau-Ponty and other figures who might also reject atomism, including both Kant and Hegel. As we noted earlier, Kant argues in the analogies that 'there is a unity of nature in the connection of all appearances' (Kant 1929: A216/B263). Here, Kant argues that this unity of nature has to be understood as something internal to experience, rather than being simply a metaphysical or psychological principle. 'Taken together, the analogies thus declare that all appearances lie, and must lie, in *one* nature, because without this *a priori* unity no unity of experience, and therefore no determination of objects in it, would be possible' (Kant 1929: A216/B263). While Kant's claims in the analogies point to the need to understand nature as a unified system, the notion of unity here is at best organic, with each object a fully determinate entity in reciprocal relations with other objects. For Merleau-Ponty, too, our experience of the world is one of a unity, but this unity is between a determinate object and a field of indeterminacy. Returning to the theme of attention, Merleau-Ponty writes, 'the act of attention is, however, at least rooted in the life of consciousness, and we can finally understand that it emerges from its indifferent freedom to give itself a present object. The passage from the indeterminate to the determinate, this continuous taking up again of its own history in the unity of a new sense, is thought itself' (Merleau-Ponty 2012: 33). There is no equivalent notion in Kant's thought. While his *Critique of Judgment* does include the notion of indeterminacy, this is only as a yet-to-be-completed determination achieved through reflective judgement.

We can also relate this question of determinacy to Hegel's thought.[18] In Chapter 1, we noted that Hegel's account of the finite and the infinite

[18] Berendzen 2009: 165 is wrong to argue that Merleau-Ponty 'obviously falls' into the Hegelian tradition of overcoming Kantian dualisms. In fact, Merleau-Ponty's brief but pivotal reference to Kierkegaard in defining objective thought (Merleau-Ponty 2012: 74) suggests that Merleau-Ponty is better situated in the tradition of reaction to Hegel's approach to philosophy.

involved demonstrating that each category implied the other. This is a specific instance of a more general claim asserted in Hegel's work: that determination requires mediation. In *The Phenomenology of Spirit*, Hegel begins by showing that an immediate relationship to an object, while appearing to be the most determinate relationship we can have, is actually the most bare universal conception of it. Similarly, in the *Science of Logic*, Hegel begins with the notion of pure being. As he demonstrates, such a conception of being lacking in all determinations turns out to be unstable. 'Being, the indeterminate immediate, is in fact *nothing*, and neither more nor less than *nothing*' (Hegel 1989: 82). Since nothing also lacks all determination or content, it proves to be indistinguishable from being. With 'no diversity within itself nor any with a reference outwards' (Hegel 1989: 82), we have an immediate transition between the two terms. We can take from this the implication that the kind of atomism we introduced as the target of Merleau-Ponty's thought is also one of the targets of Hegel's speculative thought. When Hegel writes that 'being – does not pass over but has passed over – into nothing, and nothing into being' (1989: 82–3), he is drawing out an implication that we cannot make sense of these categories. In fact, we must already think them in relation to one another, since 'their truth is, therefore, this immediate vanishing of the one into the other' (Hegel 1989: 83). In claiming that being and nothing can only be thought in terms of their relationship to one another, does he anticipate Merleau-Ponty's account of determination?

The reference to the wider problem of determinate being makes clear that there is a sharp divide between Merleau-Ponty and Hegel here, and that the figure/background structure is something that departs radically from what we find in Hegel's thought. To develop a sense of these differences, we can turn to the dialectic which precedes the dialectic of the finite and the infinite: the dialectic of something and other. This dialectic emerges from the fact that determinate being for Hegel proves to be more than the simple unity of being and nothing (or reality and negation). Rather, these two terms need to be in relation to one another. As Hegel somewhat cryptically puts it, 'something is the *first negation of negation*, as simple self-relation in the form of being' (1989: 115). By this, Hegel loosely means that as well as the negative moment that gives determinacy to determinate being, there is a second moment, whereby this difference inherent to determinate being is negated, or overcome. Now, as Hegel notes,[19] understanding something as the relation of being and negation

---

[19] I am here following Houlgate's (2006: 321–3) interpretation of some very difficult passages in Hegel 1989: 116.

can be understood in two different ways, depending on whether we see the difference of being from nothing overcome, or the difference of nothing from being. Thus, as well as something, we develop its negative image of an other. As we can see from the fact that something and an other are each determined by a difference in emphasis, an other is also a self-relating determinacy. As the dialectic progresses, what at first is merely an indifferent relation between the two concepts becomes one that is intrinsic to them. Given they share the same structure, each is both something and other. We eventually realise that this relation is a necessary relation:

> But their truth is their relation; being-for-other and being-in-itself are, therefore, the above determinations [of something and other] posited *as moments* of one and the same something, as determinations which are relations and which remain in their unity, in the unity of determinate being. Each, therefore, at the same time, also contains within itself its other moment which is distinguished from it. (Hegel 1989: 119)

We can note here a trait of the dialectic that we have seen previously. Here, the categories of something and other prove to contain one another, just as being and nothing proved to be identical to one another, and the finite and infinite showed themselves to contain one another. There is a key difference from Merleau-Ponty in that in the case of something and other, while something does indeed require a relation to that which it is not in order to become determinate, and hence falls outside of the atomism we dealt with earlier in this chapter, the relation is one that is reciprocal. We have here the same essential difference from Merleau-Ponty that we found with Kant's philosophy.

A figure, therefore, is not perceived against other objects, but against a horizon that remains indeterminate. This is a necessary feature of perception, which always occurs from a perspective, and thus always requires that the space of perception has a direction, and hence a horizon:

> Thus, since every conceivable being relates directly or indirectly to the perceived world, and since the perceived world is only grasped through orientation, we cannot dissociate being from oriented being; there is no reason to 'ground' space or to ask what is the level of all levels. (Merleau-Ponty 2012: 264)

This explains the experience of the child with colour. It is not the case that they are simply inattentive to the nature of colour. Such an interpretation wrongly characterises a previous indeterminacy as a determinate but unattended to characteristic of the object, and hence falls prey to the experience error. Rather, certain features of the object that are initially a part of the indeterminate horizon of the object are actively constituted as the object itself. Attention therefore constitutes a new determination of the object, and this new determination is then read back into the previous relations with the object. What Merleau-Ponty is proposing, therefore, is an asymmetric relationship between a figure and background, rather than simply the reliance of a figure on other figures for its determination. This different account of the nature of experience necessitates a different notion of synthesis.

4.9   The Constitution of Experience

How does this alternative view of the nature of experience affect its constitution? Merleau-Ponty notes that Kant 'starts [the transcendental deduction] with the principle that if a perception is able to be my own, it must from the start be one of my "representations"' (1968: 43). We have already seen how various claims Kant makes in the transcendental deduction form a network of mutually supporting assumptions, and Merleau-Ponty notes that this assumption that experience is to be understood in terms of judgement is key. Once we make this claim, we are left in a position whereby it must be the understanding that unites within the object the aspects under which the object presents itself. Kant notes, in turn, that 'we can reduce all acts of the *understanding* to judgments, and the understanding may therefore be represented as a *faculty of judgment*' (Kant 1929: A69/B94). In relating a series of passive representations to the concept of an object, Kant therefore draws on the kind of synthesis we use when making judgements:

> By *synthesis*, in its most general sense, I understand the act of putting different representations together, and of grasping what is manifold in them in one [act of] knowledge. (Kant 1929: A77/B103)

Thinking of perceptions in terms of representations that are amenable to a model of synthesis based on judgement shows a sharp difference from the account of perception Merleau-Ponty introduces. For Merleau-Ponty, perception involves the determination of a figure against an indeterminate ground. The kind of synthesis one finds in judgement involves bringing together representations that are in themselves distinct into a unity. To use Kant's example:

> In every judgment there is a concept which holds of many representations, and among them of a given representation that is immediately related to an object. Thus in the judgment, 'all bodies are divisible', the concept of the

divisible applies to various other concepts, but is here applied in particular to the concept of body, and this concept again to certain appearances that present themselves to us. (Kant 1929: A68–9/B93)

Here, whilst the judgement itself is based on the reciprocal determination of these representations through the structure of the subordination of the predicate to the subject, the two representations, in themselves, are still fully determined. As each is determinate and self-sufficient, they require the agency of the subject in order to bring them together. This leads to the result that the unity of the object is governed by the categories, and hence, as Kant shows in the second analogy, that this unity in turn implies that the object be understood as participating in a field of objective determinate objects systematically integrated into a set of relations of cause and effect.[20] Once the nature of the world is understood in terms of relations of knowledge, it is no surprise that there is no place for perception as something prior to the objective and universal structures of the categories.[21] The world becomes 'an invariable system of relations to which every existing thing is subjected if it is to be known … like a crystal cube, where all possible presentations can be conceived by its law of construction and that allows its hidden sides to be seen in its present construction' (Merleau-Ponty 2012: 342).

If we accept Merleau-Ponty's claim that the simplest structure of perception is a figure against a background, and hence a mixture of the determinate and indeterminate, then perceptions do not form the kinds of determinate entities that are amenable to categorial synthesis. They

[20] Merleau-Ponty discusses this implication in the *Phenomenology of Perception*: 'Nevertheless, two sorts of reflections are possible here. The first – intellectualist reflection – thematises the object and consciousness, and, to repeat a Kantian expression, it "raises them to the concept." The object thus becomes *what is*, and consequently what is for everyone and for all times (even if only as an episode that is fleeting, but of which it will always be true that it existed in objective time). Consciousness, thematised by reflection, *is* existence for itself. And, with the help of this idea of consciousness, and this idea of the object, it is easy to show that every sensible quality is only fully an object within the context of the relations of the universe, and that sensation can only be on condition of existing for a central and unique I' (Merleau-Ponty 2012: 226–7).

[21] We might at this stage return to Kant's initial distinction between perception and experience and ask whether perception, which was not defined by Kant as entailing a reference to objects, escapes from categorial synthesis. Towards the end of the deduction, however, Kant notes that in fact even perception is structured according to the categories insofar as it requires the space that perception takes place in to be determined according to the category of magnitude. In the *Prolegomena*, Kant similarly notes that sensation falls under magnitude, since 'for indeed between every given degree of light and darkness, every degree of warmth and the completely cold, every degree of heaviness and absolute lightness … ever smaller degrees can be thought … therefore no perception is possible that would show a complete absence' (Kant 1997: §24). '[A]ll synthesis, therefore, even that which renders perception possible, is subject to the categories' (Kant 1929: B161). This synthesis operates according to a 'rule of apprehension', operating through the imagination (see Allison 2004: 185–201). I will return to the significance of the imagination at the end of the section.

simply do not stand on their own as distinct elements to be combined into the form of a judgement. Furthermore, the fact that there is a sense, or organisation, to perception that differs in kind from that of judgement implies that there may be another form of synthesis that differs in kind from categorial synthesis. In accepting that perception has an irreducible sense within itself, Merleau-Ponty considers that sense may not simply be bestowed on a collection of passive givens by an active subject.

Rather than the categorial synthesis we find in transcendental idealism, it is organised according to a synthesis, 'if one can still speak here of a synthesis' (Merleau-Ponty 2012: 344), that Merleau-Ponty calls a transition synthesis. This notion of synthesis has two key characteristics. First, as its name suggests, the transition synthesis operates through the transformation of a perspective rather than the constitution of one. Second, rather than relying on a series of determinate elements, it relies on the relationship between the determinate and the indeterminate. If we turn to Merleau-Ponty's account of the determination of directionality in space, for instance, he claims that without an originary presence in space, it is impossible to explain why one set of directions is privileged over another:

> It is easy to show that a direction can only exist for a subject who traces it out, and although a constituting mind eminently has the power to trace out all directions in space, in the present moment this mind has no direction and, consequently, it has no space, for it is lacking an actual starting point or an absolute here that could gradually give a direction [*sens*] to all the determinations of space. (Merleau-Ponty 2012: 258)

Since the Kantian synthesising subject is prior to the constitution of this space, we cannot explain its orientation within it. Rather, Merleau-Ponty claims that synthesis moves us from one set of 'anchorage points' which 'invite us to constitute another space in the midst of a certain space to which they owe their stability' (Merleau-Ponty 2012: 259–60). As such, we are always already within a system of direction, or sense, which means that we can always account for our present perspective on the world as being a transition from a previous orientation. Merleau-Ponty gives the example of approaching the town of Chartres. When we look away, then return our gaze to the town, we do not have the experience of two perspectives which need to be reunited by an 'invariant' (Merleau-Ponty 2012: 344). We can abstract two moments from perception in order to make the judgement, 'It's Chartres', only because they are both drawn from a single perception of the world, which cannot consequently admit the same discontinuity (Merleau-Ponty 2012: 344). For Merleau-Ponty, the question of synthesis is not about the constitution of space. Merleau-Ponty's claim is, rather, that the subject is always already found within a spatial milieu. The question is not one of how space is constituted, but rather of how a subject that is always already encountered in relation to a spatial world comes to change the directionality of that world.

The second claim is that synthesis does not operate in terms of determinate moments. As Merleau-Ponty notes, when we perceive a scene, our perception cannot be understood as a series of representations that require an external synthetic act of unification to be united. 'The perceiving body does not occupy different points of view in turn beneath the gaze of a consciousness who has no place and who thinks these perspectives' (Merleau-Ponty 2012: 344). Rather, the different perspectives of my perception are only distinguished from one another through my reflection on them. It is only when I transpose my perspectival experience into the structures of reflection that it becomes individuated into moments.[22] When we looked at Merleau-Ponty's claim that perception was organised according to *Gestalt* structures, we noted that individual impressions pointed beyond themselves, implying borders or connections that were not strictly given. As such, there was a fundamental indeterminacy at the heart of perception, since spatial structures were determined by context. This holds true for temporal structures as well, and individual perspectives on the objects (to use the language of reflection) pass into one another without definite borders. 'The diversity of points of view is only suspected through an imperceptible slippage, or through a certain "indeterminacy" of the appearance' (Merleau-Ponty 2012: 344). This claim that perception is self-organising eliminates the need to posit a transcendental unity of apperception and a transcendental object. If perception organises itself, then there is no need to posit a transcendental subject responsible for the organisation of experience. In this sense, perception is primary, and prior to the subject.[23] Merleau-Ponty's alternative conception of experience,

---

[22] In *The Visible and the Invisible*, Merleau-Ponty argues that our natural tendency to talk of perceptions means that to avoid falling into this illusion, we need to introduce a new way of talking about the subject's relation to the world: 'We exclude the term perception to the whole extent that it already implies a cutting up of what is lived into discontinuous acts' (Merleau-Ponty 1968: 158).

[23] Merleau-Ponty sees the subject and object as abstractions from a prior phenomenal field that tends to but never reaches distinct structures of subject and object (cf. Bell 1998: 127–8). In the *Phenomenology of Perception*, the lived body is often taken to be the centre of synthesis, frequently as playing the same functional role as the transcendental unity of apperception. As Merleau-Ponty makes clear in *The Visible and the Invisible*, however, the *Phenomenology of Perception* fails as a project because it begins from the '"consciousness"–"object" distinction' (Merleau-Ponty 1968: 200; cf. Merleau-Ponty 1968: 183). *The Visible and the Invisible* argues that the lived body and object are rather themselves subsequent to a primordial moment he calls 'vision'. This strong thesis of the

therefore, points to a different conception of the kind of synthesis that makes this experience possible. Since the figure-background structure differs in kind from the structure of judgement, a different form of synthesis is needed.

In this section, I have focused on the role of the understanding and judgement in Kant's account of the constitution of experience. As Matherne (2016) notes, however, Kant also gives a prominent role to the imagination in the 'A Deduction'. Here, the imagination mediates between the synthesis or intuition and the synthesis of the understanding. Kant notes that it is a 'merely empirical law' that 'representations which have often followed or accompanied one another finally become associated' (Kant 1929: A100). He then argues that this empirical law requires a regularity in the appearances themselves. This is provided by the transcendental synthesis of the imagination, which organises the manifold of intuition in such a way that past moments in time or in a sequence are preserved to be related to present moments.

> [I]f I were always to drop out of thought the preceding representations (the first parts of the line, the antecedent parts of the time period, or the units in the order represented), and did not reproduce them while advancing to those that follow, a complete representation would never be obtained: none of the above-mentioned thoughts, not even the purest and most elementary representations of space and time could arise. (Kant 1929: A102)

The imagination therefore lays the ground for the synthesis of recognition in the concept by the understanding by providing a sequence of

---

ontological primacy of perception, even over the lived body, runs throughout *The Visible and the Invisible*. For instance:

> [Bergson] evokes, beyond the 'point of view of the object' and the 'point of view of the subject,' a common nucleus which is the 'winding' [*serpentement*], being as a winding (what I called 'modulation of the being in the world'). It is necessary to make understood how that (or any *Gestalt*) is a perception 'being formed in the things'. This is still only an approximative expression, in the subject-object language (Wahl, Bergson) of what there is to be said. That is, that the things have us, and that it is not we who have the things. (Merleau-Ponty 1968: 194)

Merleau-Ponty discusses this 'event of the order of brute or wild being which, ontologically, is primary' (1968: 200) in his work on aesthetics, where he argues that '[w]e speak of "inspiration," and the word should be taken literally. There really is inspiration and expiration of Being, action and passion so slightly discernible that it becomes impossible to distinguish between what sees and what is seen, what paints and what is painted' (Merleau-Ponty 1964a: 167). It is an open question as to whether the later work is a break with the *Phenomenology of Perception*, or a clearer formulation of its aims outside of the language of consciousness. I favour the latter interpretation, but Merleau-Ponty's criticisms of Kant remain broadly the same between the two texts so we can note that even if the former holds, it is at least compatible with both philosophies.

representations that can be brought together by judgement. In the 'B Deduction', Kant argues that '[i]t is one and the same spontaneity, which in the one case, under the title of imagination, and in the other case, under the title of understanding, brings combination into the manifold of intuition' (Kant 1929: B162n). As Allison (2004: 196-7) argues, it therefore performs its functions according to the categories, albeit not in a subsumptive manner. As such, it falls under Merleau-Ponty's critique of Kant's model of synthesis. Nonetheless, even if we focus on the 'A Deduction', we can note that the two features of Kant's synthesis that Merleau-Ponty attacks are both present in the synthesis of the imagination. First, the imagination still plays a constitutive role in giving time a sense, and thus precedes it, rather than developing the sense of time within time itself. Second, as with the understanding, the imagination relates together determinate representations, whether representations of moments of time or numbers when counting. As such, even in this instance, synthesis for Kant still fails to recognise indeterminacy. I now want to raise a final question – why does Kant mischaracterise something that should be as immediately transparent as experience?

4.10   Kant's Mischaracterisation of Experience

To answer this question, we need to turn to the question of how we characterise the world as a whole. The first thing to note is that the world for Merleau-Ponty is not something like a totality of objects. In keeping with his claim that all perception has a figure-horizon structure, it is rather a background against which objects make themselves manifest. What Merleau-Ponty wants to make clear is that the unity of the world is not the unity of something like a system of appearances that we find in Kant's analogies, or of a fully determinate (and in principle, knowable) set of relations, such as we might find in naturalism. Rather, Merleau-Ponty argues that the unity of the world is more like the unity of style of an individual that is recognisable, yet unspecifiable:

> I experience the unity of the world just as I recognise a style. Moreover, the style of a person or of a town does not remain constant for me. After ten years of friendship, and without even taking into account changes from growing older, it seems to be a relationship with a different person; after ten years of living in a neighbourhood, it seems to be a different neighbourhood. Yet it is only the *knowledge of things* that varies. Almost unnoticeable upon my first glance, this knowledge is transformed through the unfolding of perception. (Merleau-Ponty 2012: 342)

As he writes elsewhere, 'the natural world is the horizon of all horizons, and the style of all styles, which ensures my experiences have a given, not a willed, unity beneath the ruptures of my personal and historical life' (Merleau-Ponty 2012: 345).

As the horizon of all horizons is the ultimate horizon of our world, it cannot itself be made a figure, since there is no horizon against which it could appear. At the heart of Merleau-Ponty's critique of determinate being is the claim that Kant has fallen prey to a transcendental illusion that the style of this ultimate horizon can be thematised as an object, but such a thematisation breaks with the principle that every figure appears against a background. This illusion has some basis in the nature of the transition synthesis, which allows us to shift between perspectives and hence change those aspects of an object that are foregrounded as determinate:

> Each object, then, is the mirror of all the others. When I see the lamp on my table, I attribute to it not merely the qualities that are visible from my location, but also those that the fireplace, the walls and the table can 'see' …. Thus, I can see one object insofar as objects form a system or world, and insofar as each of them arranges the others around itself like spectators of its hidden aspects and as the guarantee of their permanence. (Merleau-Ponty 2012: 71)

While there is a tendency to see the lamp as a unity, in fact, in attending to aspects of the object, others fall away into the indeterminate horizon. In this sense, perception gives us a constant transitional interplay between determinacy and indeterminacy. The implication of this is that the object cannot be given in its absolute density, as attending to one moment of the object involves others falling back into indeterminacy. Furthermore, given the natural world is a horizon of all horizons, the world itself remains 'an open and indefinite multiplicity where relations are reciprocally implicated' (Merleau-Ponty 2012: 73).

The error emerges when we fail to recognise this necessary horizonal nature of perspectives, and see each effectively as a possible representation of the object. This is effectively to see these perspectives as individual atoms, the totality of which 'condensed into a strict coexistence' (Merleau-Ponty 2012: 72) would give the absolute object. While it appears that by comparing representations in memory, we could reach this density, in doing so we have already transposed perception to the categories of reflection. We here assume something like an 'immense World-Memory' (Merleau-Ponty 2012: 73) as the source of our perspectives. The world is thus seen to contain all perspectives simultaneously. Once we have intellectually constructed the notion of an absolute object, we see this as the basis of our perception of the world, and thus in turn deduce our experience from the relations between objects.

Here we have the structure of the transcendental illusion at the heart of Kant's account of perception. There is a tendency in perception to give us a determinate object. While it appears to reflection as if the object can be given all at once by a synthesis of all perspectives, 'my human gaze never *posits* more than one side of the object, even if by means of horizons it intends all the others' (Merleau-Ponty 2012: 72). The actual transition from perspective to perspective entails a continual shift in the horizon: it is a presumptive synthesis. Reflection takes this process of interplay as a series of moments, all of which could be potentially given at once, and in this forgets the object-horizon structure of perception. It is only by effectively treating perspectives as things that can be placed alongside each other that we can make sense of simultaneously occupying a number of different perspectives. It effectively sees perception as a series of representations which could simultaneously be thought by an 'I think' in the same way that a number of propositions could be related together by the same subject. Whereas for Merleau-Ponty, the openness of the world is a result of the necessity of the horizon structure, for the philosopher of reflection, we have what Merleau-Ponty calls the universe, which is 'a completed and explicit totality where relations would be reciprocally determined' (Merleau-Ponty 2012: 73). Thus, by taking a tendency within perception for an absolute state, reflection thereby develops what Merleau-Ponty calls 'the objective thought' of common sense and science. What is 'the result and the natural continuation' (Merleau-Ponty 2012: 74) of perception in the end becomes forgetful of its initial perspectivism, and is forced to reconstruct our experience through the categories of causal sequences or judgement. In this respect, Merleau-Ponty notes ironically that while Kant's analogies suggest the kind of closed view of the world we find in the model of objective thought, or reflection, in the antinomies, Kant rightly denies the possibility of thinking of the world as a totality.

4.11   Conclusion

For Merleau-Ponty, therefore, traditional accounts of thinking as judging fail to account for our relationship to the world because they cover over the presence of organisation and sense within perception itself. In making perception primary, Merleau-Ponty further suggests that judgement emerges out of perception, before the former illegitimately reformulates the latter as a relation of representation. In this process, whereby the division into subject and object emerges from a prior field of unity, we may see something of a response to Hölderlin's effort to think of judgement in terms of that which lacked any of its determinations. Hölderlin was unable to account for the emergence of determination because his concept of being was undifferentiated. Here, however, perception contains its own logic that differs in kind from that of judgement, providing a proper account of genesis. Nonetheless, in his final, unfinished work, *The Visible and the Invisible*, Merleau-Ponty hints that in starting from the consciousness–object distinction, the problems he poses in that work are insoluble (Merleau-Ponty 1968: 200). Earlier, he makes explicit that the difficulties with such terms are that 'they are more often than not only correlates or counterparts of the *objective* world' (1968: 157). Even the central term 'perception' from the early work is left to one side:

> We exclude the term perception to the whole extent that it already implies a cutting up of what is lived into discontinuous acts, or a reference to 'things' whose status is not specified, or simply an opposition between the visible and the invisible. Not that these distinctions are definitively meaningless, but because if we were to admit them from the start, we would re-enter the impasses we are trying to avoid. (Merleau-Ponty 1968: 158)

The Visible and the Invisible lays out a more explicitly ontological programme than that of the *Phenomenology of Perception*, but while the notes and draft chapters are suggestive, it is still unclear in what direction Merleau-Ponty would have taken this new ontology. In the next chapter, we will turn to the work of Derrida, but we will see that despite the change in emphasis in Derrida's work, the claim that thinking operates prior to the constitution of categorial judgement will still be maintained.

CHAPTER 5

Derrida and Différance

5.1 Introduction

In this chapter, we will turn from phenomenology to poststructuralism, taking up the work of Jacques Derrida. Derrida's work differs from those philosophers we have looked at so far in that he situates his concerns much more centrally within the history of philosophy itself, and so questions about the nature of thinking tend to be worked through in relation to the tensions we find in philosophers' texts. Nonetheless, we find in Derrida's work the same rejection of understanding thinking as judging that we have seen running through Bergson and the phenomenologists. We also find the claim that what gives sense to the claims we make operates according to a logic that differs in kind from judgement, and that this logic of sense is covered over by the structures of judgement themselves. Rather than exploring the nature of experience itself, Derrida looks at the way in which philosophers deploy their categories to attempt to make sense of the world around us. As such, Derrida's approach involves showing the way in which philosophers institute categorial structures, while at the same time covering over the non-categorial ground of these structures. Derrida has a number of names for both the surface structures of thinking and their non-categorial grounds, but in this chapter we will focus on two ways in which this difference is played out: the concepts ('concepts' understood loosely) of presence and *différance*, and the place of speech and writing in philosophy, with the traditional privileging of the former.

Presence, then, is the name Derrida gives to the traditional manner of organising determinations presupposed by philosophy. In his late work, *Limited Inc.*, Derrida sets out two 'indications' of metaphysics that show the essential structures of presence. The first indication is that presence presupposes a pure origin for philosophical thought, such as we find in Schelling's identity philosophy, or Hegel's notion of pure being. The second indication shows how this origin is differentiated to give rise to a variety of categories, or properties we find in the world. Here, we find a number of the characteristics of judgement:

> The hierarchical axiology, the ethical-ontological distinctions which do not merely set up value-oppositions clustered around an ideal and unfindable limit, but moreover subordinate these values to each other (normal/abnormal, standard/parasite, fulfilled/Void, serious/nonserious, literal/nonliteral, briefly: positive/negative and idea/non-ideal). (Derrida 1988: 93)

To begin with, we have a series of distinctions that operate in terms of oppositions that are used to determine the nature of something through a positive term and its negation. Returning to the first indication, we here can see the need for a pure origin, since a nested series of such determinations will move towards greater and greater determination, and conversely will presuppose a point of absolute generality to be differentiated. Derrida here makes two further claims about this manner of determination. First, the establishment of the structures of judgement is an inherently ethical procedure, since the oppositions that form the hierarchies inevitably privilege one term. We shall see this with the opposition between spoken and written language. We will also see that there is a tension between the sharp determinations we find within judgements and the ambiguities and problem cases we find when we actually attempt to categorise the world itself in terms of these judgements. We will see this in terms of Plato's privileging of the speaking subject, Husserl's account of consciousness that attempts to move from a reading of the indefinite to the universal, and Hegel's efforts to show that philosophy presupposes a phonetic conception of language. In each case, we find that rather than the terms emerging from the analysis, they are presupposed by it in order to allow the analysis to go forward. Derrida here explicitly refers to Kant's notions of transcendental ideas and ideals as principles that allow the organisation of our judgements through a *focus imaginarius*. For example, the idea of a purely phonetic language functions as a transcendental ideal for Hegel that allows him to set up a clear opposition between philosophical and non-philosophical language. In taking this distinction to be more than simply an organising principle, Derrida is effectively arguing that Hegel falls into the same kinds of difficulties Kant found with the transcendental realists.

Underlying presence is what Derrida calls *différance*. *Différance* has what Derrida calls 'conceptual effects', but is not itself a concept. Rather, it is

Derrida and *Différance*

something like the condition for the possibility of concepts.[1] As we shall see, Derrida's account of *différance* is difficult to tease out, primarily because it escapes conceptual determination while making such determinations possible. Nonetheless, Derrida insists that *différance* is not the object of a negative theology, since it is in effect closer to rather than further away from conceptual determinations. We can note that *différance* can be understood in opposition to both the clear delineation of conceptual determinations, as well as in opposition to the idea of a pure origin. Given the difficulty in getting a clear understanding of what Derrida means by *différance*, we will look at a number of different accounts of the operation of difference in the history of philosophy. In the first part of the chapter, I want to look at Derrida's essay, 'Plato's Pharmacy', where we see Derrida's claim that philosophy has privileged speech over writing is played out. As we will see, Derrida makes two claims here. First, he notes that while speech appears to be the privileged term, in an important sense writing is privileged, with this privilege subsequently covered over. Derrida will introduce a second sense of writing which is equivalent to *différance* and is responsible for the constitution of the speech-writing opposition itself. We will then look at how these themes are developed through Derrida's reading of Hegel's relationship to language. Here we shall see that Hegel is forced to cover over his own acknowledgement of the non-phonetic elements of his own language in order to sustain the necessary relation of subject and Spirit. We will then turn to Husserl to look more closely at the relationship between consciousness and judgement in Derrida's philosophy. Finally, we will draw together the results of this analysis to develop an account of *différance* itself.

5.2   Plato

'Plato's Pharmacy' provides a detailed analysis of Plato's criticism of writing, focusing on the *Phaedrus*.[2] Plato's rejection of writing is a well-accepted part of the interpretation of his thought, and the following, for instance, is typical of Plato's considerations of writing:

> Anyone who leaves behind him a written manual, and likewise anyone who takes it over from him, on the supposition that such writing will provide something reliable and permanent, must be exceedingly simple-minded; he

---

[1] See Wood 1988 for a justification of the transcendental reading of Derrida. Similarly, Gasché 1988 develops what he calls a 'quasi-transcendental' reading of Derrida's thought.
[2] Zuckert 1996: 216–25 provides a helpful summary of the broader themes of Derrida's text. Derrida's analysis in 'Plato's Pharmacy' covers a great deal of ground, and so here we will focus on a couple of key moments in his analysis that show the relationship between speech, writing, and *logos*.

must really be ignorant of Ammon's utterance, if he imagines that written words can do anything more than remind one who knows that which the writing is concerned with. (Plato 1997c: 275c)[3]

Derrida's concern is less with Plato's arguments themselves than with those aspects of his texts that first appear to be inessential in comparison with them. His aim is to show through these elements of the text that important aspects of its constitution fall outside of categorial thought. It is here that the ground is laid for the kinds of oppositions such texts rely upon. As such, Derrida takes as central to his analysis Plato's use of an Egyptian myth concerning the invention of writing (Plato 1997c: 274c–275c). In the myth, the god, Theuth, brings forward a series of inventions to the king-god of all Egypt, Thamus. Theuth is responsible for inventions, such as geometry, number, astronomy, gambling, and writing. As he brings each invention before Thamus, he argues why each should be given to the Egyptians. Thamus in turn either agrees with Theuth's assessment or argues against it in various ways. When writing is brought forth, Theuth claims that writing will allow the Egyptians to improve their memories, and to develop wisdom. He claims, thereby, that what he has invented is a recipe (*pharmakon*) for memory and wisdom.

---

[3] Plato's argument here that writing is of little service to humanity since it can only remind us of what we already know rather than teach us something novel bears a striking similarity to Meno's paradox, which purports to show the impossibility of learning:

> Do you realise that you are bringing up the trick argument that a man cannot try to discover what he knows or what he does not know? He would not seek what he knows, for since he knows it there is no need of the inquiry, nor what he does not know, for in that case he does not even know what to look for. (Plato 1997a: 80d3–e5)

Dillon 1988 argues that solving this paradox is at the heart of the motivation for Merleau-Ponty's project of developing a logic of perception that differs in kind from that of judgement and is constitutive of the field of reflection. He argues that the paradox arises from empiricism and rationalism covering over this pre-reflective constitution of sense. For empiricism, thinking is understood in causal terms, which covers over the need for an account of sense. For intellectualism, sense is explained by an internal connection between the data of experience, insofar as what is presented to us is constituted by judgement. This means, however, that insofar as what is presented to us is constituted by judgement, it is already known to us. 'What intellectualism lacks is the contingency of the opportunities for thought' (Merleau-Ponty 2012: 30). In the first case, meaning is entirely beyond us, and in the second, meaning is always already present to us. As Merleau-Ponty puts it:

> Consciousness is too poor in the first case, and too rich in the second for any phenomena to be able to *solicit* it. Empiricism does not see that we need to know what we are looking for, otherwise we would not go looking for it; intellectualism does not see that we need to be ignorant of what we are looking for, or again we would not go looking for it. (Merleau-Ponty 2012: 30)

Derrida's argument that writing ultimately has to be understood as differing in kind from our reflective categories and constitutive of them can therefore be seen as having a close affinity with Merleau-Ponty's thought here.

Thamus instead claims that writing, rather than promoting memory, will simply promote memorising. It simply teaches how to repeat words that we have learnt by heart, and thus gives those who read the writing merely the appearance of having knowledge, rather than knowledge itself. Derrida here points to another possible translation of *pharmakon* as drug, as opposed to remedy. His claim will be that the ambiguity that we find in the positive and negative connotations of the word drug can also be applied to writing more generally.[4] Furthermore, Derrida will argue that this ambiguity points to an equivocation between the category of writing and a deeper, non-categorial characterisation of it. Now, as Derrida notes, the relationship between Theuth and Thamus is much like the relationship between a father and a son. In fact, we can push this notion of a relationship between father and son further. We can also understand the models of speech and writing in terms of relationships between the father and the child:

> [T]he origin of *logos* is *its father*. One could say anachronistically that the 'speaking subject' is the *father* of his speech. And one would quickly realise that this is no metaphor, at least not in the sense of any common, conventional effect of rhetoric. *Logos* is a son, then, a son that would be destroyed in its very presence without the present *attendance* of his father. (Derrida 1981a: 77)

What distinguishes speech from writing is that whereas for speech, the father (the speaking subject) is present, writing has in a sense been orphaned. We can see in this a more general criticism of writing offered by Plato, which once again revolves around presence: that writing should be seen as secondary to speech, since speech operates in the presence of the speaker, who is able to correct any misinterpretations of what has been said, whereas with writing the writer is normally absent, and thus is not able to clarify any misreadings. More broadly, this privileging of the presence of the subject will, for Derrida, characterise the development of Western philosophy, and we will see the emphasis on presence at play in both Hegel and Husserl.

---

[4] While we will be focusing on the connection of writing and the *pharmakon* in this chapter, Derrida's analysis brings in a broad range of acceptations of the word, arguing that each plays a role in the development of Plato's text. Brogan 1989: 8 gives the following summary of the different meanings of the term used by Derrida: 'Among these are included: a drug, a healing remedy or medicine, an enchanted potion or philter, a charm or spell, a poison, a means of producing something, a dye or paint. Although, as Derrida points out, Plato never uses the word, *pharmakon* is related to the word *pharmakos* which means a scapegoat sacrificed for atonement and purification. It is also related to the word *pharmakeia* which means pharmacy or sorcery and is also the name of the maiden with whom Orithyia was playing in the myth of Boreas that Plato relates in the *Phaedrus*.'

In the background in Plato's criticism of writing is the connection between speech as the living word and writing as the dead letter. In this regard, the discussion of speech and its relationship to the father is connected, Derrida argues, with another metaphor at play in Plato's text: the idea of *logos* as animal. One of Socrates' criticisms of writing, particularly the speech of Lysias that is the initial focus of the *Phaedrus*, is that it lacks any organic structure. Rather, the parts of Lysias' speech are entirely interchangeable. Socrates therefore makes the following claim:

> Every discourse (*logos*) must be put together like a living creature, with a body of its own; it must be neither without head nor without legs; and it must have a middle and extremities that are fitting both to one another and to the whole work. (Plato, *Phaedrus*, quoted in Derrida 1981a: 80)[5]

It might seem that Derrida's introduction of these metaphors is somewhat arbitrary, but we can see in the introduction of this case of speech as a living creature a move towards the kind of organicism that Hegel takes to be the structure of Spirit, where each moment is determined by its relation to the whole, and the whole by its relation to the parts (as we saw in Hegel's characterisation of the good infinite in the first chapter). We can also note that these familial relations are explicitly taken up by Plato to define the logical relations between the Forms and the empirical world. As such, what appears to be a contingent aspect of the text serves to determine relations between key terms of Plato's philosophy. Thus, Plato in the *Republic* writes as follows:

> It was the sun, then, that I meant when I spoke of that offspring of the Good (*ton tou agathou akgonon*), which the Good has created in its own image (*hon tagathon egennesen analogon heautoi*), and which stands in the visible world in the same relation to vision and visible things as that which the good itself bears in the intelligible world to intelligence and to intelligible objects. (Plato, *Republic*, quoted in Derrida 1981a: 82)

What interests Derrida in all of these cases is the question of the relationship between the father and the son. At first, it seems that the structure of the metaphor is clear, but when we look closer we see tensions that threaten to disrupt the logic of Plato's distinctions themselves. Derrida's claim is that the father/son relationship is intimately bound up with *logos*. It is only through *logos* as speech or reason that we can distinguish the human relationship of father/son from other relationships such as 'mere cause/

---

[5] As Brogan (1989: 11) notes, Derrida's own text subverts Plato's criteria for the text in 'Plato's Pharmacy' by providing neither a clear conclusion nor a preface that introduces the text.

effect or generator/engendered' (Derrida 1981a: 80). 'Living beings, father and son, are announced to us within the household of logos' (Derrida 1981a: 81). As such, it is only once the consequent is in place that we can represent the origin as an origin, thus leading to a paradox. *Logos* can only give an account of its origin in terms that emerge with *logos* itself, thus presenting a situation where the true, non-categorial origin is by necessity covered over. When we turn to Husserl, we will see a similar structure in terms of judgement, where Derrida will claim that the characterisation of experience itself as proto-juridical will be introduced retrospectively by his analysis of language itself as focused on judgement. Derrida therefore argues that there is a tendency for a juridical model of thinking to present its conditions of genesis as themselves juridical.

As Derrida's analysis develops, he adds a further dimension to his analysis of writing for Plato. He returns to the theme of the metaphors of familial relationships that were in the background of his account. Originally, while the subject is the father of speech, writing was an orphan. Derrida now points to a further Platonic metaphor:

> And once a thing is put in writing, the composition, whatever it may be, drifts all over the place, getting into the hands not only of those who understand it, but equally of those who have no business with it; it doesn't know how to address the right people, and not address the wrong. And when it is ill-treated and unfairly abused it always needs its parent to come to its aid, being unable to defend itself or attend to its own needs. (Plato, *Phaedrus*, in Derrida 1981a: 143)

This statement reiterates the absence of the father, but it also points to another way of reading the status of writing. Derrida notes that we could also understand the position of writing to be that of the illegitimate child – the bastard. In this sense, the father is once again not present, as it cannot affirm its relationship to the son, who falls outside of the law. In this sense, writing would be seen as a 'false brother' to speech.

If we accept Derrida's claim that Socrates considers writing to be an illegitimate child, then we are pushed towards understanding speech itself as the brother of writing. We began with an analysis of the relationship between speech and writing, but as Derrida develops his account, he begins to show that these terms cannot be separated as much as they first appear to be for Plato. This represents a crucial shift in Plato's texts. Previously, we were trying to distinguish speech from writing. Now, however, the metaphors Plato introduces see speech and writing instead as two different species of writing: good writing and bad writing. We have moved, therefore, from a difference in kind to a difference in degree. Socrates, for instance, uses the following metaphor about the scattering of seeds to distinguish speech from writing. In this case the difference isn't a difference in kind, but a difference between the good farmer and the bad farmer:

> Socrates: . . . and now tell me this. If a sensible farmer had some seeds to look after (*hon spermaton kedoito*) and wanted them to bear fruit, would he with serious intent (*spoudei*) plant them during the summer in a garden of Adonis, and enjoy watching it produce fine fruit within eight days? If he did so at all wouldn't it be in a holiday spirit (*heortes . . . Kbarin*) just for fun (*paidias*)? For serious purposes wouldn't he behave like a scientific farmer, sow his seeds in suitable soil, and be well content if they came to maturity within eight months? . . . . And are we to maintain that he who has know-ledge of what is just, honorable, and good has less sense than the farmer in dealing with his seeds? . . . . Then it won't be with serious intent (*spoudei*) that he will 'write them in water' (*en hudati grapsei*, an expression equivalent to 'writing in sand') or in that black fluid we call ink, using his pen to sow words (*melani speiron dia kalamou meta logon*) that can't either speak in their own support (*boethein*) or teach the truth adequately. (Plato, *Phaedrus*, in Derrida 1981a: 150–1)

As Derrida notes, the idea that speech is a form of writing is a metaphor that runs all the way through the Western metaphysical tradition, and we frequently find references to thinking as a kind of writing on the soul, or as an imprint in the wax of the soul, etc. As such, Plato prefigures much of the Western tradition in understanding thinking in terms of writing whilst at the same moment denigrating writing. What are the implications of this new relationship between speech and writing?

First, it means that the essence of speech is now understood in relation to what it is supposed to overcome. Speech is understood as the opposite of (bad) writing, while writing is tied to thought itself. Thus, the hierarchy of speech and writing is inverted. As we shall see, Derrida will argue that this inversion of terms in a hierarchy of values, together with a demonstration of their interdependence, is a fundamental moment of the deconstructive method, and represents the first step in the analysis. We can see the parallels here with Hegel's dialectical method, which also begins by show-ing the interdependence of terms that are opposed to each other. Derrida himself recognises this affinity, but also notes that while for Hegel, this dialectical moment opens out onto a new category which sublates the previous opposition, the final phase of Derrida's analysis is to move beyond this hierarchy entirely. Derrida turns to the *Timaeus* to show this move in 'Plato's Pharmacy'. Here, when Plato gives an account of the origin of the world, he is also forced to posit something prior to the distinction between Forms and copies that allows them to be distinguished from one another – 'the "place", "the locus", "that in which" things appear' (Derrida 1981a: 160). As this place is what makes the activity of distinguishing possible, it itself cannot be distinguished:

> Wherefore the mother and receptacle of all created and visible and in any way sensible things is not to be termed earth or air or fire or water, or any of their compounds, or any of the elements from which these are derived, but is an invisible and formless being which receives all things and in some mysterious way partakes of the intelligible, and is most incomprehensible. (Plato, *Timaeus*, in Derrida 1981a: 159)

It is in the *Sophist* that the significance of this notion of Being prior to differentiated being is recognised. There, Plato relates the question of how to respond to the sophists to the question of Parmenides' conception of Being. Parmenides held that Being was pure and entirely undifferentiated. If there is only pure being, then it would be impossible to say that something 'is not'. This presents a problem, as we want to be able to say that the doctrines of the sophist are false. For this reason, it is necessary to cover over this origin of undifferentiated being in order to allow us to present the kinds of distinctions and oppositions that allow us to develop the dialectic. The condition of the dialectic, therefore, is that we cover over the nature of being with the name of being. Thus, writing, as the effacing of the origin, becomes the condition of the possibility of overcoming the sophist. What makes possible Plato's project of the search for truth is therefore precisely what prevents it ever reaching that truth: writing as *pharmakon*.

As he accepts in an interview with Henri Ronse (Derrida 1981b: 7), Derrida uses two senses of writing – one for what one might call the empirical use of the term writing, for that which is opposed to speech, and one for what Ronse calls the 'common root of writing and speech'. More than simply seeing the *pharmakon* as something which escapes from the various oppositions with which Plato attempts to define it, Derrida goes on to claim that, in fact, the *pharmakon* is responsible for providing the space within which the kind of oppositions Plato relies upon can be constituted:

> And if one got to thinking that something like the *pharmakon* – or writing – far from being governed by these oppositions, opens up their very possibility without letting itself be comprehended by them; if one got to thinking that it can only be out of something like writing – or the *pharmakon* – that the

strange difference between inside and outside can spring; if, consequently, one got to thinking that writing as a *pharmakon* cannot simply be assigned a site within what it situates, cannot be subsumed under concepts whose contours it draws, leaves only its ghost to a logic that can only seek to govern it insofar as logic arises from it – one would then have to bend [*plier*] into strange contortions what could no longer even simply be called logic or discourse. (Derrida 1988: 103)

Derrida's analysis of Plato captures his method when analysing a philo-sophical text, which he calls deconstruction. Within Plato's text, we find a fundamental opposition between the categories of speech and writing. This opposition takes the form of the priority of one of the terms over the other: in this case, speech over writing. As we have seen, these two features of thinking, opposition and hierarchy, are fundamental structures of categorial thought. Derrida gives several definitions of deconstruction,[6] but here we shall focus on the earliest definition given in *Positions* as the later definitions focus more on deconstruction's aims in developing an ethico-political position. Derrida writes that 'the [general strategy of deconstruction] is to avoid both simply neutralising the binary oppositions of metaphysics and simply residing within the closed field of these oppositions, thereby confirming it'[7] (Derrida 1981b: 41). In order to meet these goals, deconstruction introduces the two phases that we saw in 'Plato's Pharmacy'. First, we have the reversal of the hierarchy itself, so Derrida shows that despite the immediate impression of a priority of speech over writing, in fact we can interpret Plato's text as understanding speech as derivative from writing. Derrida's account here has acknowledged affinities with Hegel, since for Hegel, too, we have a method that operates by showing the mutual dependence of opposites. As such, deconstruction main-tains 'relations of profound affinity with Hegelian discourse (such as it must be read)' (Derrida 1984: 14).

Nonetheless, Derrida rejects the second moment of Hegelian dialectics whereby these opposed terms are reunited in a higher form of unity, since as Derrida's second criterion of deconstruction makes clear, such a unity, and the dialectic of negation, would continue to operate within the framework of opposition: 'I fear, precisely, that the category of "negation" reintroduces the Hegelian logic of the *Aufhebung*. It has happened that

[6] Lawlor 2019 provides an excellent analysis of Derrida's various definitions of deconstruction.
[7] Zuckert 1996: 215 argues that Derrida's project can be seen as 'bring[ing] metaphysics to closure by revealing its limits'. I take this closure not to involve the rejection of thinking in terms of judgement, but rather the incorporation into this thinking of the recognition that its genesis is in a transcendental field that differs in kind from it, rather than a finite synthetic or infinite analytic subject that operates according to analogous structures.

Derrida and *Différance*

I have spoken of nonpresence, in effect, but by this I was designating less a negated presence, than "something" (nothing, indeed, in the form of presence) that deviates from the opposition presence/ absence (negated presence), with all that this opposition implies' (Derrida 1981b: 95). We will explore these relations directly later in the chapter, but for now we can note that Derrida argues for 'a kind of infinitesimal and radical displacement' (Derrida 1984: 14) of Hegelian discourse. In effect, what Derrida argues for, therefore, is that this opposition between terms opens out onto a moment that falls outside of the oppositions themselves and in fact is generative of them. As Derrida's reading progresses, however, we see that this oppositional form of writing is replaced by what appears to be a transcendental form of writing which differs in kind from normal writing and speech, and functions as something like a ground for them. In this sense, Derrida is perhaps closer to Kant than to Hegel, with the discovery of an antinomy showing that an implicit assumption, in this case presence, has been in play within the metaphysical system. As such, Derrida here shows an affinity with Bergson, Sartre, and Merleau-Ponty, each of whom in their own way returns to Kant to find a way to diverge from Hegel. We can also note an affinity with the method of Bergson, where, for instance, free will and determinism are shown to be related to one another, and then are overturned in favour of a non-juridical model of thought as process that differs in kind from both categories. As we shall see, for Derrida too, what opens up the space for metaphysics is a movement[8] that itself cannot be understood in the categories of metaphysics.[9]

5.3 Hegel

I want to now explore in more detail deconstruction's relationship to the dialectic, as it is here that Derrida shows his proximity to the post-Kantian

[8] 'What is written as *différance*, then, will be the playing movement that "produces" by means of something that is not simply an activity – these differences, these effects of difference' (Derrida 1984: 11).
[9] 'Only a little further on, Socrates compares the written texts Phaedrus has brought along to a drug (*pharmakon*). This *pharmakon*, this "medicine," this philtre, which acts as both remedy and poison, already introduces itself into the body of discourse with all its ambivalence. This charm, this spellbinding virtue, this power of fascination, can be – alternatively or simultaneously – beneficent or malevolent. The *pharmakon* would be a *substance* – with all that word can connote in terms of matter with occult virtues, cryptic depths refusing to submit their ambivalence to analysis, already paving the way for alchemy – if we didn't eventually come to recognise it as antisubstance itself: that which resists any philosopheme, indefinitely exceeding its bounds as non-identity, nonessence, nonsubstance; granting philosophy by that very fact the inexhaustible adversity of what funds it and the infinite absence of what founds it' (Derrida 1988: 70).

tradition, and his rejection of its implicit commitment to a juridical model of thinking. As we have just seen, Derrida believes himself to be close to Hegel in developing an immanent method that shows the interrelation of our categories of thought. We have already seen that Derrida's method differs from Hegel's, and in his analysis of Hegel we can see why Derrida believes that Hegel himself covers over the role of *différance* in the formation of his system. In his essay, 'The Pit and the Pyramid: Introduction to Hegel's Semiology' (Derrida 1984: 69–108), Derrida sets out his account of Hegel's own relationship between speech and language. As with Plato, we shall see that while Hegel accords a place to writing, this is only on the basis of writing being subordinated to speech, and only on the basis of writing being understood as phonetic writing. As Hegel himself puts it in his discussion of writing in the *Philosophy of Mind*:

> While on the subject of spoken language (which is the original language), we can also mention, but here only in passing, written language; this is merely a further development within the particular province of language which enlists the help of an externally practical activity. Written language proceeds to the field of immediate spatial intuition, in which it takes and produces signs. (Hegel 2007: §459 Rem.)

If we turn to the final moment in Hegel's *Phenomenology of Spirit*, Absolute Knowing, we can see that reflexivity and self-presence are at the heart of Hegel's equation of substance and subject.[10] This will involve a privileging of the kind of writing that will preserve this equation. Derrida notes that Hegel's theory of the sign occurs in his discussion of psychology, 'the science of spirit determining itself in itself as a subject for itself' (Derrida 1984: 75). Hegel displays an ambivalence towards the notion of the sign,[11] but Derrida argues that the sign plays a central role in Hegel's metaphysics. For Hegel, the voice, in its use of signs, unites nature and Spirit, since the voice uses natural sounds, but the natural existence of these signs is sublated in order for them to be given the significance found in Spirit. In other words, the voice, in organising sound into language, demonstrates the commensurability of reason and nature. The voice also brings the inner world into alignment with the outer through expression in language: 'Sound articulating itself further

---

[10] Cf., for instance, Hegel 1977: §793: 'These are the moments of which the reconciliation of Spirit with its own consciousness proper is composed; by themselves they are single and separate, and it is solely their spiritual unity that constitutes the power of this reconciliation. The last of these moments is, however, necessarily this unity itself and, as is evident, it binds them all into itself.'

[11] Cf. Derrida 1984: 83.

for determinate representations, speech, and its system, language, give to sensations, intuitions, representations a second, higher reality than their immediate one, in general an existence that carries weight in the realm of representation' (Hegel 2007: §459). Language therefore allows consciousness to be present to itself, and is the way in which consciousness integrates itself into a community by allowing itself to become determinate, and thus enter the sphere of reason. We can note too that once this criterion of presence has been accepted, writing will naturally take on a subordinate role as a moment at one remove from the proper presence of speech. Given the *Phenomenology of Spirit*'s span of the history of Spirit, writing will be essential in transmitting the voice beyond the individual's death, but only on condition that it has the same structure as the voice itself – that it thus takes on the form of phonetic writing. Writing therefore is understood as structurally analogous to speech, but also as subordinate to it. In this manner, writing, as the non-categorial ground for the categories of speech, is covered over by Hegel's dialectic.

Derrida explores this claim by looking at Hegel's response to those languages that do not appear to have this structure of relating speech and writing, namely non-phonetic languages such as Egyptian and Chinese. Now, Hegel's claim is that the 'alphabetic writing is in and for itself the more intelligent form' (Hegel 2007: §459 Rem., quoted in Derrida 1984: 95), and that 'the Eastern form must be excluded from philosophy . . . . Philosophy proper commences in the West' (Hegel 1974: 99, quoted in Derrida 1984: 101). This distinction between two kinds of language is essential for Hegel, since it allows him to preserve the connection between the voice and writing in the philosophical tradition, while excluding those non-phonetic forms of writing that would disrupt the close connection between the voice and its transcription. The difficulty with this approach is that while there is de facto a connection between philosophy and phonetics, Hegel posits a necessary connection between philosophy and phonetic writing. Derrida makes two sets of claims against Hegel here. First, Derrida argues that the notion of a phonetic language is simply a 'teleological ideal' for Hegel, given the non-existence of purely phonetic languages. While Hegel takes the non-phonetic aspects of language to be accidental, Derrida argues that they represent 'the example of an essential law that limits the achievements of the teleological ideal' (Derrida 1984: 96). Second, Derrida argues that despite Hegel's attempts to show that there is an inherent problem with non-phonetic language, his account in fact shows a series of non-dialectical contradictions in Hegel's own relationship to such languages.

Turning to the first point, Derrida argues that at the heart of Hegel's account of phonetic writing is something analogous to a Kantian transcendental ideal. This ideal would make possible metaphysics by guaranteeing the relationship between speech and writing. In the *Critique of Pure Reason*, Kant introduces transcendental ideals in the transcendental dialectic in Kant's discussion of the notion of transcendental illusion. Transcendental ideals are a form of transcendental idea, and emerge through reason's efforts to systematise knowledge. As we saw in Chapter 1, Kant argues that human thought is discursive, and hence relies on the relation between the faculties of intuition and the understanding. If thought for Kant just operates in terms of the understanding, however, we would be limited to particular empirical judgements about intuition, whereas knowledge involves systematising these individual judgements. Kant describes this process as '[finding] the unconditioned for the conditioned cognitions of the understanding, by which its unity will be completed' (Kant 1929: A307/ B364). Kant gives an example of how reason operates in terms of the judgement, 'Caius is mortal.' We *could* simply derive this judgement from experience, but in order for reason to understand this judgement in a systematic fashion, reason rather seeks the condition for the statement, 'all men are mortal'. Now, Kant's claim is that in order for reason to systematise the particular judgements of the understanding, it needs to have an idea of the complete totality of the conditions for the particular judgement. Since all of the conditions of the judgement cannot be given in experience, this idea of a totality of all conditions goes beyond experience, and is merely a heuristic device that reason uses in order to carry out its operation of synthesis; what Kant calls a *focus imaginarius*. The transcendental illusion emerges when reason confuses this project of moving back through the conditions which govern an object with the cosmological principle that 'when the conditioned is given, then so is the entire series of conditions subordinated one to the other, which is also given (i.e. contained in the object and its connections)' (Kant 1929: A307–8/B364). In doing so, reason introduces a transcendental idea as something that can actually be given. The three transcendental ideas Kant discusses are God, the self, and the world, and in each case these ideas make possible a form of enquiry while leading reason into error if they are taken to be real objects. As such, we can see that transcendental illusions themselves are unavoidable, and Kant compares them to examples such as the moon appearing larger at its rising (Kant 1929: A297/B354). Error emerges when we fail to recognise that transcendental ideas are conditions of synthesis rather than given objects of experience. As Kant notes, the astronomer cannot avoid seeing the moon as larger at its rising, but he is nonetheless not deceived by it.

While ideas are general concepts, the ideal is a particular that is entirely determined by the idea (Kant 1929: A568/B596). Kant gives the following analogy of a transcendental ideal:

> Virtue, and therewith human wisdom in its complete purity, are ideas. The wise man (of the Stoics) is, however, an ideal, that is, a man existing in thought only, but in complete conformity with the idea of wisdom. As the idea gives the rule, so the ideal in such a case serves as the archetype for the complete determination of the copy. (Kant 1929: A569/B597)

The ideal is here essentially normative, and allows us to put to practical use the ideas of wisdom and purity. The ideal of the stoic sage gives us a model against which to judge conduct. Thus, it provides reason 'with a concept of that which is entirely complete in its kind, and thereby enabling it to estimate and to measure the degree and the defects of the incomplete' (Kant 1929: A570/B598). In effect, the transcendental ideal therefore institutes a distinction between the essential and the accidental by giving us an archetype that allows us to determine an object as an imperfect copy of it. It is by bringing an object into relation with this archetype that we can qualify the object as lacking certain properties, rather than simply having different properties.

Understanding Hegel's philosophy of language as governed by an ideal means that Derrida sees it as operating according to a principle not given in experience or through the immanent development of our concepts. It is this principle that allows Hegel to systematise our account of language. Thus, rather than operating through an immanent method, Hegel's account of language would presuppose a transcendent theory of language which governs the way in which the empirical is synthesised. We can relate this back to the question of resemblance that we have dealt with throughout this volume. As we have seen, each of the philosophers we have dealt with so far has noted the inability of a system of judgement to determine which resemblances we take to be essential and which are accidental. We can see here that on Derrida's account, the constitution of these categories, which will involve *différance*, is covered over for Hegel by the introduction of an ideal that is a presupposition that falls outside the system itself, and is the result of what Derrida calls a moment of radical freedom that cannot be explained within the domain of the dialectic itself. As such, the essence of writing would be its phonetic elements, and those features that do not conform to the phonetic structures would be merely accidental. Such an account runs into difficulties when dealing with languages that do not operate on a phonetic basis, such as Egyptian and Chinese. In discussing Leibniz's efforts to develop his *character-istica universalis*, a universal language of science based on a set of rationalised principles inspired by Chinese characters, Hegel even recognises in passing the essential role of non-phonetic language in a range of Western disciplines:

> Leibniz's practical mind (*Verstand*) misled him to exaggerate the advantages which a completely written language, formed on the hieroglyphic method (*and hieroglyphics are used even where there is alphabetic writing, as in our signs for numbers, the planets, the chemical elements, etc.*), would have as a universal language for the intercourse of nations and especially of scholars. (Hegel 2007: §459 Rem., in Derrida 1984: 96, Derrida's italics)

Whereas for Kant, the transcendental ideal provides a framework for unifying and expanding our empirical knowledge, and so gives sense to a set of acknowledged empirical facts, for Hegel here, the transcendental ideal instead functions as a way of instituting a distinction between essential and accidental facts, thus allowing us to disavow portions of our empirical knowledge. As such, the privileging of a form of writing that can be subordinated to speech in a simple manner is a presupposition of Hegel's method, rather than a result of it.[12]

Second, in Hegel's reading of non-phonetic language, Derrida argues that Hegel finds himself embroiled in a series of contradictions that are fundamentally non-dialectical, and which emerge from Hegel adopting something like a Freudian 'kettle logic', whereby a number of mutually incompatible disavowals are presented that point to a deeper motivation to the rejection. For instance, in analysing the Chinese script, Hegel argues that Chinese is a precursor of the kinds of logical systems Leibniz envisages, which would allow for meaning to emerge simply through the grammatical structure of the words themselves. As such, Hegel characterises Chinese as operating as a purely formal language of abstraction, and hence as divorced from Spirit. Conversely, he also criticises Chinese for lacking a properly formulated grammar, and hence being divorced from Spirit. Similarly, while Hegel praises German for its polysemic nature, which makes it

---

[12] In this regard, Derrida can be understood as re-inverting Hegel's own account of Kant's transcendental ideas. As Maybee 2016 argues, the self-driving nature of reason can in large part be derived from Kant's notion of the transcendental idea. While Kant sees the transcendental realist use of transcendental ideas as resulting in contradiction, Hegel sees these contradictions as proof that contradiction itself is an objective feature of the world. Derrida is instead arguing here that Hegelian reason is not in fact self-driving, but relies on a pre-existing transcendental to begin its development. To this extent, Derrida sees Hegel himself as taking an idea that allows reason to systematise experience, phonetic language, as something actually given.

conducive to dialectical inversions, he criticises Chinese for the same trait. Contradictions such as these lead Derrida to argue that Hegel's criticisms of non-phonetic writing are not based on an immanent analysis of these languages themselves, but on the need to protect a certain relation between speech and writing:

> The nature of [the Chinese] written language is at the outset a great hindrance to the development of the sciences . . . . They have, as is well known, beside a spoken language, a *written language*; which does not express, as ours does, individual sounds – does not present the spoken words to the eye, but represents the ideas themselves by signs. This appears at first sight a great advantage, and has gained the suffrage of many great men – among others, of Leibniz. In reality, it is anything but such. (Hegel 1974: 134–5, in Derrida 1984: 103)

As such, for Derrida, 'speculative metaphysics permits itself to be separated neither from *logos* nor, simultaneously, from the *logos* which never thinks or presents itself except in its historical complicity with the voice and phonetic writing' (Derrida 1984: 104). In effect, therefore, once again the *logos* of the voice becomes the *logos* of metaphysics itself. When we realise the contradictory nature of the privileging of one term of an opposition such as speech and writing, we are not led to a more adequate conceptual form, but rather to the rejection of the implicit presupposition of the form of *logos* itself. As such, there is no *Aufhebung* to a higher concept for Derrida, but rather a recognition that what makes possible the conceptual oppositions is itself of a radically different nature to that which it makes possible. Rather, Derrida argues that what he calls the 'quasi-concept' of *différance* is what makes possible the kind of conceptual operations that characterise presence.[13]

While this movement of alternation between moments in an opposition, followed by a rejection of both moments, appears to have the same structure of the dialectic, we can see that, in fact, Derrida's account of contradiction is closer to Bergson's account of intuition, where contradiction between different conceptual schemas does not lead to a more adequate system of categories, but to the rejection of the structure of categories themselves. As such, while Derrida claims to be infinitely close to Hegel, this claim is in fact rather misleading. *Différance* is not contradiction, the sublation of the

---

[13] See Derrida 1988: 118–19 for his discussion of the quasi-concept. Patton also takes up this notion, and notes its proximity to Deleuze and Guattari's analysis of philosophical concepts (Patton 2000: 15–16). Gasché 1988 deals extensively with this notion of the quasi-concept in chapters 8 and 9. Derrida argues that while *différance* is not a concept, it produces 'conceptual effects' (Derrida 1981b: 40).

existing categories, and Derrida rather describes it as a moment of 'dissonance' (Derrida 1981b: 42) introduced into the text.

5.4 Husserl

The final figure I want to look at in this chapter is Edmund Husserl. The analysis of speech and writing in Plato's thought is mirrored closely by the reading Derrida gives of Husserl. What this reading brings out clearly is the connection between presence and predication and the structure of thinking. We can begin looking at Derrida's reading of Husserl by noting that much as Plato and Hegel privileged the presence of the speaker, Husserl's phenomenology begins from a 'principle of all principles' that establishes the same priority: 'every originary presentive intuition is a legitimizing source of cognition, that everything originally (so to speak, in its "personal" actuality) offered to us in "intuition" is to be accepted simply as what it is presented as being, but also only within the limits in which it is presented there' (Husserl 1982: §24). In effect, as Derrida notes in 'Form and Meaning', at the heart of phenomenology is the analogy of an object being present to us as it is to sight (Derrida 1984: 158). Sense is here understood within the constraints of the visual.

Given the centrality of presence for phenomenology, Derrida turns to Husserl's *Lectures on Internal Time Consciousness*, since it is here that Husserl analyses the structure of the 'now', the moment when the object is intuited by consciousness that guarantees its legitimacy as a ground for cognition. The central structure of time consciousness for Husserl is what he calls the 'living present', and we can note at the outset that while this living present gives us the intuitive presence of the object in time, Husserl's concern is not simply with this moment of intuition in itself, since a focus purely on my own intuition would lack universality. Husserl instead considers the living present to be a universal form of experience thus capable of providing a ground for science. Derrida's claim in analysing the living present is therefore going to be once again to show that underlying this moment of presence is a moment that differs in kind from it, which Derrida will call *différance*. As such, the living present in fact becomes an effect of a deeper process, and as with Plato, Husserl is forced to cover over this deeper process to prepare the way for science.

Husserl's account of consciousness in *Lectures on Internal Time Consciousness* is capable of explaining the phenomenology of extended temporal events such as listening to a melody. Such an account needs to recognise first that a melody unfolds over time, and so our consciousness of the melody must involve us being at a given point within it, so there must be a 'now'. Second, our understanding of melody needs us to be able to relate the sound we are hearing now to those we have heard previously. As we saw in our analysis of Bergson, this retention of the past cannot simply be an intellectual recognition, since the previous notes of the melody affect the perception of the present note, rather than simply sitting alongside it. This suggests that as well as a 'now', we also need to understand time as having a thick present. As such, consciousness retains its past moments, and also anticipates its immediate future. For Husserl, there is a distinction between this process of retention, which operates passively and in terms of incomplete temporal objects, and the active process of memory, which operates on complete objects. Nonetheless, Derrida will argue that both are in fact representations, and that this difference in kind cannot be maintained.[14] We saw Sartre's claim in Chapter 3 that the transcendental ego that Husserl takes to constitute the organisation of time consciousness is in fact constituted by the organised structure of temporality. For Sartre, therefore, the ego is constituted by the structure of temporality, rather than temporality emerging from the constituting synthesis of a prior transcendental ego. At the heart of Derrida's account is an analogous claim: that the transcendental ego is a surface effect of a deeper process (though Derrida fails to acknowledge his debt to Sartre until his later years[15]). Rather than this being the effect of a transversal interplay of consciousnesses as it is for Sartre, for Derrida we need to understand this process of constitution in terms of his quasi-concept of *différance*.

For Husserl, phenomenology represents the completion of the original intentions of metaphysics, without the degeneracy that emerges through its later 'blindness before the authentic mode of ideality' (Lawlor 2002: 168). Husserl's account of the living present therefore includes two moments: presence as immediate intuition and presence as form. We cannot understand presence purely in terms of the intuition of the individual, since the individual will die. The authentic mode of ideality that Husserl sees at the heart of metaphysics must meet two criteria. First, it must be infinitely repeatable. This repeatability gives the mode the characteristic of universality. Second, this mode must not originate from an other-worldly source,

---

[14] 'The difference between retention and reproduction, between primary memory and secondary memory, is not the difference – not the radical difference Husserl would want – between perception and non-perception, but between two perceptions of non-perception' (Derrida 2011: 56). See Lawlor 2002: 180–8 and Cisney 2014: 127–9 for analysis of this argument.

[15] Cf. Baugh 1999 for an analysis of the similarities between *différance* and Sartre's account of consciousness. Baugh here highlight's Derrida's later admission of an 'immense debt' to Sartre (70).

as we find in the metaphysics of Plato. Rather, ideality emerges from the very repeatability of the mode itself. Now, a mortal being can only repeat a mode indefinitely because of their mortality. In order to bridge the gap between the indefinite and the infinite, Husserl presupposes the living present to be the 'ultimate form of ideality' (Lawlor 2002: 169):

> Presence has always been and will always be, to infinity, the form in which – we can say apodictically – the infinite diversity of content will be produced. The opposition – which inaugurates metaphysics – between form and matter finds in the concrete ideality of the living present its ultimate and radical justification. (Derrida 2011: 6)

Derrida can be seen as reading the question at the heart of Husserl as being about how these two different moments of form and intuition can be related to one another. On the one hand, this connection can be read as the question of how we relate the genetic aspects of the emergence of ideal forms, the account needed to escape from Platonism to the intuitionist account of our relationship with the ideal. This is the issue that Derrida addresses in his *Introduction to Husserl's Origin of Geometry*, where he looks at Husserl's account of the genesis of the geometrical understanding of the world. The second issue is one of a fundamentally Kantian nature, namely how we can relate these two moments of presence, which are different in kind, to each other. Just as the problem for Kant is how to relate two faculties that differ in kind to each other, for Husserl, on Derrida's model, we need to understand how intuition can be related to form. Just as with Kant, Derrida argues that this connection occurs through an element that shares qualities of both intuitional and formal characteristics. For Plato, we saw that there was an initial privileging of speech, and we find the same in Husserl on Derrida's account, with the voice as the moment that is able to unite the particular and the universal just as it united the natural and the rational for Hegel.

The process of hearing oneself speak, particularly when it comes to internal monologue, seems to relate purely to the subject, and bypasses any necessary reference to the body that we find in our sensory relations with others. Rather, it appears to be a pure moment of self-relation. Within this self-relation, however, we have the structures of language that connect this immediate self-relation with structures of universality that operate beyond the indefinite:

> The living act, the act that gives life, the *Lebendigkeit* that animates the body of the signifier and transforms it into an expression that wants to say, the soul of language, seems not to separate itself from itself, from its presence to

itself. The soul of language does not risk the death in the body of a signifier abandoned to the world and to the visibility of space. (Derrida 2011: 67)

The voice has three moments for Derrida.[16] First, it is produced either in the head or through the vocal cords. For this reason, we can understand the voice as an element of the world itself. Despite this presence in the world, the voice is not subject to the kinds of enquiry that we find in the mundane empirical sciences. As such, we can find a strong parallel here between the voice in Derrida's analysis and Hegel's account of the voice we looked at earlier in this chapter. Finally, in the process of hearing oneself speak, one still exteriorises one's thoughts, but this exteriorisation does not require any 'detour through the world' (Lawlor 2002: 192). This moment of self-relation, then, escapes from the limitations of relation to worldly objects, with their indefiniteness, and thus provides a foundation for the movement from intuition to form. It also allows a relation that shows the emergence of the form of ideality from a structure that is prior to it. Derrida also argues that this act of speaking to oneself for Husserl operates in terms of expression, and hence operates in terms of judgement: 'the "speaking to oneself" that here Husserl wants to restore is not a "speaking-about-oneself-to-oneself," unless the latter can take the form of a "speaking to oneself that S is P"' (Derrida 2011: 63).

Derrida argues that once we recognise that the voice is the moment of self-presence, this voice is, or is the origin of, self-consciousness. '[S]tructurally, and in principle, no consciousness is possible without the voice. The voice is being close to itself in the form of universality, as con-sciousness' (Derrida 2011: 68). This identification of the auto-affection of the self by itself with consciousness leads to an issue, however, once we realise that while auto-affection in this case operates without reference to space, it does necessarily operate in terms of time. Auto-affection requires a separation between the voice as speaking and the voice as hearing. As such, as with a melody, to form a unity, it requires the retention of the moment of speaking at the moment we are affected by our own voice. This, however, puts us in the odd position that self-consciousness begins on the basis of a repetition, since in order for the voice to hear itself, it must first speak, then be re-presented by memory. As Lawlor notes, memory therefore precedes perception on Derrida's reading of Husserl (Lawlor 2002: 193). For Derrida, this means that at the heart of self-consciousness is a moment of *différance* that makes self-presence possible. Derrida here draws close to Kant's claim, taken up by Deleuze, that

---

[16] See Lawlor 2002: 191–2 for a more detailed reading of Derrida's analysis of the voice.

what makes possible the foundational project of the *cogito* in Descartes' work is the removal of time from the *cogito*.[17] We can therefore see a connection between the moves made here and Kant's account of the paralogisms we looked at in Chapter 3, with Kant also showing the limitations of self-presence once we take time seriously. Much as with Sartre, the result of Derrida's analysis is the claim that we have to understand self-consciousness on the basis of a structure that differs in kind from it:

> The movement of différance does not supervene upon a transcendental subject. The movement of différance produces the transcendental subject. Auto-affection is not a modality of experience that characterises a being that would already be itself (*autos*). Auto-affection produces the same as the self-relation in the difference with itself, in the non-identical. (Derrida 2011: 71)

We can note a further parallel between Kant and Derrida here. Since *différance* occurs prior to the emergence of the subject, then just as with Kant's transcendental unity of apperception, we cannot apply categorial determinations to it. As Lawlor puts it,

> [T]his difference is not a difference between two beings; there is no ontic duplication that would place this auto-affection outside of the world . . . . Here we have the same yet different, yet not a *substantial* difference. (Lawlor 2002: 195)

As we shall see, this leads to the *différance* itself falling outside the realm of conceptuality.

In a later essay, Derrida sets out some more diagnostic claims showing the parallels between his reading of Husserl and Plato.[18] Here, we find a relationship between sense and judgement analogous to that which we have found in Plato. As Derrida notes, Husserl wishes to show how experience, present as sense, can be the ground for science, understood in terms of judgement. Husserl initially sees these two realms as independent of each other, and the stratum of expression, which is the basis for science, is introduced after an analysis of experience, or sense. Nonetheless, Derrida argues that in understanding the living present as the transcendental form of experience, Husserl has presupposed the notion of form. Just as in our reading of Plato, the relation between the father as subject and the child as

---

[17] 'Descartes could draw his conclusion only by expelling time, by reducing the Cogito to an instant and entrusting time to the operation of continuous creation carried out by God. More generally, the supposed identity of the I has no other guarantee than the unity of God himself' (Deleuze 1994: 86).
[18] 'Form and Meaning: A Note on the Phenomenology of Language', in Derrida 1984: 155–74.

logos can only be framed in terms of father and child once *logos* is in force, so the relation between sense and its expression in judgement can only be understood from the stratum of expression itself. Similarly, just as with Hegel, Derrida notes that Husserl characterises this process whereby we move from intuition to its ideal form in terms of 'Ideas in the Kantian sense' (Derrida 1989: 134n),[19] a structure we can now see as already present in Plato's own familial metaphors of *logos*. This means that the nature of sense, as experience, is always already understood according to the categories of expression: 'the description of the infrastructure (of sense) has been guided secretly by the superstructural possibility of meaning' (Derrida 1984: 171).

Derrida therefore argues that there is a 'complicity' between the structure of predication and the notion of presence in the living present that Husserl takes to be the founding moment of his philosophy (the form of experience). '[W]e may ask, here, to what extent the reference to the expressive stratum, before even becoming a theme, has secretly carried out analyses of the preexpressive stratum, and permitted a kernel of logical sense to be discovered in it, in the universal and allegedly silent form of being-present' (Derrida 1984: 171). In effect, the complicity is between the 'is' of the immediate intuitive presence and the 'is' of predication within judgement. This presupposition that the form of judgement will be commensurate with the structure of our intuition of the world leads to the impossibility of recognising *différance* within our account of the world, and hence reduces thinking to judging.

I will conclude this discussion of Derrida's reading of Husserl by looking in passing at Derrida's earlier *Introduction to the Origin of Geometry*, where we find the same relation to writing in Husserl's thought as we have in Plato and Hegel. As Derrida notes, Husserl himself is dismissive of writing for similar reasons to Plato's rejection of it, arguing that it involves a 'technicist's and objectivist's alienation, which degraded science into a skill or a game' (Derrida 1989: 98). Nonetheless, as we have seen, the subject for Husserl is mortal. We have already seen that this leads Husserl to prioritise form over intuition. Even with Derrida's analysis of the voice, however, we still have a problematic relation to individual existents:

---

[19] Bernet 1989: 149–50 correctly notes that this moment of Husserl's thought, which occurs in the *Origin of Geometry*, is at the heart of *Speech and Phenomena*, where the possibility of indefinite repetition in intuitive presence is converted into infinite presence by taking what is a task of consciousness as an actually given object, thus falling for a transcendental illusion. Bell 1998 in his reading of Husserl (in particular 65–75) explores Husserl's use of the Kantian notion of idea in order to account for objectivity.

'Speech [*langage oral*] has freed the object of individual subjectivity but leaves it bound to its beginning and to the synchrony of an exchange within the institutive community' (Derrida 1989: 87). Rather, it is writing that gives true objectivity to science by moving away from a relation to a particular subject to a relation to a subject in general, which Derrida will equate with the transcendental subject. Thus, by moving from a writing that will always relate to a particular empirical individual to a writing that is addressed to the individual in its generality, science becomes possible. Once again drawing close to Sartre in his analysis of the transcendental field, Derrida posits this transcendental field of writing as the constituting moment of the particular subjectivities for whom speech is a possibility:

> Jean Hyppolite invokes the possibility of a 'subjectless transcendental field,' one in which 'the conditions of subjectivity would appear and where the subject would be constituted starting from the transcendental field'. Writing, as the place of absolutely permanent ideal objectivities and there-fore of absolute Objectivity, certainly constitutes such a transcendental field. (Derrida 1989: 88)

5.5   *Différance*

Strictly speaking, there is no 'concept' of *différance*, and Derrida argues that since *différance* does not involve the rigid limits we might assume for a concept, it is 'pulled through' and bleeds into a series of other Derridean concepts that in other texts will play roles related to *différance*.[20] The lack of conceptual structure means that we cannot define *différance*, though Derrida does write that '[i]f there were a definition of *différance*, it would be precisely the limit, the interruption, the destruction of the Hegelian *relève* wherever it operates' (Derrida 1981a: 40–1). As such, *différance* refers to this moment that falls outside of conceptual determinations. For this reason, we can begin our analysis of the term '*différance*' by noting the obvious point that it differs in one letter from the word 'difference'. While

[20] 'Since it cannot be elevated into a master-word or a master concept, since it blocks every relationship to theology, *différance* finds itself enmeshed in the work that pulls it through a chain of other "concepts," other "words," other textual configurations. Perhaps later I will have occasion to indicate why such other "words" or "concepts" later or simultaneously imposed themselves; and why room had to be left for their insistence (for example, gram, reserve, incision, trace, spacing, blank-sens blanc, sang blanc, sans blanc, cent blancs, semblant-supplement, pharmakon, margin-mark-march, etc.). By definition the list has no taxonomical closure, and even less does it constitute a lexicon' (Derrida 1981b: 40). See also Derrida 1984: 12.

we have a written *différance* here, this difference cannot be expressed phonetically (in French at least), since the pronunciation of the two words is identical. Derrida's aim in setting out this quasi-concept of *différance* is therefore to put forward a moment that escapes from a privileging of the voice, and with it from the structures of presence, by using an element that cannot be successfully distinguished by the voice. We can note first that this rejection of presence means a rejection of the whole structure of the sign. As Derrida notes, a sign relies on the notion of absence, and thus at first glance appears to share something with *différance*. While the sign relies on the notion of absence (we only require signs for things that are not present), this absence can only be understood in terms of an originary presence, and in terms of a future presence that the sign attempts to reappropriate. The absence of presence in the sign is therefore secondary and provisional. *Différance* differs from the sign in operating in terms of neither presence nor absence. In effect, therefore, this puts it outside of the realm of presence, and representation, and as we shall see, *différance* operates much like a transcendental ground for presence. What, then, is *différance*?

Instead of a concept or a word, Derrida calls *différance* a 'sheaf' that assembles different significances:

> [T]he word sheaf seems to mark more appropriately that the assemblage to be proposed has the complex structure of a weaving, an interlacing that permits the different threads and different lines of meaning – or of force – to go off again in different directions, just as it is always ready to tie itself up with others. (Derrida 1984: 3)

What ensures that *différance* isn't a concept isn't the fact that it has several meanings; many concepts do, and this possibility is a central aspect of, for instance, Hegel's account of dialectics. Rather, what prevents *différance* from being a concept is that it is what allows us to have meaningful concepts. As such, it acts as a transcendental condition for the possibility of conceptual thought. If *différance* is going to explain how concepts get their meaning, then *différance* itself cannot be a concept, at the risk of circularity. Derrida argues that *différance* weaves together two 'lines of meaning'. These are *différance* as deferral and *différance* as spacing. Derrida refers to the first of these as follows:

> The Greek *diapherein* does not comport one of the two motifs of the Latin *differre*, to wit, the action of putting off until later, of taking into account, of taking account of time and of the forces of operation that implies an economic calculation, a detour, a delay, a relay, a reserve, a representation – concepts

I would summarise here in a word I have never used but that could be inscribed within this chain: temporization. (Derrida 1984: 8)

This first sense of *différance* is as the point of difference within the subject between the call of the voice and its repetition. It is thus the moment of difference that makes possible the subject while incorporating a fracture within them that cannot itself be understood by categorial thought. Derrida's claim here is that rather than presence grounding this difference, in fact it is *différance*, as a moment of non-presence, that makes presence possible. Returning to *Speech and Phenomena*, Derrida writes of this moment that '*différance* is what makes the movement of signification possible only if each element that is said to be "present," appearing on the stage of presence, is related to something other than itself but retains the mark of a past element and already lets itself be hollowed out by the mark of its relation to a future element' (Derrida 2011: 142–3).

In the *Différance* essay, Derrida extends this claim beyond Husserl, noting Descartes' effort to understand the subject as the foundation of philosophy. Derrida's claim is that such an approach doesn't work for a number of reasons. First, if we recognise that language can be understood apart from the subject, then there is a sense in which rather than language being a function of the subject, the subject could be a function of language. Second, and following on from this, Derrida claims that if we try to understand the notion of a subject that is purely present to itself, then we tend to fall back on the notion of the self as a substance. This is what Descartes does in the *Meditations* when he makes the claim that the self is a thinking thing. We cannot ground the notion of presence in a substance, however, as presence itself is supposed to be the ground for metaphysical categories such as substance. Finally, as Derrida notes, just as the meaning of words contains references to past and future uses, there is no moment of self-presence which is outside of time. Since consciousness is always anticipating the future, and retaining the past, there is no moment where the self can purely relate to itself.

We can now turn to the second sense of *différance*, which is of spacing:

The other sense of *différer* is the more common and identifiable one: to be not identical, to be other, to be discernible, etc. When dealing with *differen(ts)(ds)*, a word that can be written with a final *ts* or a final *ds*, as you will, whether it is a question of dissimilar otherness or of allergic and polemical otherness, an interval, a distance, *spacing*, must be produced between the element's other, and be produced with a certain perseverance in repetition. (Derrida 1984: 8–9)

In *Positions*, he writes, '*différance*, as that which produces different things, that which differentiates, is the common root of all of the oppositional concepts that mark our language, such as, to take only a few examples, sensible/intelligible, intuition/signification, nature/culture, etc.' (Derrida 1981b: 9). In what way does *différance* achieve this?

The first thing to note is that spacing is not space, but is that which renders possible space. Why is space important for language? As we have already seen in our analysis of Bergson, if we are going to understand words or concepts as external to each other but as determined in relation to one another, we need something like a conception of space. Space, whether real or metaphorical, allows us to see two things as differing as being 'this and not that', by effectively being in different locations in our conceptual system. When we 'map out' a language, we need some kind of space within which to chart the relative positions of concepts in relation to one another. We could also view this aspect of spacing from another perspective. Spacing is what allows the rupture between concepts that opens the way for different concepts to be distinguished from each other. As with Bergson, Sartre, and Merleau-Ponty, therefore, Derrida's *différance* operates through a process of dissociation to generate a field of meaningful terms. As the genesis of the space within which meaning is deployed, through the differential relationships of concepts, *différance* therefore is prior to the kinds of oppositions that require the notion of space to give them meaning. Thus, spacing is both active and passive – it is an active sundering of conceptual unities into different concepts, but also a passive providing of a space for concepts. Similarly, Derrida claims that *différance* falls outside of another key opposition between sensibility and intellect. We cannot distinguish between *différance*-with-an-a and difference-with-an-e sensibly. We also cannot intellectually distinguish *différance*, as it is prior to conceptual determination. The conclusion of this is that what makes possible the system of meaning is something that is radically unsystematisable.

We have seen that Derrida equates presence with predication, and so we find in Derrida's account of *différance* some themes we have already found in the work of Hölderlin. In rejecting presence, we are also forced to reject the standard oppositions that metaphysics relies upon when characterising *différance*, just as Hölderlin sees being as entirely indeterminate since it exists prior to the *Ur-teilung*. As such, *différance* is understood neither as presence nor as lack, and fails to be captured by the active/passive opposition. Rather, *différance* operates as an 'origin' that has none of the traits of the structure of judgement:

> A determination or an effect within a system which is no longer that of presence but of différance, a system that no longer tolerates the opposition

of activity and passivity, nor that of cause and effect, or of indetermination and determination, etc. (Derrida 1984: 16)

As we have already seen, however, the notion of a pure origin in the work of Hölderlin emerges from the inability to think an alternative to judgement. Thus, the diversity of the world is opposed to a moment of unity prior to determination by judgement. Derrida's claim, therefore, would be that Hölderlin's position, with an indeterminate moment of origin, is itself a moment within the metaphysics of presence. Hölderlin's aim of understanding the world as emerging from an originary division is precisely what Derrida rejects when he puts into question a 'rightful beginning, an absolute point of departure' (Derrida 1984: 6). He sets this out most clearly in his discussion of negative theology.

As Derrida notes, since *différance* 'derives from no category of being', and hence is outside of the structures of judgement, we cannot use either form of the copula to evaluate it. To use 'is' to make a claim about its existence, or to attribute a property to *différance*, would be to reintroduce *différance* into the realm of metaphysics and hence to prevent it from giving an account of the genesis of judgement. Derrida argues that a traditional negative theology operates by denying God finite categories of essence and existence only to posit that God can only be captured by categories of existence that transcend finite experience. Derrida is quite clear that this isn't the correct understanding of *différance*. Negative theology still effectively treats the ground of the world, God, as an object, albeit one that is unknowable. *Différance* isn't to be understood as some kind of beyond to the world, but rather as the operation of generating the differential nexus within which names gain significance. The unnameability of *différance* therefore in a sense comes from its closeness to rather than its distance from us:

> The unnameable is not an ineffable Being which no name could approach: God, for example. This unnameable is the play which makes possible nominal effects, the relatively unitary and atomic structures that are called names, the chains of or substitutions of names in which, for example, the nominal effect *différance* is itself enmeshed. (Derrida 1984: 26–7)

For Derrida, the organisation of *différance* differs in kind from the structures of judgement. Rather than the combinatory logic of judgement, we find *différance* operating according to a logic of dissociation, where concepts such as difference represent provisional coagulations of an underlying transcendental field. As Derrida puts it, deconstruction operates 'according to lines of force and forces of rupture that are localizable in the discourse to be deconstructed' (Derrida 1981b: 82).

Derrida's claim is therefore that philosophy has tended to operate in the thrall of a conception of origin that privileges identity over difference. As such, returning to Hölderlin once more, we can see Derrida's claim as being that philosophy is drawn to the kind of model Hölderlin presents, of an undifferentiated unity that develops into determinate form through the supplementary introduction of difference:

> The enterprise of returning 'strategically', 'ideally', to an origin or to a priority thought to be simple, intact, normal, pure, standard, self-identical, in order then to think in terms of derivation, complication, deterioration, accident, etc. All metaphysicians, from Plato to Rousseau, Descartes to Husserl, have proceeded in this way, conceiving good to be before evil, the positive before the negative, the pure before the impure, the simple before the complex, the essential before the accidental, the imitated before the imitation, etc. And this is not just *one* metaphysical gesture among others, it is *the* metaphysical exigency, that which has been the most constant, most profound and most potent. (Derrida 1988: 93)

We might note at this point that despite Derrida's explicit claim to be writing against the phenomenological tradition, this notion of the privileging of a pure origin is difficult to reconcile with a figure such as Merleau-Ponty, for whom the basic element of perception is always already complex and ambiguous. Hence, if presence is equated with predication, we can see traces of the deconstructive approach as operative prior to Derrida, in, for instance, Merleau-Ponty's move to a logic of perception, and to a synthesis of transition.

5.6   Conclusion

In specifying the locus of Derrida's enquiry, he talks of a '"thought-that-means-nothing," the thought that exceeds meaning and meaning-as-hearing-oneself-speak by interrogating them – this thought, announced in grammatology, is given precisely as the thought for which there is no sure opposition between outside and inside' (Derrida 1981b: 12). Here, then, we have the claim that at the heart of Derrida's philosophy is the attempt to think a thought that precedes the structures of determination we encountered in presence. We can understand Derrida's analysis as having two moments. First, we have an account of the constitution of judgement through a prior moment that differs in kind from it. In this analysis, the key term here is *différance*, which Derrida claims 'is thus no longer simply a concept, but rather the possibility of conceptuality, of a conceptual process and system in general' (Derrida 1984: 11). Difference is that which gives sense to juridical thought whilst being itself incompre-hensible to it. Second, we have the transcendental dialectic whereby *différance* is covered over. Here, Derrida argues that the move to categorial thought emerges through a transcendental illusion. Whether in terms of the transparency of speech in Plato, phonetic language in Hegel, or the form of the living presence in Husserl, something which can only be given as a task is taken as a complete object for analysis. The error that emerges from this illusion, which grounds representation and effaces the role of *différance* in constituting the grounds for judgement, is an act of 'radical and irruptive freedom' (Derrida 1989: 134). It is in this manner that we can understand Derrida as one of the 'responsible guardians of the heritage of transcendental idealism' (Derrida 2005: 134).

We have also seen throughout this analysis a number of affinities with the philosophers we have already looked at. *Différance*, in its characterisa-tion as spacing, bears a resemblance to Bergsonian duration, in its role as constitutive of the space where oppositional determinations become think-able, and its constitution of localisable but ambiguous centres of action. *Différance* as deferral shares many structural parallels with Sartre's account of consciousness in its aim to show the constitution of consciousness from a prior transcendental field, an account which in turn borrows from Bergson's characterisation of an interpenetrative multiplicity. Finally, *différance* does not operate through the constitution of determinations from a prior pure origin, but rather is a continuous operation. In this regard, we can see a parallel between Derrida's rejection of the notion of an origin and Merleau-Ponty's move from synthesis as a process of constitu-tion to synthesis as transitional that does away with the idea of such a pure beginning. In the next chapter, we will turn to the work of Michel Foucault, who also, at least on the surface, represents a break with phe-nomenology. As we shall see, however, this break itself operates within the framework of a post-Kantianism without judgement.

CHAPTER 6

Foucault, Power, and the Juridico-Discursive

6.1 Introduction

In the last chapter, we saw how Derrida attempted to develop a philosophy that entailed both rejecting the structure of judgement and rejecting the central place of the subject. This project was already implicit in Sartre's adoption of a transcendental field governed by transversal rather than centralised connections, and in Merleau-Ponty's account of transition synthesis. The result of this was the conclusion that sense was different in kind from judgement, and that the subject was constituted by a pre-individual transcendental field understood in terms of *différance*. Foucault presents a similar project: 'to think of knowledge as an historical process before any problematic of the truth, and more fundamentally than the subject-object relation. Knowledge (*connaissance*) freed from the subject-object relations is knowledge (*savoir*)' (Foucault, quoted in Elden 2017: 35). As we shall see, while Foucault is hostile to many aspects of the Kantian project in his explicit statements, this hostility centres on taking as essential to transcendental philosophy two related claims. These are that transcendental philosophy relies on the subject as a central organising principle, and that the organisation of thought is structured by judgement. Once we accept that transcendental philosophy does not have to be bound to these assumptions, we find a much more ambivalent relationship to it. We find the claim that what needs to be analysed is the sense underlying the categorial claims of our discourse, as well as how the objects of that discourse are constituted. Presenting a single account of Foucault's work is exceptionally difficult, since he frequently revises his approach, often reinterpreting earlier writings in the light of these new approaches. In this chapter, I will follow the relatively accepted division into an early archaeological period and a later genealogical period, though it is important to recognise that there are shifts in approach throughout his work.[1] In the first period, Foucault sets out his account of the structure of representation in the history of ideas, and the manner in which the space that organises our knowledge claims is contingent, yet determines what can and cannot be said within a given form of discourse. The second introduces the notion of power into Foucault's analysis. This allows Foucault to show the interrelation of discourse and the non-discursive. As we shall see, *The History of Sexuality* attempts to analyse a moment prior to the formation of the visible and the invisible, and to show how the body that Merleau-Ponty takes as the locus of sense is itself constituted by deeper processes operating above and below the body itself.[2] I want to begin by looking at Foucault's relationship with Kant through the origin of Foucault's term for his method in the early work, 'archaeology', before turning to the three epistemes which Foucault thinks characterise the structure of knowledge. As we shall see, the same problem of resemblance, and ultimately the same solution, in terms of the development of a logic of dissociation governs Foucault's thought, as we have found in previous thinkers.

6.2 Foucault's Relationship to Kant

Foucault holds an ambivalent relationship to Kant. While Foucault takes up aspects of the transcendental, he nevertheless sees Kant's formulation of it as inherently unstable, and as presupposing a constituting subject. Such a presupposition puts the origin of the subject out of question, since the subject becomes the condition for enquiry itself. His ambivalence comes through in his assertion of a need to break radically with Kant,[3] but also in a recognition that his own project has a Kantian origin. When a review of *The Order of Things* in the *New York Times Book Review* attributed Foucault's key term 'archaeology' to Freud, Foucault responded by claiming a Kantian lineage of the term.[4] Kant's use of the term can be found in

---

[1] See, for instance, Han 2002 and Oksala 2005 on the development between *The Order of Things* and *The Archaeology of Knowledge*. While understanding these developments is clearly significant for a full understanding of Foucault's work, we will leave them to one side here given the more circumscribed domain of our reading.

[2] As Foucault puts it, 'I believe that the political significance of the problem of sex is due to the fact that sex is located at the point of intersection of the discipline of the body and the control of the population' (Foucault 2002e: 125).

[3] Schmidt and Wartenberg 1994 provide the strongest reading of early Foucault as straightforwardly rejecting Kant. See Han 2002: 17–37 for a more balanced reading.

[4] See McQuillan 2010a: 39.

a late incomplete paper, 'What Real Progress Has Metaphysics Made in Germany Since the Time of Leibniz and Wolff?', written but never submitted for the Berlin *Académie Royal des Sciences et des Belles-Lettres* 1790 prize essay contest (Kant 2002). In this essay, Kant argues that the history of philosophy cannot be understood in terms of empirical historical knowledge, since such knowledge deals with contingent facts, and philosophy, as a rational science, deals with necessities. The science that deals with the history of philosophy is named 'archaeology' by Kant. Since the history of philosophy is the history of the systematicity of philosophy, Kant ties archaeology to the faculty of reason.

Kant claims to have shown in the aesthetic and analytic of the *Critique of Pure Reason* that the understanding takes appearances, and unifies them according to rules (Kant 1929: A302/B359). As we saw in the last chapter, these faculties on their own would only give us a fragmentary knowledge of phenomena. We therefore need a further synthesis, whereby these different cognitions of the understanding are unified into a system. It is this second step which is carried out by reason. Reason therefore serves to unify the rules of the understanding according to principles. When dealing with the history of philosophy, we find reason playing the same role in unifying our metaphysical claims as it does with claims of empirical knowledge. As Kant puts it in the prize essay, 'there must have been a need of reason (theoretical or practical) which obliged it to ascend from its judgments about things to the grounds thereof, up to the first, initially through common reason' (2002: 417). Archaeology thus traces the process whereby reason systematises our metaphysical judgements about the nature of the world.

The history of philosophy for Kant therefore 'establishes facts of reason, it does not borrow them from historical narrative, but draws them from the nature of human reason, as philosophical archaeology' (Kant 2002: 417). It is important to note here that the facts of reason are not for Kant necessarily truths, but rather those principles that reason gives rise to in order to allow judgements to be united together. Thus, in the *First Critique*, Kant cites as a fact of reason the 'objective validity of the concept of efficient cause' (1929: A760/B788), rightly brought into doubt by Hume. Archaeology is thus for Kant a procedure whereby the presuppositions of reason, which are taken as givens by transcendental realist philosophy, are derived from an analysis of the systematising activity of reason. It is a study of the architectonics of knowledge that only becomes possible with the advent of a critique of reason itself, where it becomes possible 'to subject to examination, not the facts of reason, but reason itself, in the whole extent of its powers' (Kant 1929: A761/B789). Archaeology for Kant is not therefore concerned with objective truth, but with systematicity, and can only emerge once the transcendental philosophy has made possible this study of reason itself. We can note one further aspect of Kant's account of archaeology. As we have seen, reason for Kant operates according to the same categories as the understanding, since 'reason does not really generate any concept. The most it can do is *free* a concept of *understanding* from the unavoidable limitations of possible experience' (Kant 1929: A409/B435). As such, an understanding of the principles that allow knowledge to be systematised will be an analysis that claims that knowledge is structured in terms of judgement.

Foucault's account of archaeology shares many of the traits of Kant's account. Foucault brackets the question of the historical development of systems of knowledge in his account of archaeology. His concern is not with reasons why a particular set of principles came to systematise knowledge at a time, but rather with those principles themselves. Similarly, his concern is not with the truth of our systems of knowledge, but with the systematicity by which they relate together different claims. In fact, Foucault's project goes even further, arguing that to understand this systematicity, we must also bracket the meaning of the terms we are looking at. As we shall see, this means that Foucault's concern is with the way in which statements within a system of knowledge are connected together. If such a bracketing of sense and truth is possible, it makes possible an analysis of the nature of meaning and knowledge claims of a given historical era or epoch without presupposing either of those concepts.[5] Finally, as with Kant, archaeology for Foucault is 'a domain that has not so far been made the object of any analysis' (Foucault 2002a: 229). As follows from this claim to originality, however, there are some substantial differences between Foucault's account of archaeology and Kant's account. Here, I want to note three. First, while Kant implies that there is a single trajectory that reason follows in its systematisation of knowledge, for Foucault there are a variety of different ways in which knowledge claims can be tied together. In *The Order of Things*, Foucault calls these different systematisations *epistemes*, and divides the history of our ways of understanding the world into three epistemes. Second, while Kant limits archaeology to philosophy, Foucault sees epistemes as pervasive throughout the intellectual and practical attitudes of their times. Finally, whereas at the root of the systematisation of knowledge for Kant we find

---

[5] See Dreyfus and Rabinow 1982: 44–52 for a comparison of Foucault's method with the phenomenological method. As they note, this parallel with phenomenology lays the early work open to something analogous to Foucault's own criticisms of transcendental philosophy.

facts of reason that are judgements, for Foucault we find, at least in *The Archaeology of Knowledge*, statements, which do not share the structure of judgements. We will return to an analysis of these non-categorial structures later in the chapter. In moving away from judgement, we find the same parallel move away from the subject as the locus of philosophy that we found in Derrida, since we no longer require an organising subjectivity to hold together the autonomous moments of the judgement. As such, the kind of synthesis Foucault discovers will not be logically dependent on the subject that finds meaning within the structures governing knowledge in the given epoch.

Much as we saw with Derrida, therefore, Foucault has an ambivalent relationship with the transcendental. Insofar as the transcendental is seen as fundamentally related to a constituting subject, and to the structure of judgement, Foucault is opposed to it. *The Archaeology of Knowledge* concludes with a polemic against the 'transcendental narcissism' (Foucault 2002a: 224) of relating knowledge to the transcendental unity of apperception or its translations in the phenomenological tradition. As Colin Koopman notes, despite Kant's problems being central for Foucault, Foucault at many points attempts to distance himself from the transcendental.[6] Nonetheless, in characterising the *episteme*, which for Foucault plays the role of organising knowledge in a given historical period, as 'defin[ing] the conditions of possibility of all knowledge' (Foucault 2002b: 183) at a given moment in a given society, or as the 'historical *a priori*' (Foucault 2002b: 375), Foucault shows a substantial debt to transcendental philosophy. As we have already seen throughout this volume, transcendental philosophy does not have to rely on the notion of the constituting subject, however, or on the claim that organisation implies judgement, and McQuillan points out that Kant's own definition of the transcendental ('I entitle *transcendental* all knowledge which is occupied not so much with objects as with the mode of our knowledge of objects in so far as this mode of knowledge is to be possible *a priori*. A system of such concepts might be entitled transcendental philosophy' [Kant 1929: A11–12/B25]) does not explicitly refer to a constituting subject (McQuillan 2010b: 146). As such, Foucault's relationship to Kant is complex, but I will argue that Foucault's more polemical rejections of the transcendental rest ultimately on an illegitimate conflation of transcendental philosophy and a constitutive subject, which fails to capture these deeper debts to Kant's

---

[6] Koopman (2010) attempts to discover in Kant a distinction between transcendental critique and critique more generally, arguing that while Foucault follows Kant in terms of the latter, he opposes him in terms of the former. McQuillan 2010b: 150–1 provides good textual evidence to cast doubt on this reading.

thought. This is true whether we are looking at the earlier archaeological work or the later genealogical work, such as *The History of Sexuality*, where power operates above and beneath the level of the subject.[7] In the next section, I want to look at Foucault's own account of archaeology, beginning with *The Order of Things*. As we shall see, despite Foucault's own claim not to be concerned with the notion of sense (once again because of his belief that it implies an organising subject), several of the structures which are central to debates we have already considered are at play in Foucault's work.

6.3 Sense in Foucault

Foucault's *Order of Things* opens with a brief discussion of Borges' essay, *The Analytical Language of John Wilkins* (2000), which, Foucault claims, 'shattered all the familiar landmarks of my thought – *our* thought, the thought that bears the stamp of our age and our geography' (Foucault 2002b: xvi). Aristotle attempted to develop a taxonomy that would allow any term to be defined through a nested series of determinations, with each further determination more precisely circumscribing the nature of the object under consideration. This Aristotelian hierarchical mode of determination relies on the subsumptive logic at the heart of judgement. John Wilkins took the Aristotelian approach further in the seventeenth century, attempting to produce a universal language whereby the series of determinations from genus to species are incorporated into the structure of words themselves. Thus, the first two syllables of a word would be its genus (of which Wilkins claimed there were forty), followed by further syllables determining the precise species of the object. To take an example, 'salmon is a species of Za or Fish, a particular kind of fish called N, namely, the squamous river fish. This class ZaN is subdivided into lower classes, and the lower class salmon is called A, which means the red-fleshed kind of squamous river fish, and so a salmon is a ZaNA' (Wright Henderson 1910: 87–8). Salmon swims would in turn be 'ZaNA GoF', where 'Go' is the category of motion and 'F' represents the particular motion of swimming. In this system, therefore, the sense of a term is present within the structure of the word itself.

Borges brings in the fictitious example of a Chinese encyclopaedia entitled the 'Celestial Empire of Benevolent Knowledge' as a counter-example to this

---

[7] I will argue something similar in regard to the notion of sense itself – that while Foucault rejects the category of sense, this is because he sees sense as traditionally operating in terms of a constituting subjectivity. Foucault is here close to Deleuze in arguing that the sense of the world is constituted by a prior signifying field.

account of categorisation, to illustrate the arbitrariness of our classifications of the world. In the Chinese encyclopaedia, Borges states that animals can be classified according to the following categories:

> (a) those that belong to the emperor; (b) embalmed ones; (c) those that are trained; (d) suckling pigs; (e) mermaids; (f) fabulous ones; (g) stray dogs; (h) those that are included in this classification; (i) those that tremble as if they were mad; (j) innumerable ones; (k) those drawn with a very fine camel's-hair brush; (l) etcetera; (m) those that have just broken the flower vase; (n) those that at a distance resemble flies. (Borges 2000: 231)

Now, this categorisation clearly departs from the Aristotelian scheme that operates in terms of oppositions. Foucault argues that what Borges is presenting here is not simply comical, but is uncanny, in that it disrupts structures we use to make sense of the world. Foucault notes two different forms of disruption, the targets of which roughly correspond to Deleuze's categories of good sense and common sense. Foucault notes that the first level of disruption is provided by the arbitrary nature of characteristics that the hierarchy relies on (what Deleuze will call a failure of good sense, and Foucault calls the *incongruous* nature of the categories). There is a deeper problem, however. This second more fundamental issue Foucault raises is what he calls the *heteroclite* nature of the determinations – what Deleuze will call a failure of common sense. The heteroclite emerges through the presence of the category 'included in this classification', which proves paradoxical by both being on the same level in the hierarchy of determinations as other categories and containing them. As such, 'we shall never succeed in defining a stable relation of contained to container between each of these categories and that which includes them all' (Foucault 2002b: xviii). The deeper issue, therefore, is not the arbitrariness of this categorisation, but that it is impossible to lay out this table of categories in a consistent logical space, or to present them in a diagram such as the tree of Porphyry.

At the heart of Foucault's project in *The Order of Things* is an analysis of the nature of this space which makes ordering possible, and the way in which different rules for relating statements organise this space. For Foucault, different historical epochs will be defined by differences in the way they see determinations as connected together within this space. The basis for Foucault's enquiry is the question of discourse, as Foucault highlights by noting that aphasics often lack the ability to successfully order physical objects within a space on the basis of their properties:

> Within this simple space in which things are normally arranged and given names, the aphasiac will create a multiplicity of tiny, fragmented regions in

which nameless resemblances agglutinate things into unconnected islets; in one corner, they will place the lightest-coloured skeins, in another the red ones, somewhere else those that are softest in texture, in yet another place the longest, or those that have a tinge of purple or those that have been wound up into a ball. But no sooner have they been adumbrated than all these groupings dissolve again, for the field of identity that sustains them, however limited it may be, is still too wide not to be unstable; and so the sick mind continues to infinity, creating groups then dispersing them again, heaping up diverse similarities, destroying those that seem clearest, splitting up things that are identical, superimposing different criteria, frenziedly beginning all over again, becoming more and more disturbed, and teetering finally on the brink of anxiety. (Foucault 2002b: xx)

Bergson also introduces the example of the aphasic, but while for Bergson aphasia is just a specific case of perception in general, for Foucault aphasia is used to support the claim that discourse is prior to the sense we make of the material world. As such, the failure of the aphasic to use language leads to an inability to order space more generally. In *The Order of Things*, therefore, we find a focus on the nature of discourse that will open out in Foucault's later works to provide a double genesis, not simply of discourse, but also of the objects that discourse relates to from a field that is prior to both language and its referent. *The Order of Things* can be read as an enquiry into how the space which makes possible the kinds of orderings we take for granted in language is possible. In this sense, Deleuze is right to note that Foucault shares with Bergson a desire to determine the non-juridical operations that make the space of judgement possible.[8]

Central to Foucault's approach, therefore, is an examination of the nature of this space that is prior to particular judgements, and determines the structures that make science possible. It is a 'history of the Same – of that which, for a given culture, is both dispersed and related, therefore to be distinguished by kinds and to be collected together into identities' (Foucault 2002b: xxvi). As we noted earlier, the core concept that grounds this early project is the episteme, which Foucault defines as follows:

[W]hat I am attempting to bring to light is the epistemological field, the episteme in which knowledge, envisaged apart from all criteria having reference to its rational value or to its objective forms, grounds its positivity

---

[8] Cf. Deleuze 1988b: 4, where Deleuze equates the statement in Foucault's work with memory in Bergson's philosophy. As we saw in Chapter 2, Bergson argues that memory is what provides the sense of terms by allowing us to determine which relation between terms is actualised. For Foucault, as we shall see, the statement also has the function of determining the sense of propositions. In both cases, as they provide the sense of the judgement, memory and the statement differ in kind from the judgements they relate to.

and thereby manifests a history which is not that of its growing perfection, but rather that of its conditions of possibility; in this account, what should appear are those configurations within the space of knowledge which have given rise to the diverse forms of empirical science. Such an enterprise is not so much a history, in the traditional meaning of that word, as an 'archaeology'. (Foucault 2002b: xxiii–xxiv)

Since the episteme is the 'fundamental network defining the implicit but inevitable unity of knowledge', Foucault excludes the possibility that order is a posteriori or emerges from perception itself. As Han (2002: 40–1) notes, Foucault is here once again following Kant in arguing that since the episteme makes possible empirical knowledge, it cannot be explained in terms of it. Once again with Kant, we cannot see order as something that is simply given or discovered, but must see it as something which is constituted: 'there is nothing more tentative, nothing more empirical (*superficially, at least*) than the process of establishing an order among things' (Foucault 2002b: xxi, my italics). As such, at least in *The Order of Things*,[9] we have a strong correlation between the transcendental categories and the episteme, which Foucault entitles the historical a priori to capture the sense in which it determines the range of claims that can be made within a discourse while also being fixed to a given historical period. Nonetheless, we have a difference here, since rather than having something like a logical space which contains juridical facts of reason, we have the constitution of a space itself, which, as we shall see, will depend on non-categorial elements.

   We can once again find here a parallel with Bergson on memory in that we do not see time – in this case, historical time – as a series of periods as they would be, for instance, for Hegel's Absolute Idealism, that develop in sequence from the contradictions in the surface structure of the previous structure. Rather, the surface structure of the organisation of objects refers back to a space beneath the surface structure – what Foucault refers to elsewhere as the 'unconscious' (2002b: xi) of the time period. The obvious question, given each episteme offers a geometry of the space underlying the relationship between words and things, is what leads to the transition between different epistemes? In response to this question, Foucault argues against the dialectical analysis that would hold that each episteme is more adequate than the preceding one. Rather, Foucault essentially brackets the question of the reasons for a move from one episteme to another. This allows him to concentrate on the analysis of the structure of discourse itself, independent

---

[9] Cf. Han 2002: 60. As she notes, the episteme and the historical a priori diverge from one another in *The Archaeology of Knowledge*.

of its causes, and also to emphasise the contingency of the reasons why a particular mode of discourse comes to prominence. As we shall see later in this chapter, Foucault's introduction of power will ultimately allow him to provide an account of how discourses are formed that continues to leave a place for their contingency.

6.4 The Three Epistemes

The Order of Things presents three different ways in which this space which defines our categorisation of the world has historically been organised. Each of these ways specifies the geometry according to which our taxonomy of the natural world is constructed. Foucault does not simply take the episteme to determine how words relate to objects, but argues for the more radical claim that the episteme determines what constitutes something as an object in the first place. In fact, the episteme solves the same problem we have dealt with in relation to each of the philosophers we have looked at so far in this study: how do we determine which resemblances should be drawn together in order to give us the properties needed to make judgements? As Foucault notes, pure perception cannot give us the basic qualities needed to make judgements, as we need a criterion with which to distinguish essential and accidental qualities of things. Mirroring Derrida's claim of a transcendental ideal within Hegel, this criterion is provided by the rules of the episteme: 'In fact, there is no similitude and no distinction, even for the wholly untrained perception, that is not the result of a precise operation and of the application of a preliminary criterion' (Foucault 2002b: xxi).

Each era in history involves the development of a consistent set of rules for what counts as an object of knowledge. 'In any given culture and at any given moment, there is only one episteme that defines the conditions of possibility of all knowledge, whether expressed in a theory or silently invested in a practice' (Foucault 2002b: 183). The episteme therefore forestalls the possibility of something like Borges' Chinese encyclopaedia by providing the space within which objects of knowledge can be given with consistency. Foucault outlines three epistemes: the Renaissance, the classical, and the modern. I want to run through them briefly here. As we shall see, each episteme is governed by rules that allow resemblances to be related together into structures of knowledge.[10] As such, they precede judgement by determining what kinds of things are going to be categorised as subjects and predicates.

---

[10] For more detailed readings and assessments of the epistemes, see Gutting 1989: ch. 4–5.

The Renaissance episteme has explicitly at its heart the concept of resemblance. Knowledge of the world is understood through a web of resemblances and similitudes across various domains. As May (2006: 46) notes, one of the most influential examples of this kind of reasoning is found in Plato's *Republic*, where Socrates' explicit goal in the text is to explore the nature of justice, as it relates to individuals. Since Socrates argues that attempting to understand the soul directly would be too challenging, he suggests relying on the analogy between the structure of the city and the structure of the soul. Thus, we take the soul to be a microcosm of the city as macrocosm. What makes this possible is an understanding of the world as a 'network of similitudes' (Oksala 2005: 24) where philosophical enquiry entails discerning these similitudes through signs present in the world. These resemblances span a number of domains, and Foucault classes together the resemblances Belon draws between the structure of man's arm and the structure of the wing of a bird, and between man's baser parts and hell, where the damned souls 'are like the excrement of the universe' (Foucault 2002b: 25). There are a number of implications of the model of knowledge operating through resemblance. First, knowledge involves a process of interpretation, whereby similarities are found in the world and tied together into chains of relations. These similarities themselves are not immediately apparent, but must be deciphered, using the visible world as a means to determine the invisible relations between terms. This process of interpretation is what allows us to distinguish 'juxtaposed fragments, some identical, some different' (Foucault 2002b: 29) from significant similarities. 'Resemblance was the invisible form of that which, from the depths of the world, made things visible; but in order that this form may be brought out into the light in its turn there must be a visible figure that will draw it out from its profound invisibility' (Foucault 2002b: 30). Second, words themselves are signs that are a part of the world itself. This is particularly the case in relation to Hebrew, where words retain fragments of their original relationship to the world. 'And those words pronounced by Adam as he imposed them upon the various animals have endured, in part at least, and still carry with them in their density, like an embedded fragment of silent knowledge, the unchanging properties of beings' (Foucault 2002b: 40). Third, this conception of the world in terms of interpretation of hidden signs means there is no difference between knowledge grounded in authority, verifiable facts, and knowledge grounded in superstition.

The Renaissance episteme gives way to the classical episteme at the beginning of the seventeenth century. The classical episteme operates in terms of representation, and asserts 'the formal primacy of judgement' (Foucault

2002b: 115). At the heart of this episteme are the kinds of claims we have already discussed in the models of empiricism and rationalism. Here, we find the problem of sense as we have seen in it in the work of the phenomenologists re-emerging, since the Renaissance episteme on the surface moves away from a focus on resemblance to the analysis of the relationships between representations in terms of identity and difference. What makes this possible is a move to order as the fundamental defining characteristic of knowledge: 'that the relation of all knowledge to the *mathesis* is posited as the possibility of establishing an ordered succession between things, even non-measurable ones' (Foucault 2002b: 63). Nonetheless, as we shall see, this move to order presupposes a prior moment whereby a criterion for ordering is put in place. The paradigmatic example of the thinker of the classical episteme is Descartes, from whom the 'main secret' of his method for attaining certain truth is that '[i]n order to distinguish the simplest things from those that are complicated and to set them out in an orderly manner, we should attend to what is most simple in each series of things in which we have directly deduced some truths from others, and should observe how all the rest are more, or less, or equally removed from the simplest' (Descartes 1985b: 21). The method of knowledge therefore consists in determining ideas that can be thought clearly and distinctly, and applying a set of rules to these ideas to combine them in ways that preserve their truth while developing more complex ideas. 'There exists a single, necessary arrangement running through the whole of the Classical episteme: the association of a universal calculus and a search for the elementary within a system that is artificial and is, for that very reason, able to make nature visible from its primary elements right to the simultaneity of all their possible combinations' (Foucault 2002b: 69). With this transformation of method, we also have a transformation of the nature of the sign. In contrast to the Renaissance episteme, where the sign was a natural part of the world, with language itself tracing its origin to Adam's naming of things in the garden of Eden, 'language [withdraws] from the midst of things themselves and [enters] a period of transparency and neutrality' (Foucault 2002b: 62). Nonetheless, signs and the objects they relate to operate within a field of representation, since objects themselves appear before the mind in the form of impressions. At the heart of the classical episteme, therefore, is the structure of judgement. The paradigm method of acquiring knowledge is the formation of simple identities, which are the simple elements of knowledge. Then, through their combination by rules of inference, we have the qualification of these elements.

The classical episteme holds an ambivalent relationship to resemblance. First, the move from analogy to analysis involves a rejection of authority and superstition as ways to develop knowledge of the world. As Descartes notes in the *Regulae*, for instance, error occurs through the interference of another faculty with reason, such as when the 'deceptive judgement of the imagination . . . botches things together' (Descartes 1985b: 14). In this case, we fall into error because the imagination forms connections between ideas which are not justified by the structures of judgement. Nonetheless, Foucault points to the continuing role of resemblance in the classical episteme. At the heart of the classical episteme is the idea that knowledge is ordered, and as we saw in the paradigm case of Descartes, this ordering proceeds from the simplest to the most complex. What makes possible this enumeration is a process of comparison. It is this process of comparison that thus allows us to bring order to the flux of impressions such that they can be brought into the taxonomic tables of knowledge. By this process, the initial ordering of elements that makes knowledge possible is put into play. Comparison, when it operates in terms of magnitude, presupposes a common measure, but, Foucault argues, comparison, when it operates purely in terms of order, is internal to the terms themselves. Thus, comparison is a process that is constitutive of order, and Foucault goes so far as to hint that comparison is actually responsible for the genesis, rather than simply the discovery, of the terms that form the foundation of knowledge.[11] As Descartes writes, 'in all reasoning it is only by means of comparison that we attain an exact knowledge of the truth' (Foucault 2002b: 57). Here we return once again to the problem of what underlies the ordering of terms. Once again following Descartes, Foucault notes that 'a thing can be absolute according to one relation yet relative according to others'[12] (Foucault 2002b: 60). As such, we return to the question of determining which ordering captures the essential aspects of the object under consideration, and which merely recognises accidental features.

---

[11] 'The activity of the mind – and this is the fourth point – will therefore no longer consist in drawing things together, in setting out on a quest for everything that might reveal some sort of kinship, attraction, or secretly shared nature within them, but, on the contrary, in discriminating, that is, in establishing their identities, then the inevitability of the connections with all the successive degrees of a series. In this sense, discrimination imposes upon comparison the primary and fundamental investigation of difference: providing oneself by intuition with a distinct representation of things, and apprehending clearly the inevitable connection between one element in a series and that which immediately follows it' (Foucault 2002b: 61).

[12] 'The secret of this technique consists entirely in our attentively noting in all things that which is absolute in the highest degree. For some things are more absolute than others from one point of view, yet more relative from a different point of view. For example, the universal is more absolute than the particular, in virtue of its having a simpler nature, but it can also be said to be more relative than the particular in that it depends upon particulars for its existence, etc.' (Descartes 1985b: 22).

Foucault here makes the claim that what makes possible the ordering of terms by comparison is resemblance operating in terms of the imagination: 'The power of imagination is only the inverse, the other side, of its defect' (Foucault 2002b: 77). As Foucault notes, resemblance here operates as the power that creates the affinities between terms that are later taken up and given legitimacy by comparison. Without resemblance, it would be impossible to develop a system of ordering to allow the juridical method to operate:

> And, in effect, if we suppose in the uninterrupted chain of representation certain impressions, the very simplest that can be, without the slightest degree of resemblance between them, then there would be no possibility whatever of the second recalling the first, causing it to reappear, and thus authorizing its representation in the imagination; those impressions would succeed one another in the most total differentiation – so total that it could not even be perceived, since no representation would be able to immobilize itself in one place, reanimate a former one, and juxtapose itself to it so as to give rise to a comparison; even that tiny overlap of identity necessary for all differentiation would not be provided. (Foucault 2002b: 76)

Here we find Foucault once again repeating a theme developed by Bergson. Prior to the structures that make judgement possible is a non-juridical moment that establishes the sense of the episteme, and cannot be captured within it. 'At the border of knowledge, similitude is that barely sketched form, that rudimentary relation which knowledge must overlay to its full extent, but which continues, indefinitely, to reside below knowledge in the manner of a mute and ineffaceable necessity' (Foucault 2002b: 75). While the absence of a place for resemblance in the theory of knowledge does give rise to an analytics of the imagination, or an analysis of nature, these enquiries mark a point of absence rather than a recognition of the place of man as the central constituting figure within the episteme. Thus, we have the centrality of the imagination in the *Meditations* in uniting the body and mind, a moment which defies analysis, or Hume's positing of a principle of attraction in the mind which, 'as to its causes . . . are mostly unknown, and must be resolv'd into *original* qualities of human nature, which I pretend not to explain' (Hume 1978: 1.1.4.6).

In the classical episteme, man is not an object of study in himself. While the imagination is central in providing a non-categorial moment that grounds the system of knowledge, as we have seen, the activity of constituting the episteme is something that cannot be thematised since it is prior to the categorial structures of the episteme itself. With the modern episteme, we have the emergence of man as the central category of thought.

This occurs through the gradual realisation that the table of knowledge at the heart of the classical episteme cannot be perfected. At the end of the eighteenth century, this limitation is itself turned into the foundation of knowledge. At the heart of this movement is man as the synthetic centre of knowledge. In effect, the structures of the subject that are responsible for its finitude, and the failure of the project of representation, become the foundation of knowledge through the introduction of something like the transcendental. Foucault considers Kant the first philosopher of the modern episteme: 'the Kantian critique . . . marks the threshold of our modernity; it questions representation, not in accordance with the endless movement that proceeds from the simple element to all its possible combinations, but on the basis of its rightful limits' (Foucault 2002b: 263). We have already seen how Kant formulates this finitude in terms of the discursivity thesis, which posits a difference in kind between sensibility and concepts. For Foucault, the claim is rather that we have a return to a philosophy of depth with the transcendental which makes representation possible becoming the object of enquiry. 'Kant avoids representation itself and what is given within it, in order to address himself to that on the basis of which all representation, whatever its form, may be posited' (Foucault 2002b: 262). The modern episteme falls into difficulty because of the dual nature of human beings. On the one hand, human beings are active subjects that make knowledge possible. On the other, human beings are objects of knowledge. It is the impossibility of reconciling these aspects of human nature that makes the modern episteme so problematic. In the fields of labour, life, and language, man as an object of enquiry becomes subject to 'objective "transcendentals"' (Foucault 2002b: 266) which seek to show that the structure of experience can be understood in terms of depth structures of economics, biology, and linguistics. As such, Foucault's analysis of the modern episteme concentrates as much on the transcendental conditions of man as an object as man as a subject. There is a clear tension between these two approaches, both of which emerge from seeing representation as to be understood in the light of structures which ground it. Beginning with Fichte, Foucault argues that post-Kantian philosophy struggles to reconcile these two moments by moving to a genetic transcendental philosophy. Hegel attempts to resolve this difficulty by taking back 'the totality of the empirical domain . . . into the interior of a consciousness revealing itself to itself as spirit, in other words, as an empirical and a transcendental field simultaneously' (Foucault 2002b: 269). As such, for Hegel, the transcendental and the empirical are reconciled by beginning with an empirical natural consciousness, and by showing how the categories of experience emerge immanently through the contradictions inherent to particular forms of consciousness. Finitude implies a history, and this history of man as an object of knowledge has the potential to destabilise the transcendental structures of knowledge by making them subject to the empirical.

This conflation of the transcendental and empirical begins, for Foucault, with Kant himself. Foucault's claim is that beneath the questions of transcendental philosophy is a question that refers us to anthropology. As Foucault writes:

> This had already been formulated by Kant in his *Logic*, when to his traditional trilogy of questions he added an ultimate one: the three critical questions (What can I know? What must I do? What am I permitted to hope?) then found themselves referred to a fourth, and inscribed, as it were, 'to its account': *Was ist der Mensch?* [What is man?] (Foucault 2002b: 371)

While this question originates in the *Logic*, Foucault argues that it is 'the anthropological question *par excellence*' (Foucault 2008: 87), and takes it to be the question which grounds the others. Now, while the point Foucault is making here should be read in rhetorical terms, it should be clear that if the first three questions, all of which Kant argues must be referred to his transcendental philosophy, must be answered within the framework of anthropology, which has its basis in empirical knowledge, then the strict division between the transcendental and the empirical collapses, with the transcendental now dependent on the empirical.

Foucault's secondary thesis was a translation and commentary on Kant's *Anthropology from a Pragmatic Point of View*, and it is in this text that Foucault argues for the confusion between the empirical and the transcendental in Kant's philosophy. Kant's *Anthropology* predates his critical turn, and attempts to develop a 'systematic doctrine containing our knowledge of man' from a pragmatic perspective. Such a perspective sees man as a 'freely acting being', or 'citizen of the world' (Kant quoted in Caygill 2000: 73), and Foucault sees this as a potential challenge to the critical system by incorporating an account of the genesis of the subject that operates within the empirical work. As Beatrice Han (2002) shows, Foucault offers two potential readings of Kant's *Anthropology*. The first, critical, interpretation sees the anthropology as repeating the critical philosophy but affirming its foundational role, and hence reaffirming the transcendental-empirical split at the heart of Kant's philosophy. The second is a decentred reading that reverses the relationship between the critical and anthropological projects. Foucault begins by noting that for Kant, anthropology cannot simply be the study of the kind of passive subjectivity we find determined by the categories under the form of time. Rather, anthropology, in order to give a meaningful account of human beings, requires that we understand them according to a 'living principle'. 'The only possible anthropology is that where, rather than being tied to the passivity of phenomenal determinations, the *Gemüt* [mind] is instead animated by the work of ideas on the level of the field of experience' (Foucault 2008: 62). Foucault notes that this principle that animates *Gemüt* is *Geist*, or spirit: 'The principle of the mind that animates by means of ideas is called spirit' (Kant 2007: 349). With this reference to ideas, Foucault argues that it is the same force which drives reason to systematise knowledge in the *First Critique* that also drives *Gemüt* to project itself into a field of possibilities. Just as reason synthesises experience according to a possible object that can be thought but not given, empirical experience is oriented in terms of a future that gives sense to experience without being present to it.

> Such then is the function of the *Geist*. It does not organize the *Gemüt* in such a way that it is made into a living being, or into the *analogon* of organic life, or indeed into the life of the Absolute itself; rather, its function is to vitalize, to engender, in the passivity of the *Gemüt*, which is that of empirical determin-ation, a teeming mass of ideas – the multiple structures of a totality in the process of becoming that make and unmake themselves like so many of the half-lives that live and die in the mind. (Foucault 2008: 63)

Foucault takes this analogy to disrupt the rigorous division of the transcendental and the empirical in Kant's system. *Geist* now animates both the transcendental nature of reason and the empirical nature of *Gemüt*, and thus threatens to undermine the distinction between empirical and transcendental. In effect, *Geist* operates as both a principle that allows the subject to appear as an object of knowledge and a principle that sees man as a being who actively engages with the world. For Foucault, the addition of the fourth question, *what is man?*, to the list of questions Kant concerns himself with is the locus of this confusion between levels, since it calls on us to develop knowledge of the structure of finitude within finitude.[13] Foucault thus argues that the anthropology finds Kant in a paralogism, whereby man is understood both as the object and condition of knowledge.[14] As Han (2002: 29) notes, Foucault's reading here relies on

[13] 'The values implicit in the question *Was ist der Mensch?* are responsible for this homogenous, destructured and infinitely reversible field in which man presents his truth as the soul of truth' (Foucault 2008: 123–4).
[14] '[F]rom the moment when one tries to define an essence of the man who could express himself from himself, and who would be at the same time the foundation of all possible knowledge and every possible limit of knowledge, we are in the midst of paralogism' (Foucault 1994: 453).

an equivocation of Kant's characterisation of *Geist* as a 'natural drive', drawing on the meanings of natural as either an essential aspect of an entity or as pertaining to empirical nature, and it seems perfectly possible to read the *Anthropology* as consistent with Kant's transcendental philosophy. As such, the fractured conception of the self which Kant develops so carefully in his own paralogisms is not threatened by Foucault's criticisms, but we can nonetheless see how the post-Kantian tradition, which emerges from tensions surrounding the foundations of Kant's position, may well break down the distinction between the transcendental and the empirical in the way Foucault suggests.

6.5   The Statement in *The Archaeology of Knowledge*

Before turning to Foucault's later genealogical work, I want to briefly discuss Foucault's other key archaeological work, *The Archaeology of Knowledge*. Here, Foucault introduces what he terms the statement, which shows in detail his move away from judgement. In *The Archaeology of Knowledge*, rather than discussing the epistemes, Foucault develops an account of what he calls discursive formations, a term he uses to characterise large bodies of discourse such as natural history. For Foucault, the nature of such discursive formations is governed by a set of rules that determine how what Foucault calls statements are formed and related to their objects. Now, we will explore the nature of statements shortly, but we can note that *The Archaeology of Knowledge* once again has an ambivalent relationship to transcendental philosophy. On the one hand, the rules governing the generation and relation of statements are understood as the historical a priori, in the sense that they provide the conditions for meaningful discourse within a given discursive formation:

> If one wishes to undertake an archaeological analysis of knowledge itself . . ..
> One must reconstitute the general system of thought, whose network, in its positivity, renders an interplay of simultaneous and apparently contradictory opinions possible. It is this network that defines the conditions that make a controversy or a problem possible, and that bears the historicity of knowledge. (Foucault 2002b: 75)

On the other hand, Foucault is insistent that statements provide the conditions for real rather than possible experience, in that they assume a limited corpus of propositions, and maintain a purely descriptive function:

> The fact of [a statement's] belonging to a discursive formation and the laws that govern it are one and the same thing; this is not paradoxical since the

> discursive formation is characterized not by principles of construction but
> by a dispersion of fact, since for statements it is not a condition of possibility
> but a law of coexistence. (Foucault 2002a: 131)

Furthermore, as Deleuze notes, Foucault's account here differs from the
transcendental in that the rules of synthesis 'are on the side of the "object"
and historical formation, not a universal subject (the *a priori* itself is
historical)' (Deleuze 1988b: 60). What statements, and the rules governing
their formation and relations, determine is the meaning of a given discourse. As such, Foucault argues that the nature of statements determines
what is taken to be a meaningful proposition within a given discursive
formation,[15] or rather, what meaning is to be given to a proposition within
a given discursive formation.

> The identity of a statement is subjected to a second group of conditions and
> limits: those that are imposed by all the other statements among which it
> figures, by the domain in which it can be used or applied, by the role and
> functions that it can perform. The affirmation that the earth is round or that
> species evolve does not constitute the same statement before and after
> Copernicus, before and after Darwin; it is not, for such simple formulations,
> that the meaning of the words has changed; what changed was the relation
> of these affirmations to other propositions, their conditions of use and
> reinvestment, the field of experience, of possible verifications, of problems
> to be resolved, to which they can be referred. (Foucault 2002a: 116)

As such, the meaning of a statement itself varies depending on its place
within a system of statements. We can note that this system of statements
is not organised in the same manner as propositions or juridical functions. As we have seen, judgement operates in terms of contradiction,
either seeing the avoidance of contradiction as governing the consistency
of a system of propositions, or contradiction as driving the development
of juridical sense in the case of Hegel. The statement, however, gives
sense to a discursive formation that will contain contrary claims that
together show the structure of the debate of a given epoch. Further, we
can note that Foucault's own examples of a statement do not necessarily
have the structure of a judgement. 'The keyboard of a typewriter is not
a statement; but the same series of letters, A, Z, E, R, T, listed in
a typewriting manual, is the statement of the alphabetical order adopted

---

[15] 'The statement is not therefore a structure (that is, a group of relations between variable elements,
thus authorizing a possibly infinite number of concrete models); it is a function of existence that
properly belongs to signs and on the basis of which one may then decide, through analysis or
intuition, whether or not they "make sense"' (Foucault 2002a: 97).

by French typewriters'[16] (Foucault 2002a: 96). As such, despite the rejection of the kind of transcendental account favoured by *The Order of Things*, *The Archaeology of Knowledge* preserves the idea of a field that differs in kind from judgements while giving sense to them. What is key to Foucault's logic of sense here is that the pure interrelation of statements lacking in sense gives rise to a discourse imbued with sense, and in fact determines which propositions can be seen as making sense within the discursive formation as a whole. As Deleuze puts it:

> Statements are not in any sense portrayed as a synthesis of words and things, or as composite phrases or propositions. On the contrary, they precede the phrases or propositions which implicitly presuppose them, and lead to the formation of words and objects. (Deleuze 1988b: 12)

6.6 The Status of Archaeology

Foucault's early archaeological work raises a number of questions. On the one hand, we can see the similarities with Hegel's own account of the history of ideas, with different historical periods likewise operating in terms of a transcendental that is itself open to change. Nonetheless, in this notion of change, we find a radical difference from Hegel. For Hegel, the transition between different conceptions of the world occurs immanently, as each set of categories that govern the structure of the world develop their own inherent contradictions, and, in moving beyond these contradictions, open the way to a new set of categories that resolve them. This allows Hegel to explain the transition between different categorial schemes and allows us to potentially resolve a further question about the standpoint from which we observe the development of the dialectic itself. While Hegel may at points pre-empt conclusions in his commentary on the transitions the categories go through, we can see that movement between the categories itself can be understood from a position internal to the dialectic. Foucault's position is more ambiguous on both of these points. At least in *The Order of Things* and *The Archaeology of Knowledge*, it seems no account of the transition between different epistemes is possible. This is a corollary of the fact that the archaeological method aims to bracket both the truth and the meaning of the claims it considers. Foucault would consider this in many ways a strength of the account, since it allows us

---

[16] 'Other examples, in any case, are less ambiguous: a classificatory table of the botanical species is made up of statements, not sentences (Linnaeus's *Genera Plantarum* is a whole book of statements, in which one can recognize only a small number of sentences); a genealogical tree, an accounts book, the calculations of a trade balance are statements; where are the sentences?' (Foucault 2002a: 92–3).

to recognise that such transitions rest on contingent aspects of the world. As we shall see, however, the introduction of power into Foucault's model provides a way of showing how models of discourse develop without having to see the truth or meaning of that discourse as determining the development of our conceptual scheme. Similarly, the question of where Foucault writes from is equally pressing. Dreyfus and Rabinow argue that the archaeologist occupies a position similar to the phenomenologist, with the meaning and truth of propositions bracketed, and ultimately falls into the same difficulties as phenomenology and transcendental philosophy more generally, with Foucault positing archaeology as taking place from a position outside of the empirical, and hence setting up the empirical-transcendental doublet he criticises in Kant.[17]

We could perhaps equate this early work to something like a Leibnizian phase of Foucault's development, where Foucault attempts to explain all determination in terms of discourse just as Leibniz attempts to explain all phenomena in terms of judgement. Statements for Foucault determine both the nature of discourse and the objects to which this discourse relates. As such, in this early work, 'only statements are determining and revelatory, even though they reveal something other than what they say. We are not surprised that in *The Archaeology of Knowledge* the visible is now more or less designated only negatively, as the non-discursive, but that the discursive has even more discursive relations with the non-discursive' (Deleuze 1988b: 67). As we shall see, Foucault's later work develops an account that attempts to give a more positive analysis of the non-discursive through the introduction of the notion of power in explaining why given discourses emerge. Power will function as a third moment explaining the genesis of the visible and the invisible.[18]

6.7   Foucault and Power

In an interview given in 1977, Foucault claims that the focus of his early work was power,[19] which may come as a surprise, given the lack of explicit

---

[17] See Oksala 2005: 72–3 for a critique of this view.
[18] We are once again following Deleuze here, who notes that '[w]hat the *Archaeology* recognized but still only designated negatively, as non-discursive environments, is given its positive form in *Discipline and Punish*, a form that haunted the whole of Foucault's work: the form of the visible, as opposed to the form of whatever can be articulated. For example, at the beginning of the nineteenth century masses and populations become visible, and emerge into the light of day at the same time as medical statements manage to articulate new objects (tissular lesions and the anatomophysiological correlations)' (Deleuze 1988b: 32).
[19] Foucault 2002e: 115.

engagement with this concept in the work we have considered so far.[20] Nonetheless, in *Discipline and Punish* and *The History of Sexuality*, Foucault explicitly thematises the role of power in the development of discourse. I want to focus here on *The History of Sexuality*, as here Foucault presents in detail his analytic of power. The focus on sexuality is important because Foucault makes several claims about the significance of sexuality as a discourse. First, Foucault claims that sex is the 'master key' (Foucault 1978: 78) to our self-interpretation. Beginning with the Christian confessional, but continuing through Freud and then sexual liberation, the West has managed 'to bring us almost entirely – our bodies, our minds, our individuality, our history – under the sway of a logic of concupiscence and desire' (Foucault 1978: 78). Thus, sexuality is not an arbitrary choice of discourse for Foucault. In particular, the fact that it draws together anatomical aspects of our existence together with an analysis of our nature as a member of a species (through the development of statistical approaches to population in the nineteenth century) means that sexuality provides an account of the whole range of our nature. For Merleau-Ponty, the body, as the centre of synthesis, is the locus of sense. Foucault's account operates prior to this constituted field of sense, looking at levels of organisation above and below the body in terms of population dynamics and the specific anatomy that constitutes the body. Third, much as with Borges' Chinese encyclopaedia, Foucault claims that sex is a category governed by arbitrariness in terms of its domain of analysis: 'the notion of "sex" made it possible to group together, in an artificial unity, anatomical elements, biological functions, conducts, sensations, and pleasures, and it enabled one to make use of this fictitious unity as a causal principle, an omnipresent meaning, a secret to be discovered everywhere' (Foucault 1978: 154). This arbitrariness points to the role of power in giving it such a prominent role in our self-understanding.

Foucault's claim in *The History of Sexuality*, therefore, is going to be that we interpret our own natures through the categories of sexuality, and that to understand the development of the discourse of sexuality, we need to have a proper understanding of power. Here, I want to first highlight the account of power, which Foucault calls the juridico-discursive model of power and believes has traditionally been used to explain the way power operates within society. As we shall see, this model, which sees power

---

[20] As Oksala 2005: 95 notes, *The Archaeology of Knowledge* does pose the question of power, since discourse is the object of political struggle, but Foucault does not address in this text how power and discourse are to be related.

operating in terms of law, fails to adequately capture the way power governs sexuality. To understand power, we need to move away from thinking of it in terms of judgement and see it as constitutive of our categories of thought themselves. We shall further see that Foucault argues that this notion of power tends to allow itself to be understood in categorial terms in order to operate more effectively. I want to conclude with Foucault's analysis of the positive relationship between power and the discourse on sexuality. What makes possible our discourse on sexuality, and therefore defines what claims and procedures we use to analyse ourselves are taken to be meaningful, are power relations that cannot be captured by the oppositional logic of judgement.

Foucault's account begins with an analysis of what he claims is the received narrative of the history of sexuality: what he calls the repressive hypothesis. This is the claim that the history of sexuality has been governed by the suppression of discourse about sex:

> The seventeenth century, then, was the beginning of an age of repression emblematic of what we call the bourgeois societies, an age which perhaps we still have not completely left behind. Calling sex by its name thereafter became more difficult and more costly. As if in order to gain mastery over it in reality, it had first been necessary to subjugate it at the level of language, control its free circulation in speech, expunge it from the things that were said, and extinguish the words that rendered it too visibly present. (Foucault 1978: 17)

Foucault isn't explicit about where he takes this narrative to come from,[21] but we can see in it the embodiment of the narrative that sexuality was repressed by the introduction of Victorian values, which have only been overcome through the rejection of repression through the movements of sexual liberation from the 1950s. According to the rationale Foucault provides, this shift in the nature of our relationship to sexuality is traditionally understood in terms of labour power, with sex not related to reproduction being viewed as a waste of the energy of the worker that could be better exploited in other ways: 'At a time when labour capacity was being systematically exploited, how could this capacity be allowed to dissipate itself in pleasurable pursuits, except in those – reduced to a minimum – that enabled it to reproduce itself?' (Foucault 1978: 6). As Foucault notes, however, there is something rather odd about this interpretation of sexuality in terms of labour forces that, on a Marxist reading,

---

[21] See Kelly 2013: 24–8 for a discussion of who Foucault may have in mind with his formulation of the repressive hypothesis.

would view consciousness as constituted by social structures, yet sees sexuality as an objective phenomenon that is related to power through a simple process of repression.

In fact, Foucault notes that the nineteenth century represents a multiplication of discourses on sexuality rather than their elimination. The emergence of the population as an object of study led to new ways of categorising the economic strength of a nation, and to the possibility of intervening in order to augment the labour capacity of a state. Thus, categories such as birth and death rates and fertility rates became important measures, and with them the analysis of specifically sexual categories such as 'the birthrate, the age of marriage, the legitimate and illegitimate births, the precocity and frequency of sexual relations, the ways of making them fertile or sterile, the effects of unmarried life or of the prohibitions, the impact of contraceptive practices' (Foucault 1978: 25–6). As such, a new discourse pertaining to sexuality emerges. Similarly, while we may note that on the surface, there is a silencing of discourse on the sexuality of children, we find besides an explicit effort to structure institutions and even physical spaces in order to limit the possibilities for 'youth's universal sin' (Foucault 1978: 29). Thus, 'the space for classes, the shape of the tables, the planning of the recreation lessons, the distribution of the dormitories (with or without partitions, with or without curtains), the rules for monitoring bedtime and sleep periods – all this referred, in the most prolix manner, to the sexuality of children' (Foucault 1978: 28). Finally, we have the increasing medicalisation of sexuality. Foucault introduces the example of the farmhand who 'had obtained a few caresses from a little girl, just as he had done before and seen done by the village urchins round about him' (Foucault 1978: 31). While acquitted of any crime, he is nonetheless shut away to be studied for life in the hospital at Maréville while reports on him are published.

While critics could criticise (and have criticised) the empirical detail of the history of sexuality offered in *The History of Sexuality*,[22] Foucault does appear to capture a trend of the development of power. If Foucault is right, however, that even a cursory examination of the nature of discourse about sex shows that there has been a proliferation of discourse, why is it the case that this proliferation has not been noticed? On a superficial level, Foucault notes something called 'speaker's benefit' (1978: 10). In seeing discourse about sexuality as being prohibited, the very act of speaking out against this prohibition becomes transgressive. As such, raising the repressive hypothesis shows

---

[22] See, for instance, Bartky 2002 for a critique of Foucault's empirical account.

the speaker to be standing up to power. More profoundly, Foucault claims that the structures of the repressive hypothesis, and the future of liberation from the repressive prohibitions that it heralds, are themselves an *image* of power that emerges to mask a more subtle operation of power behind the simplistic model of prohibition proposed by the repressive hypothesis. Thus, the claim that power is simply that which prevents discourse, and the corollary that discourse itself is a mode of liberation from power, is a myth that allows power to operate more effectively: 'power is tolerable only on condition that it mask a substantial part of itself. Its success is proportional to its ability to hide its own mechanisms' (Foucault 1978: 86). In the next two sections, I therefore want to analyse the differences between the scheme of power that is presupposed by the repressive hypothesis and the model of power Foucault instead takes to be operating. As we will see, this model of power eschews the structures of judgement in favour of seeing power as operating according to a patchwork of different modalities and relations.

6.8   Juridico-Discursive Power and Biopower

So, let us begin with the conception of power that Foucault argues is operating within the repressive hypothesis. Foucault sees the model that is operative as originating within the structures of monarchical power. The origin of the model of power is the monarchy's emergence as a single point of unity over the multiplicity of power relations in the feudal world. The monarchy allows these various forces to be subordinated to a single point of power. The monarch unifies the law with their own being, such that a transgression of the will of the monarch is a transgression of right. As with sexuality, we can see the monarchy itself as an expression of power, such that 'law was not simply a weapon skilfully wielded by monarchs; it was the monarchic system's mode of manifestation and the form of its acceptability' (Foucault 1978: 87). Thus, when the monarchy itself is overturned in France, the model of power, the law, is preserved, in that it is the legitimacy of the monarchy that is called into question. What does this representation of power in terms of law entail?

Foucault claims that the model of power found in the repressive hypothesis is what he calls a juridico-discursive model of power. Such a model takes judgement as central, in the two forms of legal judgement, and, underlying this, the taxonomical structures of judgement we have discovered throughout this enquiry. Foucault presents a brief summary of this model of power, compressing it into five key tenets:

(i)   That it operates in terms of negation.
(ii) That it operates in terms of a rule.
(iii) That it operates in terms of prohibition.
(iv) That it censors that which is prohibited.
(v)   That it operates in the same way at all power levels.

When understanding sexuality in terms of the law, the reference to negation implies that power on this model is entirely negative. Power here does
nothing except prevent the expression of what is a pre-existing sexuality.
Second, power operates in terms of the insistence of a rule. This has two
separate implications. Power will operate in terms of the kinds of dualities
we have seen to characterise judgement more generally: 'licit and illicit',
'permitted and forbidden' (Foucault 1978: 83). It also means that power
will operate in terms of language on this model, insofar as rules or laws can
be given a determinate sense. Third, power operates purely by giving this
prohibition to the individual, thus forcing sex to renounce itself. Fourth,
power operates through positing the non-existence of that which is prohibited. Finally, at all levels of power, power operates in the same manner,
notably by the subordination of the individual to the law.

Such an account of power that privileges the law naturally rests on an
account of judgement. We could draw an analogy here with Hegel's theory
of Greek tragedy, which sees the characters within the tragedy themselves
as simply manifestations of an underlying law.[23] Just as for Hegel, this
understanding of drama in terms of law makes art 'the sensuous appearance
of the Idea' (Houlgate 2005: 213); understanding power as the manifestation of law makes power the appearance of judgement in the world. Given
this model, where power has a negative relationship to sex and does not
determine its nature, but simply prevents its expression, it is reliant on
a framework that will provide an account of the determinations that power
will rely on. This account of determination will need to mirror that of
power itself in order for it to provide a scaffold for power to operate. This is
inevitable to the extent that the law must be made determinate through
language to be effective on this model. We can see that power has all of the
characteristics of a judgement. First, it operates through a process of
conditioning rather than positive creation. Judgement here operates only
on a pre-existing subject, just as judgement operates to add determinations
to a subject whose existence cannot be understood within the juridical

---

[23] See Hegel 1975: 1208–20 for Hegel's paradigmatic analysis of *Antigone* in terms of the Idea. Deleuze
1994 discusses this connection between law and judgement in drama in relation to Rosenberg 1994.

framework itself. Second, this subject is determined through a nexus of determinations that are opposed to each other, just as judgement operates in terms of a hierarchy of opposed judgements. Finally, this network of opposed determinations shares the same formal structure at each level of the hierarchy, just as Aristotle's account of determination provides an account of determination through the repeated application of relations of subordination. Thus the structure of subordination under a property that occurs in judgement is mirrored by submission of an individual to power under the law.

We can see how such a model of power leads naturally to the repressive hypothesis. If power is seen as only operating by constraint, then our account of the history of sexuality will be one of constraint and liberation from constraint.[24] While our representation of power may operate in terms of judgement and constraint, Foucault argues that such a model of power fails to capture the complexities of how power itself operates. As we have seen, Foucault's account suggests that power does not simply constrain, but has a far more creative role in organising situations. In each of the cases of population statistics, child sexuality, and the medicalisation of sexual deviancy, we find that rather than a prohibition on discussing sexuality, we have the emergence of a new discourse. Insofar as this model of power sees it as constituting the discourse itself, there is no moment of sexuality prior to the application of power that can be returned to, and the project of seeking to liberate an essential sexuality is therefore a project that reinforces the effects of power rather than freeing us from them. 'At bottom, despite the differences in epochs and objectives, the representation of power has remained under the spell of monarchy. In political thought and analysis, we still have not cut off the head of the king' (Foucault 1978: 88–9).

I want now to turn to Foucault's positive account of the development of the discourses on sexuality. Foucault sees modern power as originating in the Catholic confessional. The move away from juridical power entails a move away from the act as locus of power in relation to the law to the individual as locus of power. Thus, we have the movement from the punishment of the act of sodomy to the description of the homosexual in medical literature of the nineteenth century. While Catholic confession is concerned with the confession of sins, from the outset it seeks the confession not merely of transgressions, but of the desires that lead to

[24] Here, we have another parallel with the sovereign as a model of power, in that in both cases power is seen to operate from outside of its field of application, as the sovereign stands above their subjects, and power is seen as an imposition on a natural sexuality. Cf. Rouse 2005: 103.

these transgressions. Given the centrality of these desires to the subject, we already have with the confession a move from acts to the subject. So what are the central characteristics of the confession? First, it is a ritual for producing truth about oneself, but we can note at the outset that this truth emerges within a power relation to one's confessor. This production of truth involves a transposition of desire into discourse in such a manner that both its own nature and the nature of the subject (through rituals of purification, etc.) are transformed. Confession also involves the idea of concealment. As well as the obligation to confess, there is also a duty to conceal aspects of our desires in order to later be able to confess them. Thus, the hermeneutical structure that leads us to attempt to seek authenticity beneath the effects of power is itself an effect of the way power constitutes discourse on sexuality, with essence an illusion of the structure of discourse.

This confessional structure forms the basis for the development of the scientific model of sexuality in the nineteenth century. Medicalisation shifts the central axis of the discourse of sexuality from sin and redemption to pathology and normality. The aim of the medicalisation of sexuality was not simply to bring it within the remit of scientific enquiry, but also to justify the kinds of intrusions into the lives of patients that medical intervention involved. Foucault lists the following claims. First, there is a 'clinical codification of the inducement to speak' (Foucault 1978: 65). Set categories are developed, as well as techniques to allow the quantification of qualities that are constituted to determine sexuality, such as questionnaires. Second, a 'general and diffuse causality' (Foucault 1978: 66) is posited whereby excesses or deficiencies in the characteristics produced by codification are seen as potentially being the causes for a wide variety of other physical and psychological conditions. This justifies medical intervention, or concern over the living arrangements of schoolboys. Third, there is the 'principle of a latency intrinsic to sexuality' (Foucault 1978: 66), which posits sexuality as something hidden behind appearances, and, moving beyond religious confession, perhaps unknown to the subject themselves. This allows force to be used on the subject to exact a confession. Fourth, medicalisation introduced the 'method of interpretation' (Foucault 1978: 66), whereby confessions are required to be passed through the interpretative relationship with the investigator. Thus, truths on their own are seen as 'blind', and in need of schematisation through an interpretative framework to enter discourse. Finally, the effects of confession are recodified in order to see it as a therapeutic rather than purifying exercise.

We can see the contrast between the two forms of power clearly in the contrast between the juridico-discursive prohibition on the act of incest and the biopolitical treatment of child sexuality. In the case of the act of incest, the aim of power was traditionally to prevent transgression. On that basis, it operated through an attempt to bring about an 'asymptotic decrease in the thing it condemned' (Foucault 1978: 41). In the case of child sexuality, we appear to have a similar structure. Masturbation, for instance, was treated 'like an epidemic that needed to be eradicated' (Foucault 1978: 42). What this treatment entailed, however, was a sophisticated introduction of surveillance into the milieu of the family. 'Wherever here was the chance they might appear, devices of surveillance were installed; traps were laid for compelling admissions; inexhaustible and corrective discourses were imposed; parents and teachers were alerted, and left with the suspicion that all children were guilty, and with the fear of being themselves at fault if their suspicions were not sufficiently strong' (Foucault 1978: 42). The result of this is that power isn't exercised by preventing the spread of a practice. Rather, power is exercised by using the prohibited act, masturbation, as a way of penetrating a new domain, the family, to install a particular form of discourse. Power here therefore uses the act as a support for expanding its range of activities. Power here is invested in ensuring that childhood sexuality is perpetuated, and understood in more and more nuanced terms, to ensure the further development of the structures of discourse. As such, it is essentially productive rather than negative. At root, and as with Bergson, the logic here is dissociative, with power constituting new domains of operation through the constitution of new categories and identities via a process of distinction.[25]

6.9   Power and Sense

The History of Sexuality therefore resolves one of the issues with the early work through the introduction of a positive notion of power. Discourse is fundamentally intertwined with power, and it is this that allows us to explain why particular forms of discourse prosper at particular moments

---

[25] See, for instance, Foucault's claim that 'relations of power are not in a position of exteriority with respect to other types of relationships (economic processes, knowledge relationships, sexual relations), but are immanent in the latter; they are the immediate effects of the divisions, inequalities, and disequilibriums which occur in the latter, and conversely they are the internal conditions of these differentiations; relations of power are not in superstructural positions, with merely a role of prohibition or accompaniment; they have a directly productive role, wherever they come into play' (Foucault 1978: 94).

in time. 'Discourse transmits and produces power; it reinforces it, but also undermines and exposes it, renders it fragile and makes it possible to thwart it' (Foucault 1978: 101). For Foucault, then, the entire discourse of power which understands it in terms of judgement is itself an illusion that allows power to function more effectively. Once we recognise the illegitimacy of this account of power, we open the way to what Foucault calls an 'analytics' of power: 'that is, toward a definition of the specific domain formed by relations of power, and toward a determination of the instruments that will make possible its analysis' (Foucault 1978: 82). This is because while the domain formed by relations of power may be expressible in categorial terms, the power relations themselves are not. What gives sense to the domain is therefore non-categorial. Foucault does not define power (and we cannot do so since knowledge of power itself operates within the structures of power), but he does offer four 'cautionary prescriptions' to be followed when investigating power. The first, the 'rule of immanence' (Foucault 1978: 98), maintains that there is no exteriority between knowledge and power, even if these differ in their roles. As such, there is no authentic moment prior to the imposition of power. Second, the 'rule of continual variations' (Foucault 1978: 99) states that power isn't to be understood according to an atemporal distribution. Rather, power is a process that involves a continual change in the relations it holds. Third, the rule of 'double conditioning' (Foucault 1978: 99) asserts that we do not have a simple hierarchy of forces, where at each level the structural relations are identical, as we might find with a nested series of judgements. Rather, power operates differently at different levels, each of which reciprocally conditions the others. Finally, the rule of the 'tactical polyvalence of discourses' (Foucault 1978: 101) states that we do not find sharp binary distinctions between dominant and excluded discourses. Rather, we have a multiplicity of discourses running in parallel, with different discourses coming into play in relation to different strategies power adopts. Together, these rules suggest a model of the constitution of discourses radically different from judgement.

6.10   Conclusion

As we saw, in Foucault's early work, discursive formations operated in terms of statements that gave sense to the propositions within the discourse. We also saw that the statement for Foucault had a structure that differed in kind from the judgement. Power also takes on this role of determining the structure of discourse while itself evading this structure. As with the phenomenologists' notion of sense, we can make sense of the operations of power, even though they operate outside of judgement. Foucault is explicit that power is intelligible, and operates in order to fulfil objectives, but is not wielded by individuals. As such, Foucault claims it is intentional but non-subjective.

As Oksala (2005: 97) argues, Foucault's project in *The History of Sexuality* is essentially transcendental. Foucault writes that 'two or three centuries ago, Western philosophy postulated, explicitly or implicitly, the subject as the foundation, as the central core of all knowledge, as that in which, and on the basis of which freedom revealed itself and truth could blossom' (Foucault 2002d: 3). This claim is exemplified by Kant's claim at the outset of the transcendental deduction that it must be possible for an 'I think' to accompany all of our representations (Kant 1929: B131). As Sartre noted, however, the fact that an 'I think' must be able to accompany our representations does not guarantee that the 'I' is the ground of our knowledge claims. Rather than the subject being the ground of a transcendental procedure, it can be seen as the result of it. For Sartre, what constituted the ground for the subject was a transversal field of acts of consciousness. For Foucault, however, what constitutes the subject is a transcendental field determined by structures entirely outside of consciousness: 'my aim will be to show you how social practices may engender domains of knowledge that not only bring new objects, new concepts, and new techniques to light, but also give rise to totally new forms of subjects and subjects of knowledge' (Foucault 2002d: 2). As such, the enquiry into discourse, and into power, is ultimately subordinated to the analysis of the conditions that make the subject possible. Against his earlier claims about the centrality of power for his analysis, in 1982 Foucault claims that 'it is not power, but the subject, that is the general theme of my work' (Foucault 2002c: 327). As we have seen, displacing the subject as the locus of synthesis entails a movement away from judgement as the primary form of organisation, since judgement requires a subject to organise the representations that compose it. In taking power and knowledge to be the structures that transcendentally organise the world, Foucault believes he has moved beyond Sartre and Merleau-Ponty, who retain in turn consciousness and the body as the sites of transcendental organisation. For Foucault, power itself constitutes both the body and the categories of consciousness.[26] As such, it constitutes what for Merleau-Ponty is the conduit for sense in the world. Nonetheless, we can see *The History of*

---

[26] In talking about the role of power in the proliferation of discourse on childhood sexuality, for instance, Foucault writes, 'the extraordinary effort that went into the task that was bound to fail leads one to suspect that what was demanded of it was to persevere, to proliferate to the limits of the visible and the invisible, rather than to disappear for good' (Foucault 1978: 42).

Sexuality as an extended analysis of the limitations of the logic of judgement, and of the kind of moves we need to make sense of the non-juridical polyvalent structure of discourses that together determine the sense of the world. In the next chapter, we will turn to Deleuze, who, while sharing many affinities with Foucault, recognises more clearly his debt to phenomenology.

CHAPTER 7

Deleuze and the Question of Determination

7.1 Introduction

When we looked at Hölderlin's short piece on judgement and being in the first chapter, we saw that he takes issue with one of the central claims of Kant's transcendental philosophy. In the *Critique of Pure Reason*, Kant argues that '[t]he same function that gives unity to the different representations in a judgement also gives unity to the mere synthesis of different representations in an intuition' (Kant 1929: A79/B104–5). This claim allowed Kant to demonstrate why our judgements about the world accord with the world itself – because our intuition is conditioned by the understanding prior to us making that judgement – but it also limits our possibilities for explaining the grounds for judgement themselves. Hölderlin's project was therefore to provide a ground for judgement in terms that did not presuppose the structure of judgement itself. His claim was that, following Kant's discoveries in the transcendental deduction, one of the conditions of judgement is that we are able to understand the subject as separated from the object. I can only judge something if I, as the judger, stand opposed to it as the object of judgement. For Hölderlin, the German term for judgement, *Urteil*, implies etymologically this notion of an original (*Ur*) separation (*Teilung*). So if judgement requires this notion of separation, we are going to have to seek its ground in something which is unseparated. If the ground for judgement is something that is different in kind from the structure of judgement, then this ground will be prior to this separation, and indeed, prior to all determination: pure being. As we saw, this led to the criticism that the move from being to the individuated world of judgement was unmotivated.

Deleuze raises the same concern about the reiteration of formal logic on the transcendental level in Kant's system, noting that this move forces Kant to presuppose the structure of the object at the transcendental level. A consequence of this is that Kant rules out an account of individuation, since the structure of the object is already presupposed. In other words, Kant cannot explain how objects themselves are formed, because the transcendental field is already structured objectivally. As Deleuze writes in a passage which could easily be related to Kant's conditions of possible experience, 'to the extent that the possible is open to "realisation", it is understood as an image of the real, while the real is supposed to resemble the possible. That is why it is difficult to understand what existence adds to the concept when all it does is double like with like' (Deleuze 1994: 212).

As we saw, Hegel's response to the problem of being was to bring mediation and negation within the absolute itself, and thus to reject as empty the notion of an undifferentiated being. Deleuze also wants to give an account of the conditions of judgement. For Hegel, we either view Being as empty, in which case it is no different from nothingness, or we determine it. In determining it, we judge it, and so it ceases to be a ground for judgement. That is, Being is either formless, or already formed. Deleuze wishes to oppose these options laid out by Hegel, and to retain the transcendental structure that Hölderlin's account suggests. In order to do this, he proposes a third alternative to the two put forward by Hegel, which is that what Hölderlin calls Being would be structured in a way which was different in kind from the structure of judgement. Judgement relies on the idea that the world can be understood in terms of subjects and properties. Deleuze's conception of logic will have to be one that is not based on the notion of subjects and properties, but still lets us talk about differences: 'The ultimate, external illusion of representation is this illusion that results from all its internal illusions – namely, that groundlessness should lack differences, when in fact it swarms with them' (Deleuze 1994: 277).

If the Being turns out to be what Deleuze calls an 'undifferentiated abyss', he will be unable to show how judgement comes about, as was the case for Hölderlin. Being, however, must not be determined according to any of the categories of judgement. If Being is understood in terms of judgement, then Deleuze has not really explained how judgement comes about, but has just repeated judgement at a higher level, much as he claims Kant does. In this case, once again, the transcendental will fall away. Deleuze's transcendental field will therefore not deal with a logic of objects. A consequence of this is that it will also not be a logic of subjects. 'The new discourse is no longer of the form, but neither is it that of the formless; it is rather that of the pure unformed' (Deleuze 1990: 107).

Deleuze argues that once we recognise that forms of determination are possible other than those of predication and negation, we open up the possibility of a transcendental philosophy that provides a genuine account of the genesis of judgement itself. In relation to the Idea, which for Deleuze provides a way of thinking the world prior to representation, Deleuze writes that:

> The question of the *ens omni modo determinatum* must be posed as follows: something which exists only in the Idea may be completely determined (differentiated) and yet lack those determinations which constitute actual existence (it is undifferenciated, not yet even individuated). (Deleuze 1994: 280)

We have already encountered this notion that a field of determinations that differ in kind from those of judgement gives rise to it in our examination of Bergson's logic of multiplicities. Deleuze takes up Bergson's conception of a durational world, with some reservations, but attempts to give a positive account of how we can understand determinations that are not structured in accordance with judgement. As we saw, judgement determines using opposed pairs of predicates (rational/non-rational), and hence relies on the notion of negation. Deleuze's alternative account of determination will be developed through a reading of the differential calculus, and hence he will argue that 'just as we oppose difference in itself to negativity, so we oppose dx to not-A, the symbol of difference [*Differenzphilosophie*] to that of contradiction' (Deleuze 1994: 170).

As we shall see, Deleuze's attempt to develop an account of determination that does not rest on judgement draws on a number of figures we have looked at so far in this work. Many of the central claims of Deleuze's ontology originate from Bergson's account of duration. In particular, we shall see that Deleuze's account of what it means to 'think difference', Deleuze's Idea, explicitly refers to the work of Bergson, using it to supplement Kant's account of it. Deleuze also endorses Sartre's account of the nature of the transcendental field, where categorial connections are replaced with transversal connections, and we can see in Sartre's account of the other a precursor to Deleuze's focus on the necessity of an encounter at the origin of philosophy.[1] As important as either of these is Merleau-Ponty, who, despite few explicit mentions in Deleuze's texts, plays a pivotal role in laying the groundwork for Deleuze's transcendental account of depth, and his criticisms of Kant's thought.

Given the complexity of Deleuze's thought, we can only offer a summary here, but we will address it in three stages. In the first part of this chapter, we

---

[1] Wambacq 2017: 122–3 notes that Deleuze's acceptance of Sartre's account here is prefigured by Merleau-Ponty's adoption of the notion of a transcendental field. She notes that Merleau-Ponty also prefigures Deleuze's reservations about Sartre's use of nothingness to characterise the moment of virtuality or invisibility that opens out to the world.

will look at Deleuze's image of thought. This is Deleuze's analysis of the traditional philosophical model of thought, which, as we shall see, rests on a transcendental illusion that thinking is judging. We will then move on to see how this account of thinking can be seen as emerging from a decision by Plato to ground becoming in being. We will see that Deleuze's approach inverts this model, taking intensity, as a field of processes, as the ground for being. We will conclude by looking at Deleuze's account of how we think intensity as difference. This will once again involve a return to a key structure from Kant's philosophy, the transcendental idea. Deleuze will argue that a reformulation of the transcendental idea gives us a model of how thinking is able to think the intensity and relate it to states of affairs.

7.2   The Image of Thought

In *Difference and Repetition*, Deleuze sets out his account of what he calls the image of thought. This term is to be contrasted with what he will call 'imageless thought', which characterises his own position.[2] The image of thought consists in a number of postulates that together constitute the framework of beliefs traditionally presupposed by philosophers. Deleuze lists eight of these postulates, but here we shall just concentrate on the first four, which together give Deleuze's account of how philosophy finds itself engaged with a world it considers amenable to judgement. Deleuze's claim will be that at the heart of philosophy is a paralogism whereby we conflate the conditions for representing thought with thought itself. In succumbing to this paralogism, we fall into the transcendental illusion that all determination can be understood in terms of judgement.

  The first postulate that Deleuze introduces is the assumption of good will on the part of the thinker. Deleuze relates this postulate to the question of presuppositions, using the example of Descartes' criticism of Aristotle. Aristotle defines a human being as a 'rational animal', a definition that combines a genus, 'animal', with a difference, 'rational'. If we want to explicate this definition, we can ask what an animal is, in which case we will be given the answer that an animal is a sensitive living being. A living being in turn is an animate body, and a body an extended substance, etc. While we can, therefore, explicate the meaning of any of the terms, as Descartes notes, the more we attempt to clarify the terms of our definition, the more

---

[2] In later work, the image of thought is contrasted with other images of thought that are more positive, such as the vegetal image of thought. I deal with this idea in more depth in my work Somers-Hall 2013c. Beistegui 2010 provides an excellent study of the development of Deleuze's attempt to think outside of the dogmatic image of thought in his later work.

we find ourselves dealing with terms that are abstract and removed from experience:

> What then did I formerly think I was? A man. But what is a man? Shall I say 'a rational animal'? No; for then I should have to inquire what an animal is, what rationality is, and in this way one question would lead me down the slope to other harder ones, and I do not now have the time to waste on subtleties of this kind. (Descartes 1984: 25–6)

Rejecting this account of definition, Descartes instead considers what he knows for certain, and settles on his knowledge of his own nature as a thinking thing. We can note two aspects of this brief account that are especially relevant for Deleuze. First, while Descartes is of course concerned with certainty, a key concern in coming to the definition 'thinking thing' is that the *sense* of the term is transparent to consciousness: 'I am a mind, or intelligence, or intellect, or reason – words whose meaning I have been ignorant of until now' (Descartes 1984: 27). Second, Descartes' claim here is that he has removed the presuppositions of Aristotle's method, and hence is able to instigate a proper beginning for philosophy.

Deleuze makes a distinction between two different kinds of presuppositions: objective and subjective presuppositions. We can roughly map this distinction onto that of content and form. While Descartes rejects Aristotle's objective presuppositions about the content of thought, he assumes that the way that we represent thinking to ourselves provides an appropriate model for conducting philosophy. We have already seen in Chapter 3 on Sartre that Kant showed that Descartes had mischaracterised the *cogito* by failing to realise that the category of substance was a rule for the organisation of appearances in time rather than an objective determination of the thinking thing in itself. Deleuze here makes a wider claim that the paralogism extends to the model of thinking as judging itself. At the heart of Deleuze's analysis is the claim that Descartes' analysis of thinking is one that assumes its universality (and this is further emphasised by Descartes giving the name 'Polyander' or Everyman to the figure who practises Descartes' method in his unfinished dialogue, *The Search for Truth by Means of the Natural Light*):

> We would do better to ask what is a subjective or implicit presupposition: it has the form of 'Everybody knows …'. Everybody knows, in a pre-philosophical and pre-conceptual manner … everybody knows what it means to think and to be. … As a result, when the philosopher says 'I think therefore I am', he can assume that the universality of his premises – namely, what it means to be and to think … – will be implicitly understood, and that no one can deny that to doubt is to think, and to think is to be . . ..

Everybody knows, no one can deny, is the form of representation and the discourse of the representative. (Deleuze 1994: 129–30)

In explaining what these subjective presuppositions are, Deleuze turns to another post-Kantian philosopher, Ludwig Feuerbach, who he claims 'is among those who have pursued farthest the problem of where to begin' (Deleuze 1994: 319). In his essay, *Towards a Critique of Hegelian Philosophy* (Feuerbach 1997), Feuerbach analyses what the aim of a philosophical text is. As he notes, a philosophical text can only operate by being taken up by the intellect of the reader. As such, it relies on the reader to take up and link ideas together in order to follow the text, which in turn presupposes that the reader already has these ideas to hand. It is for this reason that Descartes settles on our nature as thinking things as the Archimedean point of his metaphysics, and that Deleuze claims that his subjective presupposition is that everybody knows what thinking is. Feuerbach puts the point as follows:

> For this very reason, what the person demonstrating communicates is not the subject matter itself; but only the medium; for he does not instil his thoughts into me like drops of medicine, nor does he preach to deaf fishes like Saint Francis; rather, he addresses himself to thinking beings. The main thing – the understanding of the thing involved – he does not give me; he gives nothing at all – otherwise the philosopher could really produce philosophers, something which so far no one has succeeded in achieving. Rather he presupposes the faculty of understanding; he shows me i.e. to the other person as such – my understanding only in a mirror. (Feuerbach 1997: 105)

If we stopped at this point, then in a manner Descartes would be justified in taking thinking as judging to be the foundation of our philosophical system. Deleuze, however, will follow Feuerbach in making the further claim that in taking thinking as judging, we are taking a representation of thinking for thinking itself. The tendency of thinking to fall for this paralogism is what leads Deleuze to claim that we presuppose that 'there is a natural capacity for thought endowed with a talent for truth or an affinity with the true, under the double aspect of a *good will on the part of the thinker* and an *upright nature on the part of thought*' (Deleuze 1994: 131). How does this paralogism arise?

Feuerbach makes two claims about the communication of thought that are relevant here. First, in order to communicate my thought to another person, I need to 'strip my thought of the form of "mine-ness"' (Feuerbach 1997: 104), since only those elements that are shared by the reader will be accessible to them for the purposes of communication. This means that philosophy operates at the level of the species and at the expense of the particularities of individual experience. Second, Feuerbach notes that communication takes place in time. As such, in order to be able to present my ideas, the complex nature of internal thinking needs to be simplified into a sequence of terms that can be expressed successively:

> And yet, systematic thought is by no means the same as thought as such, or essential thought; it is only self-presenting thought. To the extent that I present my thoughts, I place them in time; an insight that contains all its successive elements within a simultaneity within my mind now becomes a sequence. (Feuerbach 1997: 101)

Here, we have the origin of Deleuze's idea of an *image* of thought, which is prefigured by Feuerbach's notion of an 'image of reason' (Feuerbach 1997: 106). For Deleuze, this image of thought is to an extent unavoidable, much as transcendental illusion was for Kant, but we fall into error (hence Deleuze's introduction of the term the 'dogmatic image of thought' [1994: 167]) when we take this presentation of thought for thought itself. We can note a close parallel here with Bergson's account of consciousness in *Time and Free Will*, where we had a similar transposition from an interpenetrative multiplicity that resisted expression into a discrete multiplicity, once again to admit communication of internal states. Merleau-Ponty also makes the same argument in relation to Kant's account of the transcendental deduction, which he takes to rest on an account of 'mutilated thought' (Merleau-Ponty 1968: 35). Just as Deleuze here takes thinking to be illegitimately understood according to the structures of representation, we saw in Chapter 4 that Merleau-Ponty reads Kant as treating the various perspectives of consciousness as elements analogous to those of judgement, thus falsifying our experience of the world.

We can draw three implications from this claim that will be important for the development of Deleuze's philosophy. First, if this analysis is correct, then there is indeed a subjective presupposition to philosophies such as Descartes',[3] namely the process of abstraction and transposition of thinking that makes the communication of thought possible. Second, if philosophy begins from within the paralogism of thought, then it will be unable to create any new concepts, since it will be restricted to what is

---

[3] The critique developed by Feuerbach is wider than Descartes' philosophy, and in fact Feuerbach sees Hegel as the main target of his critique, as the figure who develops the most perfect image of reason. Deleuze 1994: 129 makes a similar claim, noting that while Descartes begins with an abstract notion of thought, Hegel himself begins with a conception of being itself abstracted from concrete being.

already present in the mind of the reader.[4] Finally, if thinking is to move beyond the transcendental illusion of representation, it must begin with an encounter that does not operate in terms of the structures of communication. We will explore these implications throughout the chapter, but for now, I want to look in more detail at how this paralogism plays out in the work of Descartes and Kant.

7.3 Common Sense and Recognition

In what sense does philosophy prevent an encounter with the world? Deleuze's claim is that the encounter is in fact made impossible by the structure of representation. In order to explore this claim in more detail, I want to briefly look at a couple of key passages from Descartes' *Meditations*, before looking at how these structures also play out in the work of Kant. In doing so, we will bring in three more of Deleuze's postulates of the image of thought: these postulates are 'the postulate of the ideal, or common sense', 'the postulate of the model, or recognition', and 'the postulate of the element or representation' (Deleuze 1994: 207).

We have already seen one use of common sense, in the claim by Feuerbach that the communication of reason operates at the level of the species. We can also find the idea of common sense within Descartes' wax example, where he attempts to show that the *cogito* is better known than the objects we relate to. Descartes makes this claim as follows:

> Let us take, for example, this piece of wax. It has just been taken from the honeycomb; it has not quite yet lost the taste of honey; it retains some of the scent of the flowers from which it was gathered; its colour, shape and size are plain to see; it is hard, cold, and can be handled without difficulty; if you rap it with your knuckles, it makes a sound. In short, it has everything which appears necessary for a body to be known as distinctly as possible. But even as I speak, I put the wax by the fire, and look: the residual taste is eliminated, the smell goes away, the colour changes, the shape is lost, and the size increases; it becomes liquid and hot; you can hardly touch it, and if you strike it, it no longer makes a sound. But does the same wax remain? It must

---

[4] In Chapter 5, we noted that both Derrida and Merleau-Ponty could be understood as developing an account of thought that did not succumb to Meno's paradox. We can see here a similar moment in Deleuze's thought, where the diagnosis of the inability to acquire knowledge we find in the paradox is taken to be falling into this transcendental illusion where the presentation of thinking is taken as thinking itself. A concern with this problem is one of the motivations of Deleuze moving from a focus on knowledge to a focus on learning (see Deleuze 1994: 164–7). Deleuze and Guattari 1994 argue for the importance of the centrality of the concept of creation for philosophy. Bell's (2016) excellent study relates this to learning.

> be admitted that it does; no one denies it, no one thinks otherwise. So what
> was it in the wax that I understood with such distinctness? Evidently none of
> the features which I arrived at by means of the senses; for whatever came
> under taste, smell, sight, touch or hearing has now altered – yet the wax
> remains. (Descartes 1984: 30)

Descartes here argues that we know ourselves better than we know objects
in the world by showing that we do not perceive objects at all. Rather, we
perceive a series of properties that can alter while the underlying unity itself
is maintained. In a later paragraph, Descartes argues that this unity is in
fact supplied by us, as can be seen in the case of error, when we hold
together different properties under an object that does not in fact exist. As
such, Descartes institutes the model of judgement in relation to a world of
substances and properties. Descartes calls common sense, or *sensus com-*
munis, the faculty responsible for relating together the different properties
of the senses. Common sense is intimately related to Deleuze's third
postulate, recognition:

> An object is recognised, however, when one faculty locates it as identical to
> that of another, or rather when all the faculties together relate their given
> and relate themselves to a form of identity in the object. (Deleuze 1994: 169)

Deleuze generalises this account of common sense, introducing the further
term, good sense, that equates to recognition, and claiming that these two
structures make judgement possible.[5] Deleuze defines good sense and
common sense as follows: 'For while common sense is the norm of identity
from the point of view of the pure Self and the form of the unspecified
object which corresponds to it, good sense is the norm of distribution from
the point of view of the empirical selves and the objects qualified as this or
that kind of thing (which is why it is considered to be universally distributed)' (Deleuze 1994: 133–4). Good sense here governs the kinds of properties we should attribute to an object, and how we distinguish the essential
and the accidental. Failures of good sense lead to the kind of errors
Descartes considers when we misrecognise hats and coats as people. In
these cases, the failure is one that is essentially empirical, and amounts to
poor judgement (the subsumption of the wrong particular under a given
universal). Common sense rather sets out the structure of judgement itself,

---

[5] Good sense and common sense in fact have a wider meaning for Deleuze, and he will argue that the
image of thought is what prevents thermodynamics from thinking the constitution of physical
systems. As it presupposes points of individuation (common sense), it tends to explore how physical
systems with given differences (good sense) tend to cancel these differences over time to return to
pure homogeneity (Deleuze 1994: 226).

and represents a transcendental condition of representation. It is by assuming a common substance that we can unify the different properties of the objects given by the senses.

In Deleuze's diagnosis of the operation of the image of thought in Kant's transcendental idealism, he introduces a fourth postulate of the image of thought: the postulate of representation. Deleuze's relationship with Kant here is once again ambivalent, and Deleuze claims that Kant 'seemed equipped to overturn the image of thought' (1994: 172), but in fact reinstates the structure of common sense. While Descartes sees God as guaranteeing the relation between thinking and its objects, for Kant objects instead 'must conform to our knowledge' (Kant 1929: Bxvi). The notion of an object now only has validity as a way of organising intuitions:

> Intuition and concepts constitute, therefore, the elements of all our knowledge, so that neither concepts without an intuition in some way corresponding to them, nor intuitions without concepts, can yield knowledge. (Kant 1929: A50/B74)

On the one hand, the implication of these claims is that there is no longer a 'natural right' on the part of reason to correspond to objects, and Deleuze rightly notes that a central aspect of Kant's thought is to replace error with the idea of internal illusions within reason (Deleuze 1994: 136). As such, thinking goes wrong not when reason is affected by another faculty, as is the case for Descartes, but precisely when reason is not operating in relation to another faculty. While the move from error (which naturally invokes the structures of truth and falsity, and through them judgement) to illusion seems a move away from the image of thought, Deleuze claims that Kant's project in fact operates by delimiting a sphere in which the image of thought can claim legitimacy. In the preface to the *First Critique*, Kant proclaims 'a call to reason to undertake anew the most difficult of all its tasks, namely, that of self-knowledge, and to institute a tribunal which will institute to reason its lawful claims, and dismiss all groundless pretensions, not by despotic decrees, but in accordance with its own eternal and unalterable laws' (Kant 1929: Axi–xii). Deleuze therefore sees Kant's project as 'at most amount[ing] to giving civil rights to thought considered from the point of view of its *natural law*' (Deleuze 1994: 173). It is one of formulating a coherent model of the image of thought that guarantees its legitimacy by limiting its domain of applicability. Whereas the problem of common sense for rationalism and empiricism is scepticism – whether our representations will conform to objects – the problem of common sense for Kant is how different faculties that differ in kind are able to relate to each other. This is the problem Kant addresses in the transcendental deduction. As we have seen, whereas the *cogito* for Descartes is an actual substance, for Kant the transcendental unity of apperception is not actually given in experience, but rather precedes it and makes it possible. While 'it must be possible for the "I think" to accompany all our representations' (Kant 1929: B131–2), therefore, in practice, the 'I think' may not be present, since it is an analytic indication of a prior synthetic moment of unity. Thus, in Kant we have what Deleuze calls a 'logical common sense' (1994: 173). Ultimately, therefore, while Kant appears to offer a radical break from Descartes, his philosophy for Deleuze is rather an augmentation of Descartes' thought:

> Therefore the real (synthetic) formula of the *cogito* is: I think myself and in thinking myself, I think the object in general to which I relate a represented diversity. (Deleuze 1984: 14)

Representation draws together the three postulates we have seen so far, and institutes our initial claim that all determination happens in terms of judgement. This is the fundamental 'site of transcendental illusion' (Deleuze 1994: 265) that is therefore responsible for the image of thought:

> There are four principal 'aspects' to reason, in so far as it is the medium of representation: identity in the form of the *undetermined* concept; analogy, in the relationship between ultimate *determinable* concepts; opposition, in the relations between *determinations* within concepts; resemblance, in the *determined* object of the concept itself. (Deleuze 1994: 37)

These can be mapped on to the various moments of the transcendental deduction as follows. First, experience requires that we relate our different representations to a central identity (this is the identity of the object that we discover in the synthesis of recognition). This in turn relies on an analogy between the rules governing our knowledge of objects and the rules governing the structure of objects themselves (the schematism). Now, in order for these various moments to be related together into a unity, they must have some kind of affinity with one another. This affinity requires that the same properties obtain in the object now and at some moment in the past (if cinnabar were not always red, 'my empirical imagination would never find opportunity when representing red colour to bring to mind heavy cinnabar' [Kant 1929: A100–1]). In order to determine whether a present object is an instance of a type, we therefore need the notion of opposition (red/not-red). Finally, in order to recognise this affinity, we need to be able to determine whether the object presented by a memory and the object presented by perception have *the same* property. As we are dealing with different representations, this is achieved by a comparison as to whether the representations resemble one another. Thus in order for recognition to function, we require the structures of representation to provide the machinery for recognising that we are dealing with the same object, through the diversity of perceptual experience.

The image of thought prevents a genuine encounter with the world, and conditions us to understand it in terms of unified subjects who make sense of the world in terms of judgements. While different philosophies will put these postulates into operation in different ways ('No doubt philosophy refuses every particular *doxa* [popular opinion]; no doubt it upholds no particular propositions of good sense or common sense' [Deleuze 1994: 170]), the postulates of the image of thought are present within most major traditions of philosophy. That is because Deleuze sees these postulates as present within our pre-philosophical account of the world. As such, an approach such as Descartes', or Hegel's,[6] will inevitably repeat the paralogism at the heart of the dogmatic image of thought:

> We may well discover a supra-temporal form or even a sub-temporal primary matter, an underground or *Ur-doxa*: We have not advanced a single step, but remain imprisoned by the same cave or ideas of the times which we only flatter ourselves with having 'rediscovered', by blessing them with the sign of philosophy. (Deleuze 1994: 134)

7.4 The Encounter

To escape from the image of thought, what is required is an encounter that draws us outside of the strictures of common sense and representation. In his writing on Proust, Deleuze sees this shock, or encounter, to be something like the affect of jealousy one might feel towards a lover.[7] While a philosopher like Descartes might call for reflection and calmness at the outset of our philosophical enquiry ('Today I have expressly rid my mind of all worries and arranged for myself a clear stretch of free time' [Descartes 1984: 7–8]), jealousy

---

[6] Smith 2012a: 59 argues that 'Deleuze's early anti-Hegelianism is primarily polemical' on the basis of Deleuze's introduction of his own conception of dialectics in *Difference and Repetition*. Once we recognise that Deleuze is claiming that Hegel's account of thinking itself rests on a paralogism, however, we can see that Deleuze's rejection of Hegel stems from an irreconcilable disagreement about the nature of thinking and the method of philosophy. We will see this especially clearly in the next section where we will look at Deleuze's argument that philosophy must begin with an encounter in direct opposition to Hegel's immanent method.

[7] Deleuze describes jealousy as 'the very delirium of signs' (Deleuze 2000: 138), which therefore draws us out of the structures of representation.

instead captures the sense of intensity that Deleuze thinks we need to have in order to be properly engaged with philosophy. Deleuze himself traces the origin of the encounter in philosophy to Plato, with Plato's claim that some experiences 'summon' the subject to a deeper investigation into the nature of the world. They do this not because of some empirical limitation, but rather through an in-principle paradox in the experience:

> The ones that don't summon the understanding are all those that don't go off into opposite perceptions at the same time. But the ones that do go off in that way I call summoners – whenever sense perception doesn't declare one thing any more than its opposite, no matter whether the object striking the senses is near at hand or far away. You'll understand my meaning better if I put it this way: These, we say, are three fingers – the smallest, the second, and the middle finger. (Plato 1997d: 523b–c)

What is important about the example of the fingers for Plato is that we cannot apply the predicates, long and short, to them reliably, since their length will depend on how they compare with other fingers. Plato gives a number of further examples, such as the presence of properties like beauty that both hold and do not hold of objects since every object 'comes into being and passes away' (Plato 1997d: 527b). We also recognise in an imperfect representation of a circle the ideal form of it, even though all circles we encounter are imperfect.

How does this account of the encounter open out into a new philosophy? Deleuze takes up something like this Platonic view of the encounter, though he will argue that we need to 'reverse Platonism' (Deleuze 1994: 59). If we return to Plato, we can see that as with Derrida, Deleuze sees Plato as standing at a philosophical crossroads. Deleuze notes that in the *Cratylus*, Plato appears to suggest that there might be 'two languages and two sorts of "names," one designating the pauses and rests which receive the action of the Idea, the other expressing the movements, or rebel becomings' (Deleuze 1990: 2). We can see these as related to the Platonic account of being and the Heraclitan account of becoming. On Plato's account, the contradictions we find in the realm of becoming force thinking to relate itself to the forms. He gives the following analogy:

> Well, you know what happens to lovers: whenever they see a lyre, a garment or anything else that their beloved is accustomed to use, they know the lyre, and the image of the boy to whom it belongs comes into their mind. (Plato 1997b: 73d)

As such, thought is returned to thought of the forms in the same way that the lyre leads to recollection of the boy. As we have seen, knowledge of the forms for Plato occurs through recollection of a moment prior to us being born. As such, contrary properties lead us to recognise that behind the becoming of appearance is a realm of atemporal, unchanging forms.

Deleuze calls this idea that the structures underlying appearance are essentially *atemporal* a sedentary distribution. Sedentary distributions understand the world in terms of judgement. As Deleuze puts it:

> A distribution of this type proceeds by fixed and proportional determinations which may be assimilated to 'properties' or limited territories within representation. (Deleuze 1994: 45)

These properties are therefore defined through relations of opposition, and there is a fixed divide or limit which separates things with one essence from things with the other. This idea of fixed, determinate structures underlying appearances is an approximation of Plato's position, and Deleuze takes it to underlie much of the philosophical tradition.[8] This is contrasted with the nomadic distribution:

> [A] nomad *nomos*, without property, enclosure or measure. Here, there is no longer a division of that which is distributed but rather a division among those who distribute *themselves* in an open space – a space which is unlimited, or at least without precise limits. Nothing pertains or belongs to any person, but all persons are arrayed here and there in such a manner as to cover the largest possible space . . . . To fill a space, to be distributed within it, is very different from distributing the space. (Deleuze 1994: 36–7)

The first thing to note about this account is that it has strong affinities with Bergson's account of duration. We can begin by noting, for instance, that instead of the 'sedentary distributions of the categories' (Deleuze 1994: 285) that we find, for instance, in Kant's thought, we have here a model whereby the distribution differs in kind from the empirical forms it gives rise to: we have a transcendental field that does not operate in terms of properties and subjects, but yet gives rise to them. Deleuze further takes up the Bergsonian distinction between the discrete multiplicity, which operates in terms of determinate elements within a fully extended space, and a confused multiplicity, which can be more or less extended. Just as with Bergson, the confused multiplicity is seen as giving rise to a discrete multiplicity.

This sense that the encounter leads us to a point where the self is dissolved, and the normal categories of reason fail to function, is what leads to Deleuze's fascination with figures such as Artaud, who disrupt the

---

[8] Williams 2003: 64–9 sets out clearly the reasons for taking the sedentary distribution as a model for all categorial models of thought.

image of thought.[9] Returning to Plato, Deleuze sums up the difference between his account of the encounter and that presented by Socrates:

> However, this Platonic response will not do: in fact, it rests upon intensive quantities, but recognises these only in qualities in the course of development – and for this reason, it assigns both the being of the sensible and contrariety to qualities. However, while the contrary-sensible or contrariety in the quality may constitute sensible being *par excellence*, they by no means constitute the being of the sensible. (Deleuze 1994: 236)

Here, Deleuze makes a distinction between sensible being and the being of the sensible. He argues that Plato recognises that existence involves becoming, but he understands this structure of becoming in terms of judgement (contrariety of properties in one subject). As such, the contrariety of properties points to a realm outside of becoming. For Deleuze, on the contrary, a paradox such as Plato's rather points to becoming falling outside of categorial thought. While sensible being and the being of the sensible have the same structure for Plato, then, they differ in kind for Deleuze.

We have come across this notion of an encounter that forces us outside of categorial thought at several points in this work. Bergson, for instance, introduces the example of waiting for sugar to dissolve in a glass of water. In this simple example, what Bergson demonstrates is not simply that consciousness takes time to unfold, but rather, as Deleuze notes, that consciousness is essentially open to the world. This openness to an encounter with the world, which, given its durational nature for Bergson, means an encounter with a world in constant qualitative flux, is what makes creativity possible. As Deleuze notes, in thinking the system of the sugar dissolving in the water, we are forced to think it in terms that escape the categories of the determinate elements of judgement, and in turn to reflect on consciousness' own durational nature:

> The glass of water is indeed a closed set containing the parts, the water, the sugar, perhaps the spoon, but that is not the whole. The whole creates itself, and constantly creates itself in another dimension without parts – like that

---

[9] Deleuze sees Artaud as attempting to open up a form of thinking beneath the dogmatic structures of representation: 'Artaud does not simply talk about his own "case", but already in his youthful letters shows an awareness that his case brings him into contact with a generalised thought process which can no longer be covered by the reassuring dogmatic image but which, on the contrary, amounts to the complete destruction of that image. The difficulties he describes himself as experiencing must therefore be understood as not merely in fact but as difficulties in principle, concerning and affecting the essence of what it means to think' (Deleuze 1994: 147). Artaud's own descriptions of his project explicitly invoke Bergson as a model of thinking.

which carries along the set of one qualitative state to another, like the pure, ceaseless becoming that passes through these states. It is in this sense that it is spiritual or mental. (Deleuze 1986: 10)

We can see this notion of an encounter played out most dramatically in Sartre's work, in Sartre's account of our relationship with others. As we saw in Chapter 3, Sartre rejects the idea that we know others through some kind of inference from the similarity of the other to us, for instance. In his criticisms of Heidegger, we saw that if we understood consciousness as containing something like a category of the other, then such a category would in fact prevent any real engagement with others at all, since, 'as the law precisely *constitutes* its own domain, it excludes *a priori* every real fact which it has not constructed' (Sartre 1978: 249). As such, our engagement with the other cannot take place within the domain of knowledge, but must involve an immediate encounter that changes our nature. Wambacq (2017: 112–13) notes that this idea of philosophy as an encounter is also at the heart of Merleau-Ponty's characterisation of phenomenology, with Merleau-Ponty citing with approval Eugene Fink's characterisation of phenomenology as an 'earthquake' that 'befalls' us.

This connection with Merleau-Ponty is also present in the resonances between Socrates' use of paradoxes and Merleau-Ponty's introduction of the paradox of symmetrical objects. As we saw, this argument was used by Kant to show that the organisation of intuition was different in kind from judgement, and by Merleau-Ponty to show that the structure of perception differed in kind from representation. Deleuze takes up this example too, presumably borrowing it from Merleau-Ponty. Deleuze glosses it as 'difference without a concept, repetition which escapes indefinitely continued conceptual differ-ence' (Deleuze 1994: 15). By this he means that the paradox of symmetrical objects suggests that some phenomena fall outside of conceptual understand-ing. Objects can repeat because while they are non-conceptually different, they are nonetheless conceptually identical. It is only on this basis that we can have two objects that are both distinct but also identical, and hence open to repetition. We will return to this argument in the next section. Deleuze's claim that the world has a structure that differs in kind from categorial thought opens up two questions which I want to look at for the remainder of the chapter. First, I want to ask how Deleuze characterises this world of intensity that makes possible the states of affairs that surround us. As we shall see, Deleuze once again borrows heavily from both Merleau-Ponty and Bergson in establishing his account of the world. Second, given the incom-mensurability of intensity to categorial thought, I want to explore the question of how we are to think difference. We will conclude by looking at Deleuze's account of the Idea, which is central to Deleuze's answer to this question.

7.5   Intensity

In this section, I want to outline what Deleuze considers intensity to be.[10] Deleuze takes intensity to characterise the world from his early work on Spinoza through to his later collaborations with Guattari.[11] In *Difference and Repetition*, Deleuze presents two key accounts of how intensity 'explicates' itself into the extensive world of objects, the first operating in terms of time, and the second in terms of space. The first can be seen as a reworking of the transcendental deduction, showing that what Kant takes to be the process of synthesis is actually a surface effect of a non-representational process, echoing Merleau-Ponty's own reading. The second account focuses on the emergence of space, but there are once again parallels with Merleau-Ponty's account. Here, Deleuze takes up Merleau-Ponty's accounts both of Kant's argument from incongruent counterparts[12] and of depth. As we saw in Chapter 4, Merleau-Ponty uses Kant's argument from incongruent counterparts to argue for a non-conceptual form of synthesis in perception. Deleuze here makes the same point, arguing that such non-conceptual differences that appear within representation are signs of pre-representational processes of synthesis:

> In the case of enantiomorphic bodies, Kant recognised precisely an *internal difference*. However, since it was not a conceptual difference, on his view it could refer only to an external relation with extensity as a whole in the form of extensive magnitude. In fact, the paradox of symmetrical objects, like everything concerning right and left, high and low, figure and ground, has an intensive source. (Deleuze 1994: 231)

Here, as with Merleau-Ponty, Deleuze effectively argues that the problem with Kant's account of the paradox of symmetrical objects is that he

---

[10]   Despite its acknowledged centrality, the place of intensity in Deleuze's system, and in particular its relation to the virtual actual distinction, is still contested. Clisby 2015 does an excellent job of setting out the various standard interpretations. Here, I argue that the virtual/actual distinction governs how one thinks intensity, and hence that these are two different sets of categories. This view is complicated by Deleuze's panpsychism, which I will not explore here, but which is dealt with in Somers-Hall 2013a: 62–5.

[11]   Smith 2012b provides a good account of Deleuze's engagements with some of the theoretical grounds for a philosophy of intensity through his study of the concept of univocity. See Widder 2009 for an exploration of Deleuze's reading of Duns Scotus, who brings in the idea of intensive difference prior to Spinoza.

[12]   See Somers-Hall 2013b for a full account of Deleuze's use of Kant's argument from incongruent counterparts.

believes it relies on space as pure receptivity. Rather, perception is a synthesis, but one that differs in kind from categorial synthesis. Deleuze follows Merleau-Ponty in this claim, and also follows Merleau-Ponty in seeing depth as the field of genesis of these non-representational moments: 'Depth as the (ultimate and original) heterogeneous dimension is the matrix of all extensity, including its third dimension considered to be homogeneous with the other two' (Deleuze 1994: 229). Deleuze's term, extensity, can therefore be equated with Merleau-Ponty's objective thought:

> It is notable that extensity does not account for the individuations which occur within it. No doubt the high and the low, the right and the left, the figure and the ground are individuating factors which trace rises and falls, currents and descents in extensity. (Deleuze 1994: 229)

Here, Deleuze references the three structures tied to perspective that we discussed in Chapter 4. Deleuze's claim is that structures such as left and right, or figure and ground, cannot be understood in terms of extension. Each of these characteristics, high and low, left and right, figure and ground, relate to a different dimension, and show that each of these dimensions are not interchangeable as they would be in a classical Euclidean space.

Merleau-Ponty argues ultimately that these structures, the high and low, left and right, and figure and ground, appear within a field of depth. For representation, depth is one dimension amongst the others. For Merleau-Ponty, on the contrary, given his perspectivism, depth was seen as the primary dimension from which the other dimensions emerged, as it was through the plane of depth that objects were able to organise themselves in relation to us. What Merleau-Ponty calls primary depth, therefore, is no longer a dimension of space as a container, but rather that which provides the genesis of space, given Merleau-Ponty's claim about the necessary relation between a figure and its ground. Deleuze sees depth as entailing a wider claim about the constitution of objects and their relations to each other: 'The law of figure and ground would never hold for objects unless the object itself entertained a relation to its own depth' (Deleuze 1994: 229). We have already seen this in Merleau-Ponty's work, to the degree that the primacy of perception entails perception's primacy over the constitution of subjects and objects; Deleuze takes this model as showing how a non-homogeneous field of depth can generate a field of extended objects. In doing so, he equates primary depth with intensity ('Depth is the intensity of being, or vice-versa' [Deleuze 1994: 231]).

The difference between Deleuze and Merleau-Ponty emerges from Deleuze's introduction of another model of synthesis which he calls an 'asymmetrical synthesis' (Deleuze 1994: 244). Rather than the transition synthesis, which operates in terms of perspective, Deleuze argues for a model of synthesis that operates between the two ontological planes of intensity and extensity. Turning to Deleuze's review of the work of Simondon gives us a sense of what this means. In this essay, Deleuze contrasts classical accounts of individuation with the model proposed by Simondon. On the classical model 'we put the individual after the individuation, in the same breath we put the principle of individuation *before* the process of becoming an individual, beyond the individuation itself' (Deleuze 2004: 86). Deleuze's criticisms here recall Merleau-Ponty's criticisms of the constitutive synthesis, which attempted to generate extensive space from a position prior to spatiality itself, and hence was unable to explain the contingencies of our position within space. Merleau-Ponty's alternative is to posit the transition synthesis, which sees synthesis as the movement from orientation to orientation. Deleuze's alternative, taken from Simondon, sees synthesis as operating simultaneously on and between two levels: 'In reality, the individual can only be contemporaneous with its individuation, and individuation, contemporaneous with the principle: the principle must be truly genetic, and not simply a principle of reflection' (Deleuze 2004: 86). We will explore the interaction of the two levels in greater detail shortly, but Deleuze's claim will be that intensity expresses itself in extensity while perpetuating its own existence: 'it maintains this difference in itself in the implicated order by which it is grounded' (Deleuze 1994: 232). Thus, whereas Merleau-Ponty's transition synthesis generates a constant shift in orientation, Deleuze's asymmetrical synthesis operates through the constant interplay of an intensity that is expressed without reducing itself to extensity. Deleuze's claim, therefore, is that intensity should be 'definable independently of extensity' (Deleuze 1994: 230). Thus, prior to depth, we have an account of 'space as a whole, but space as an intensive quantity: the pure *spatium*' (Deleuze 1994: 230). The third spatial synthesis therefore goes beyond Merleau-Ponty's phenomenological account by considering intensity independently of this process of the constitution of perspective. The aim of introducing this analysis of space prior to phenomenology is to open the way to an account of the individuation of bodies and subjects themselves.

So what is intensity? It is a field of pure process which is the ground for the states of affairs we find in extensity. Deleuze gives three characteristics that he takes to define intensity together. These are that it 'includes the unequal in itself' (Deleuze 1994: 232), it 'affirms difference' (1994: 234), and it is 'an implicated, enveloped or "embryonised" quantity' (1994: 237).

The first of these governs the relationship of intensity to extensity, the second governs the relationship of intensity to quality, and the third governs the interrelation between the two. Deleuze explains the first characteristic through a mathematical example. If we take the series of whole numbers, we can note that we frequently encounter quantities that cannot be expressed in terms of them. We deal with this problem by introducing a further series of numbers, the fractions, which are able to represent quantities that the whole numbers couldn't. In turn, there are numbers, the irrational numbers such as π, that cannot be represented by rational numbers, whether fractions or whole numbers. What happens in this sequence for Deleuze is that in each order of numbers, we discover a term that is incommensurable with that order, and this incommensurability is 'equalised' by instituting a new order of numbers. We began this sequence with whole numbers, and Deleuze asks the question of whether there is an order prior to the whole numbers themselves. We can find this order by looking at the distinction between ordinal and cardinal numbers. Deleuze argues that while cardinal numbers (one, two, three) are often given primacy over ordinal numbers (first, second, third), in fact 'natural numbers are first ordinal – in other words, originally intensive. Cardinal numbers result from these and are presented as the explication of the ordinal' (Deleuze 1994: 232). The difference between these two classes of numbers is that cardinal numbers presuppose a common measure or unit, which is what allows us to determine relations of quantitative equivalence between different sums (for example, 1+3=2+2). On the contrary, when we look at ordinal numbers, while there is a relationship between them, this relationship is not one that is metric (so, for instance, the relationship between first and third does not have to have the same magnitude as between second and fourth). Hence, while there is a notion of order, or what Deleuze calls, in a technical sense, distance, in this case this is not an order that can be measured or mapped out. Deleuze's claim is that the relationship between ordinal and cardinal numbers is a model for the relationship between intensity and extensity more generally. Just as ordinality is explicated into cardinality through the introduction of a unit of measure, an intensive field which is ordered by non-metric determinations is explicated into a world of determinate magnitudes.

Here, we can once again see a strong connection to Bergson, where we also had the constitution of an extensive understanding of the world emerging from a non-metric field. Deleuze in fact explicitly refers to

Bergson at this point, claiming that when Bergson talks of a qualitative multiplicity, he should have in fact talked of an intensive multiplicity.[13] Deleuze sees the move from intensity to extensity as being an ontological claim, and as well as the mathematical claim, Deleuze also claims that we can understand embryology, for instance, in intensive terms, where the changes in structure that occur in the development of the embryo can be made sense of topologically, in terms of the folding of tissue and the relative positions of structures, rather than metrically in terms of absolute measurements of magnitudes and distances.[14] He universalises this embryological idea by noting that 'the world is an egg' (Deleuze 1994: 216).

The second characteristic Deleuze notes is that intensity 'affirms difference', and here Deleuze explores how intensity gives rise to qualities. Deleuze takes this to mean that 'Difference is not negation. On the contrary, the negative is difference inverted, seen from below' (Deleuze 1994: 235). As we have seen, determination in terms of qualities relies on negation, so that we can divide objects according to a logic of 'this-and-not-that'. In terms of judgement, difference itself is understood in terms of negation: x differs from y means that x is not y. Deleuze's claim is going to be that what appear to be stable qualities of objects are in fact processes resting on differences in intensity. In order to make this claim, Deleuze turns to the scientific example of heat. Intensity is a central concept of thermodynamics, and the second law of thermodynamics states that 'heat does not pass from a body at low temperature to one at high temperature without an accompanying change elsewhere' (Atkins 2010: 42). A central implication of this claim is that the quality of heat rests on the difference between the temperature of two bodies. Heat, therefore, is itself a process that relies on a difference. While there can be the negation of a quality, Deleuze claims that even in extensive space we do not find the negation of intensities: 'It is said that in general there are no reports of null frequencies, no effectively null potentials, no absolutely null pressure, as though on a line with logarithmic graduations where zero lies at

---

[13] Here, I am following Lundy 2017: 184 in his claim that '[t]he invisible hand of Bergson . . . guides Deleuze in his stipulation of the three characteristics of intensity'. See Widder 2019 for a reading that sees Deleuze as moving away from Bergson in his account of intensity.

[14] Delanda 2002 provides an influential and accessible reading of Deleuze that understands his work as developing an ontology appropriate to complexity theory and systems with non-linear dynamics (where small changes in inputs can lead to large differences in the outputs of the system). Delanda's work is important in showing the relevance of what can seem very abstract arguments on Deleuze's part. Delanda has a tendency to equate Deleuze's concepts with scientific concepts rather than seeing Deleuze as providing a philosophical account of what makes the successes of these advances in science possible, however, which downplays Deleuze's connections to metaphysical and ethical thought.

the end of an infinite series of smaller and smaller fractions' (Deleuze 1994: 234). We can see several modifications from the account of intensities we find in the physical sciences in Deleuze's work. First, as we saw in the first characteristic, intensity for Deleuze is a transcendental principle that is constitutive of extensity, whereas the thermodynamic conception of intensity sees intensity as operating at a point within an already constituted extensive space. Second, while intensity in scientific terms is seen as governing a number of qualities, such as heat, Deleuze sees all qualities as the result of intensive differences. As such, Socrates' mistake, from Deleuze's perspective, is to maintain the structures of judgement and reject difference rather than see qualities themselves as products of a process of becoming. Finally, for thermodynamics, intensive qualities emerge at locations within extensity. For Deleuze, intensity itself is what gives rise to extensity. Deleuze claims that this aspect of thermodynamics as only dealing with constituted intensities, rather than constituting intensities, leads to the 'transcendental physical illusion' of the eventual heat death of the universe.[15]

Finally, 'intensity is an implicated, enveloped, "embryonised" quantity'. As we have seen, Deleuze's first characteristic explains the emergence of extensity from intensity, and his second characteristic shows the emergence of properties from intensity. This third characteristic shows intensity's difference from either of these prior characteristics. As Deleuze puts it, 'intensity is neither divisible, like extensive quantity, nor indivisible, like quality' (Deleuze 1994: 237). On the one hand, quality is not divisible – either one has the quality of being rational or one does not. Extensity clearly can be divided, and as we saw in Chapter 2, dividing extensity does not result in a change of its nature. This is because extensity is defined in terms of parts that are essentially interchangeable. Intensity is not made of subordinate parts in the same manner: 'when it is pointed out that a temperature is not composed of other temperatures, or a speed of other speeds, what is meant is that each temperature is already a difference, and that differences are not composed of differences of the same order but imply series of heterogeneous terms' (Deleuze 1994: 237). As such, much as with Bergson's conception of quality, we *can* divide intensity, but in dividing it we change its nature. We can therefore read Bergson's account of the qualitative change of the sound of a melody onto Deleuze's model, where we note the wrong note because of the difference it causes in the melody as a whole.

[15] Here again, we see Deleuze's claim that by assuming constituted entities, we are unable to explain the genesis of subjects or systems.

Intensity therefore provides an account of how a field of processes that fall outside of juridical modes of determination can generate the structures of extensity and quality that make judgement possible. There is a close parallel here between Merleau-Ponty's critique of objective thought and Bergson's criticism of extensive multiplicities, and we can see how Deleuze solves Hölderlin's problem of finding a non-categorial ground for being. Just as in these previous cases, we have a transposition of the structures into a different medium to make judgement possible. For the rest of this chapter, I want to turn to the question of how we think intensity. Given intensity gives rise to inequalities, our logic of intensity will itself not operate in terms of judgement. The aim will therefore be to develop a logic of intensity that will explain the genesis of extensity while not presupposing it. In developing this account, Deleuze turns to Kant's account of Ideas. Deleuze's analysis of the Idea will reiterate Derrida's claim that Kant's own formulation of the Idea covers over non-representational difference, but will argue that his account contains the seeds of a proper model of how we can think intensity.

7.6   Transcendental Ideas and the Calculus

As we saw in the previous chapter, for Kant knowledge does not simply involve true judgements about the world. Rather, the particular judgements of the understanding need to be connected together by reason in order to allow us to develop systematic science. In order to unify our knowledge, reason requires the idea of a total unity to guide its operations. As such, it presupposes the possibility of a final systematic way of understanding the world in order to carry on the process of systematising. These ideas cannot be given in experience, and are not a part of the understanding, and so each is what Kant calls a '*focus imaginarius*' (1929: A644/B672). There is, therefore, a natural illusion that the complete object that is the aim of our systematic enquiry is 'a real object lying outside of the field of empirically possible knowledge' (Kant 1929: 644/B672). Reason therefore presupposes a structure that cannot be given in experience, but yet allows us to makes sense of it. Kant calls this nature of the idea 'problematic', and claims that since it goes beyond experience, 'it remains a *problem* to which there is no solution'[16] (1929: A328/B384). Ideas are structures that are not

---

[16] Deleuze's distinction between problems and solutions maps onto the distinction between imageless thought and the dogmatic image of thought, with Deleuze arguing that there is a tendency to understand problems in the categorial terms appropriate to solutions. In doing so, the pre-predicative nature of problems is covered over by representation.

derived from the world of representation, but which yet make sense of the world of appearances.

For Kant, Ideas reinforce the identification of thinking and judging since reason operates with the same categories of the understanding. For Deleuze, they instead have a genetic function, relating intensity to representation, and are at the heart of his account of thinking. Deleuze's Ideas have three moments. First, our model of thinking must involve a moment that escapes representation – that is, a moment which is indeterminate with regard to actual objects. This would be the moment of pure pre-representational thought that Deleuze sees as the preceding representation. Second, this moment would have to be determinable. That is, it would have to be capable of being related to experience. Finally, the model would have to have a moment of determination itself – that is, it would have to be actually instantiated in experience. We can map these on to the Feuerbach account as seeing indeterminate thinking (from the point of view of representation) as determinable (under time – it is put into successive form) as a determined thought. These three moments describe the movement from something that is outside of representation to something that is capable of sustaining properties in general, to a particular determined object. Deleuze therefore claims that the Idea captures the interaction of thinking with the movement between intensity and extensity.

Deleuze claims that these three moments are present in Kant's notion of the Idea, but that the second two are only extrinsically connected with it. That is, they are determined from the perspective of the image of thought, rather than determining the image of thought. To take an example, Kant sees the transcendental ideal of God as making possible our notion that an object can be completely determined in terms of properties, which is a presupposition of the scientific attempt to make sense of the world. God itself is undetermined, but is determinable by analogy with our own intelligence, though only if we use this determination pragmatically 'in respect of the *employment* of our reason *in reference to the world*' (Kant 1929: A698/B726). Similarly, as we saw, the ideal of God as completely determined depends on analogical reasoning from finite things in terms of the actual properties that they are taken to possess: 'The Ideal is, therefore, the archetype (*prototypon*) of all things, which one and all, as imperfect copies (*ectypa*), derive from it the material of their possibility, while approximating to it in various degrees' (Kant 1929: A578/B606).

While Kant's Ideas are undetermined, making them determinable and determining them relies on an analogy with objects of experience (this is what Deleuze means by two of the Idea's characteristics being extrinsic). If we are going to explain how representation becomes possible, it cannot simply be the case that Ideas are *brought into* representation (by analogy), but rather they must give rise to it. Deleuze draws on the differential calculus to develop this account. Deleuze's reading of the calculus largely follows that of Leibniz, and here we will just give a very brief account of it. We can begin by noting that the calculus deals with rates of change of variables. We can make a distinction between average and instantaneous rates of change. As an example, if it takes me an hour to commute the 10-mile journey to work, then my average speed is 10 miles per hour. Unless my speed is constant, this will likely not be my instantaneous speed at any particular point, since I may well speed up and slow down at various points during my journey. We can make the average speed approximate the instantaneous speed by dividing the time of my commute into smaller segments and working out the average speed over those, but if I am slowing down or speeding up during one of those segments, then my average speed will be constant while my instantaneous speed will be changing. Leibniz's solution to problems like this, where the relations between variables themselves vary, is to consider the intervals over which we measure the rate of change shrinking until they reach an infinitesimal magnitude. As they do so, the average rate of change will itself approach the instantaneous rate of change until they coincide when the interval is effectively considered equal to zero. Nonetheless, in relation to each other, the quantities of which we are measuring the rates of change, for instance distance and time, are still considered to have miniscule quantities, so a ratio between them (the speed at the point, for instance) can be calculated. Leibniz calls these quantities, which on their own are equal to zero, but which form a ratio, dy and dx, and the calculus provides a way of developing an equation for the rate of change at any point on a line. These are the differentials of the differential calculus. So if we are given a mathematical function, we can work out the formula for the gradient at any point by differentiating it. An important point is that this process is reversible – that is, we can move from an equation in terms of dy/dx to the equation it gives the gradient for (known as the primitive function) by a process of integration.

    Central to Deleuze's account is going to be the differential itself. Deleuze explicitly sets the differential against the logic of judgement: 'Just as we oppose difference in itself to negativity, so we oppose dx to not-A, the symbol of difference [*Differenzphilosophie*] to that of contradiction' (Deleuze 1994: 217). If we return to the three moments that Deleuze argued needed to be intrinsically related for an account of the genesis of representational thought, Deleuze argues that each moment can be mapped on to the calculus. Since what gives us the gradient to a curve isn't the differentials themselves, but rather the ratio between them, each of the values, dy and dx, is on its own completely lacking in magnitude: 'dx is strictly nothing in relation to x, as dy is in relation to y' (Deleuze 1994: 218). Deleuze's claim is that whilst dx is strictly nothing in relation to x, this is not because the differential is not in a sense real, but rather because it cannot be captured by either (Kantian) intuition or the categories of quantity. In this sense, the differential, dx, as a symbol of difference, is 'completely undetermined' (at least with respect to representation), since, as the representation of the 'noumenon closest to the phenomenon' (Deleuze 1994: 222), difference, it escapes the symbolic order. The symbols, dy and dx, and their values of zero in respect to y and x, therefore represent the annihilation of the quantitative within them in favour of what Deleuze calls the sub-representational, or extra-propositional. Deleuze's claim is that it is thus that this element is the original moment of thought that is covered over by the paralogism. If differentials are indeterminate by themselves, they are nonetheless determinable. When differentials are brought into relation with one another, they together determine a curve that *is* determinable. That is, the function dy/dx allows us to work out the gradient at any point on the curve. Now, dy/dx is a ratio, but it is a very particular kind of ratio. In most ratios, such as ¾ or ½, the terms that make it up have a determinate quantity apart from the determinate quantity of the ratio itself. Even a ratio such as y/x is one where the elements, y and x, just stand in for determinate values. 'The relation dy/dx is not like a fraction which is established between particular quanta in intuition, but neither is it a general relation between variable algebraic magnitudes or quantities. Each term exists absolutely only in its relation to the other: it is no longer necessary, or even possible, to indicate an independent variable' (Deleuze 1994: 219). Finally, the function dy/dx doesn't simply give us a function for the gradient at any point on the curve; we also have the specific value of the gradient or ratio when we solve the differential for specific values of x and y. This final moment, where we are dealing with a precise value, gives us the equivalent of complete determination for a point on the curve.

While only one of the moments was an intrinsic feature of the Idea for Kant, the differential calculus provides a model where all three aspects are intrinsic features. Thus, we have the differential, dx, as an element that is simply incapable of being represented. Nonetheless, by entering into a relationship with another differential, both become reciprocally determined, giving an equation for generating the gradients at points on the curve. We also have the specific points that are determined (complete determination). Thus, we have a model that takes us from a non-spatial, non-conceptual moment, through a process of reciprocal determination, to a determinate extension, which provides just the model Deleuze was looking for in his critique of Kant. The *dx*, for Deleuze, is the moment of thinking prior to representation that Feuerbach was looking for, and that Deleuze thought Kant was missing. What are the moments of the equation and the specific value? Well, Deleuze presents them as essentially the concept of an object (determinability), and the specific object the concept relates to (complete determination). Just as the concept of humanity relates to all of the different varieties of human beings, the equation allows us to specify the gradient at each point on the curve. Deleuze argues that the structure of the Idea gives a way of thinking this process whereby the intensive is expressed in extensity, and also shows how different extensive systems may be grouped together according to the intensive forces that give rise to them. In the next section, we will look at a concrete example of the Idea to clarify how Deleuze thinks Ideas function.

7.7 Deleuzian Ideas

Deleuze recognises that 'differential calculus obviously belongs to mathematics, it is an entirely mathematical instrument' (Deleuze 1994: 226), and so we need to explore in more detail how it relates to thought more generally. We have seen that the elements that make up the Idea are differentials – these are elements that only become determinate in relation to each other. Deleuze defines an Idea as 'an *n*-dimensional, continuous, defined multiplicity' (Deleuze 1994: 182). Starting with the last term, Deleuze's use of the term multiplicity explicitly goes back to Bergson once more.[17] Deleuze considers the term multiplicity to be distinguished from a collection of 'many', in that the 'many' is an adjective (the many *x*) that defines a group of entities, while a multiplicity is a noun that defines a structure that does not presuppose extensive parts, much as the *Gestalt* is not constituted from parts. By '*n*-dimensional', Deleuze means that the Idea captures a number of variables which together define the processes of a system. We will return to this in a moment when we look more closely at Deleuze's model of an Idea, but we can note now that the Idea is supposed to capture the degrees of freedom, or the ways in which a system can vary.

[17] Deleuze 1988a: 115–18 sets out Deleuze's programmatic intention of extending Bergson's logic of multiplicities.

Deleuze gives three criteria for the nature of Ideas. First, 'the elements of the multiplicity must have neither sensible form nor conceptual signification, nor, therefore, any assignable function' (Deleuze 1994: 231). This means that the elements are determined by their relationships with each other. Since they are supposed to provide a way of thinking the genesis of experience, they cannot presuppose structures of experience such as perception or concepts. Second, 'the elements must in effect be determined, but reciprocally, by reciprocal relations which allow no independence to subsist' (Deleuze 1994: 231). Finally, 'a differential *relation*, must be actualised in diverse spatio-temporal *relationships*, at the same time as its *elements* are actually incarnated in a variety of terms and forms' (Deleuze 1994: 231). That is, just as we think extensity in terms of a universal that ranges over different objects, an Idea will range over a number of intensive processes. These three stages combine to give a genetic account of the origin of actual states of affairs. As we noted earlier, as well as the process of differentiation, which takes us from a formula to its differential equation, we can also integrate a differential equation, and, in doing so, move from a differential equation to what is known as the primitive function. Deleuze sees the Idea as capturing this process of genesis. We have a field of elements that, on their own, are entirely indeterminate with respect to representation. When brought into relation to each other, and through a process analogous to integration, we arrive at a concrete state of affairs.

Deleuze's conception of the organism as a biological Idea shows how this model works in practice. We have seen at various points in this work that organicism becomes a refuge of judgement once its limitations are discovered. The traditional model of the organism is formulated by Aristotle but, as we saw in our reading of Derrida in Chapter 5, is already prefigured by Plato. We can trace the modern philosophical understanding of this model to Kant, who argues that in order to understand an organism as more than simply a collection of matter, we need to understand it as a unity, and this in turn requires us to understand it as created by an intelligent being, which in turn means that we have to see the unity of organic life as purposive. What ultimately gives unity to the organism is that the whole is determined by the functional unity of the parts. Similarly, the parts themselves are determined by the functions they play in the whole: '[J]ust as each part exists only *as a result* of all the rest, so we think of each part as existing *for the sake* of the others and of the whole, i.e. as an instrument (organ)' (Kant 1987: §373). For Kant, this understanding of the organism is purely a heuristic that allows us to make sense of the world. With Hegel, however, it becomes a defining characteristic of reality:

> Every organised creature forms a whole, a *unified* and closed system, all the parts of which mutually correspond, and by reciprocal action upon one another contribute to the same purposive activity. None of these parts can alter without the others altering too; and consequently each of them, taken on its own, suggests and gives all the others. (Hegel 2002: §370, Add.)

As we have seen, this model of the organism is tied to judgement. Such an approach falls into difficulty if we wish to explain evolution. We understand the parts of an organism in terms of their function, and when we compare different organisms, we do so in terms of an analogy between their parts. This is appropriate in terms of limbs that perform the same function, but fails when we want to explore connections between parts that appear related, but yet perform a different function (legs and fins). Geoffroy St Hilaire, who Deleuze takes to be the key figure in the emergence of the Idea of the organism, takes a different approach of defining the organism by the relationship between the parts. Geoffroy called these relations between parts homologies. In effect, therefore, for Geoffroy what defines the basic structure of an organism is the relationship between the bones that make it up. In order to compare different creatures without relying on teleological functions, Geoffroy introduces the idea of an underlying abstract structure that is shared by different organisms. This abstract structure essentially just captures the connections between the bones of an organism, and will be actualised in different ways in different organisms. As such, we have a difference from the classical model where, for instance, when looking at the skull, what is important is the function of the bones, whereas for Geoffroy what matters is the number and relations of the bones that compose it. We can see that a functional account here has its limitations. While we might argue, for instance, that the human skull is composed of multiple bones in order to allow the skull to pass more easily through the birth canal, such an argument does not explain why birds' skulls are also composed of the same number of bones (Appel 1987: 88) when they peck their way out of their shells. Similarly, Geoffroy showed that the gill covers of fish bore the same relations to other bones as did the bones of the inner ear in mammals, showing the priority of relation over function (Appel 1987: 97). He also showed that where there were differences in the number of bones between fish and mammals, the same number of 'centres of ossification' occurred in the embryos of both creatures.

We can relate this account to the account of Ideas we looked at earlier. The unity of composition that forms the abstract structure on Geoffroy's account is composed of a set of elements that serve as differentials (the bones), and gain their sense through their reciprocal relations with other elements. They are, in effect, the dimensions that Deleuze attributes to the multiplicity. As we saw, the elements of an Idea 'must have neither sensible form nor conceptual signification', a criterion met by the unity of composition being composed of non-metric and topological elements that differ from the structures they are expressed in. Second, 'these elements must be determined reciprocally', a criterion met by the bones being defined by the matrix of relations to other bones they find themselves in. We can understand this by seeing each bone as a 'dimension' in the multiplicity. Finally, 'a multiple ideal connection, a differential *relation*, must be actualised in diverse spatio-temporal *relationships*, at the same time as its *elements* are actually incarnated in a variety of *terms* and forms'. We can see this in that the same unity of composition can be actualised into different species by the non-metric relations of the bones being actualised into specific magnitudes of bone sizes. Thus, the same set of relations between bones is shared by a giraffe and a camel, even if the size of the bones differs. In this particular case, Deleuze asks whether 'anatomical elements, principally bones [are] capable of fulfilling this role [of providing a field of differential relations]' (Deleuze 1994: 185). He suggests that the anatomical elements may have 'an actual, or too actual, existence', and so are potentially too close to actuality to give the difference required by the idea. Deleuze argues a better example may be modern genetics, where the DNA determines the structure of the organism, but does so in a manner that differs in kind from its instantiation.

We can note a number of aspects of this account of the Idea that shed light on the process of thinking. When we look at an intensive system, such as an embryo, we can see how the Idea provides a model for the ways in which the potentialities of the embryo could be actualised. Deleuze notes that the egg is a field of chemical gradients that become differentiated, and in the process bring into being the structures captured by the Idea. This process of actualisation involves transformations that simply wouldn't be possible for the creature within a field of extensity: 'Embryology already displays the truth that there are systematic vital movements, torsions and drifts, that only the embryo can sustain: an adult would be torn apart by them' (Deleuze 1994: 118). The Idea therefore captures the various ways in which an intensive field can express itself in the realm of extensity. It therefore functions like an essence, and Deleuze himself uses this language at points, noting that homologies are understood as 'the actualisation of an essence, in accordance with reasons and at speeds determined by the environment, with accelerations and interruptions' (Deleuze 1994: 184). We note a homology by recognising that the actual parts of both organisms are actualisations of the same transcendental essence, the unity of composition, rather than by a direct correlation of actual terms, as in Aristotle's modelling. The unity of composition therefore functions, according to Deleuze, as an Idea, as that which is actualised, whilst differing in kind from its actualisation. Further, we can see that the concept of essence which Deleuze attributes to Geoffroy is seen by Deleuze as in no way similar to the classical conception, but functions more like a field of accidents, with no privileged form or level of organisation. Describing the Idea elsewhere in *Difference and Repetition*, Deleuze writes, 'this, however, is precisely what is at issue: whether the notions of importance and non-importance are not precisely notions which concern events and accidents, and are much more "important" within accidents than the crude opposition between essence and accident itself' (1994: 189). Deleuze rather ironically refers to this structure as a 'concrete universal' (1994: 173), which, as it brings together all forms that the organism can take, 'possesses a comprehension all the more vast as its extension is great'. As we saw in Chapter 2, Bergson provides a similar model in terms of our notion of colour, where rather than arriving at a conception of colour by removing everything that is distinctive about different colours to arrive at an abstract universal, as occurs with judgement, we instead operate by 'taking the thousand and one different shades of blue, violet, green, yellow and red, and passing them through a converging lens, bringing them to a single point. Then appears in all its radiance the pure white light which, perceived here below in the shades which disperse it, enclosed above, in its undivided unity, the indefinite variety of multicoloured rays' (Bergson 1946: 225). Deleuze himself refers to this example from Bergson, arguing that the Idea of colour 'is like white light which perplicates in itself the genetic elements and relations of all the colours, but is actualised in the diverse colours with their respective spaces' (Deleuze 1994: 206).

Ideas therefore do not operate like judgement. If an Idea is to be understood as forming a multiplicity of interpenetrating elements, then it cannot have the same nature as states of affairs. Elements in states of affairs are determined in terms of limits (what they are not). Furthermore, we can see that just as problems were immanent to their solutions, the genetic conditions for states of affairs (Ideas) are actually simultaneous with states of affairs themselves. The unity of composition in Geoffroy's case does not simply *become* determinate, but determines while itself remaining undifferenciated. We thus have two series that differ in kind: actual events that occur within the world, and the ideal events of 'sections, ablations, adjunctions' (Deleuze 1994: 237) that engender them. This characteristic of co-existing with the states of affairs it engenders means that it also differs from possibility. We have already seen that the Idea can give rise to different actual situations, so, for instance, Geoffroy's unity of composition provides the rules for generating the anatomical structure of different animals. Deleuze defines the structure of the Idea as being *virtual*. Now, Deleuze introduces three claims about the nature of the virtual that need to be explored. It is 'real without being actual, differentiated without being differentiated, and complete without being entire' (Deleuze 1994: 266). In this section, I want to go through these different claims, contrasting them with the structure of possibility, which appears at first glance to be a closely aligned concept. In fact, Deleuze claims that 'the only danger in all this is that the virtual could be confused with the possible' (1994: 263).

Contrasting the virtual with the possible clarifies what it means to be real without being actual. When Kant discusses the possible, he notes that the only difference between the possible and the real is that the latter exists: 'A hundred real thalers do not contain the least coin more than a hundred possible thalers' (Kant 1929: A599/B627). The virtual is instead 'Real without being actual, ideal without being abstract' (Deleuze 1994: 260). Whereas we distinguish the possible from the real in terms of existence, Ideas are distinguished from states of affairs in that the structure of the two is different in kind, just as the differentials are different in kind from natural numbers. This both allows us to understand the virtual as real while maintaining its distinctness from the actual, and allows it to have a role in account for the genesis of actual qualities. 'The reality of the virtual is structure' (Deleuze 1994: 260), in that it provides an account of the field of relations that together will generate the actual state of affairs. In this, it is a part of the object. Jumping to the final qualification in Deleuze's list, it is 'complete without being entire'. What Deleuze means by this is that it is possible to give an account of the structure of the virtual without any reference to actual states of affairs. Such an account would be complete in itself, since it would require no reference to actuality but would not be entire, since a complete account of the object would require us also to describe the actual state of affairs, just as for Descartes we can give a complete account of extension without this being an account of the entirety of the world.

Returning to the second qualification, the virtual is 'differentiated without being differentiated'. What Deleuze means by this is that the way determination operates in the virtual differs in kind from categorial determinations. As Deleuze puts it, 'one [the possible] refers to the form of identity in the concept, whereas the other designates a pure multiplicity in the Idea which radically excludes the identical as a prior condition' (Deleuze 1994: 263). We have seen this characterisation of the possible, and its determination in terms of judgement, where we understand determination in terms of the qualification of a constituted subject. The Idea operates rather in terms of the reciprocal determination of elements that together constitute subjects for predication. Deleuze explains this interrelation of levels by taking up a quote from Leibniz, where Leibniz presents the view that perception of objects is made up of microperceptions operating underneath the threshold of the senses. Leibniz gives the following analogy which Deleuze will take up for his own purposes:

> To give a clearer example of these minute perceptions which we are unable to pick out from the crowd, I like to use the example of the roaring noise of the sea which impresses itself on us when we are standing on the shore. To hear this noise as we do, we must hear the parts which make up this whole, that is the noise of each wave, although each of these little noises makes itself known only when combined confusedly with all the others, and would not be noticed if the wave which made it were by itself. (Leibniz 1997: 54)

Deleuze argues here that Leibniz's analogy shows 'two languages which are encoded in the language of philosophy and directed at the divergent exercise of the faculties' (Deleuze 1994: 266) that represent the two descriptions that in themselves are complete, but do capture the entirety of the object. We can describe the actual state of affairs we find, which is the roar of the sea. In this case, I take up a field of constituted objects, or the sea itself, which is clear, insofar as I see it as an object, but confused, because the elements that together combined to constitute it cannot be distinguished once we are thinking in terms of the individuated. We could also focus on the waves themselves that make up the roar of the sea. In themselves, these waves are distinct, but within this language this distinctness comes at the cost of our language operating prior to objects such as the sea. In contrast to Descartes' notion of clear and distinct ideas, Deleuze's claim is that 'the clear is confused by itself, in so far as it is clear' (Deleuze 1994: 316). Here we can draw a sharp distinction between Deleuze's project and Descartes' project. Descartes built his argument on the notion of clear and distinct ideas. What this implies is that the nature of the thing (its clarity) was the same as the elements that made it up (its distinctness). We can see this claim as essentially being that the appearance of a thing as an extended body is equivalent to its essence as an extended body. For Deleuze, the appearance of a thing (insofar as it is a representation) is different in kind from what makes it up. This allows for the possibility of conceptualising the genesis of the thing itself.

We can finally turn to the nature of thinking itself. In the *Regulae*, Descartes conceives of thinking as a process that moves from proposition to proposition. For Deleuze, rather, the process of thought involves a move between the world of representation and the intensive field that gives rise to it. In determining the similarities between two animals, we do not think by drawing an analogy between the two forms. Rather, we operate by moving between the actual forms and the virtual Idea from which they are both instantiated, and then back to their actual forms. Deleuze gives a similar analysis of thinking a social revolution:

> [E]very Idea has two faces, which are like love and anger: love in the search for fragments, the progressive determination and linking of the ideal adjoint fields; anger in the condensation of singularities which, by dint of ideal events, defines the concentration of a 'revolutionary situation' and causes the Idea to explode into the actual. (Deleuze 1994: 190)

Here, we have an initial process whereby we move back from the actual to the virtual by a process of condensing together different actual forms of society to constitute an idea that gives the sense of the social in general. Once we have this idea, the revolutionary attempts to develop a situation whereby the idea can actualise itself into the future society by providing the appropriate situation of speeds and slownesses. Thought is thus a process that operates between two levels, and Deleuze writes that the I is 'split from end to end by the form of time which runs through it, it must be said that Ideas swarm in the fracture, constantly emerging on its edges, ceaselessly coming out and going back, being composed in a thousand different manners'[18] (1994: 169). As such, Deleuze relies on a structure much like Kant's paralogism, with a split between the noumenal and the world of representation. For Deleuze, however, we can think difference, provided we accept that difference cannot be determined according to the structures of representation.

7.8 Conclusion

When Deleuze is discussing the nature of the subject, he writes that:

> The great discovery of Nietzsche's philosophy, which marks his break with Schopenhauer and goes under the name of the will to power or the Dionysian world, is the following: no doubt the I and the Self must be replaced by an undifferenciated abyss, but this abyss is neither an impersonal nor an abstract Universal beyond individuation. On the contrary, it is the I and the self which are the abstract universals. They must be replaced, but

[18] Lord 2012 provides a detailed account of this fracture in the self and its relationship to Kant.

in and by individuation, in the direction of the individuating factors which consume them and which constitute the fluid world of Dionysus. (Deleuze 1994: 258)

The subject is thus governed by the asymmetrical synthesis of individuation, existing in the interplay between intensity and extensity. At the heart of the subject, therefore, is a process whereby intensity individuates itself according to degrees of speed and slowness that in turn actualise its Idea. We discover this moment beneath representation through a shock that disrupts our normal self-characterisation. While all thinking, even Descartes' own thinking, though he covers it over, moves between the actual and virtual in giving sense to our thought, the highest thought for Deleuze is the Eternal Return. This is the thought of intensity itself, within which all reference to categorial thought is dissolved:

> Moreover, if the eternal return reduces qualities to the status of pure signs, and retains of extensities only what combines with the original depth, even at the cost of our coherence and in favour of a superior coherence, then the most beautiful qualities will appear, the most brilliant colours, the most precious stones and the most vibrant extensions. (Deleuze 1994: 244)

Concluding Remarks

We have now come to the end of our exploration of sense and judgement in the French tradition. We have seen that throughout the French tradition, there has been a preoccupation with developing an account of thinking that moves away from judgement. All of the philosophers we have examined develop this account within the context of an ambivalent relationship with Kant's thought. In Kant, they find the paradigm thinker of judgement, for whom metaphysics is itself a form of logic. Nonetheless, in Kant they find a thinker for whom the limitations of his account of thinking are matched by a nuanced account of how reason itself conflates the conditions for the representation of the object with the conditions of the object itself. Kant therefore inaugurates the movement of German idealism, whilst at the same time pointing to how his own legacy can be overcome.

For Kant, we fall into difficulties when we apply reason beyond its normal bounds. Reason, whose task is to make sense of the individual claims of the understanding, takes as a focal point the idea of a total systematic view of the world whereby we could situate the claim we are considering. Transcendental realism emerges when we combine this claim with the working of the understanding, which 'represents things *as they are*, without considering whether and how we can obtain knowledge of them' (Kant 1929: A498/B526). Once we accept this assumption of the understanding, however, we effectively remove any distinction between the thing in itself and its presentation. Since everything now takes place on one plane, we assume the totality of the conditions of the object are also in principle available to us. We now have no way to make a distinction between the task of reason to trace back conditioned phenomena to their conditions and the actual givenness of those conditions, and so when we encounter a contradiction within representation, it is 'analytical' (Kant 1929: A504/B532) and hence insoluble. This is in effect the root of what Kant calls the 'indirect proof of the transcendental ideality of appearances' (1929: A506/B534), since it is only once we recognise a distinction between representations and things as they are in themselves that we are able to resolve this dilemma: 'If two opposed judgements presuppose an inadmissible condition, then in spite of their opposition, which does not amount to an opposition strictly so-called, both fall to the ground, inasmuch as the condition, under which either of them alone is maintained, itself falls' (Kant 1929: A503/B531). As such, we might recognise that rather than assuming the world is either finite or infinite in magnitude, in fact the world as it is in itself is such that the categories of magnitude do not apply to it, and hence both disjuncts are false (Kant 1929: A503–4/B531–2).

If, by some temporal paradox, the *Critique of Pure Reason* had appeared after Hegel's *Science of Logic*, such an argument may have been seen as a response to Hegel's own account of contradiction. In what appears to be a firmly transcendental realist position, Hegel argues that the systematicity of reason is something that can be given. As such, he is forced to accept the antinomies that Kant presents. His solution to this is to expand his logic to include contradiction, claiming that 'as many antinomies could be constructed as there are Notions' (Hegel 1989: 191). It is thus 'spirit which is so strong that it can endure contradiction' (Hegel 1989: 237–8). We have seen this approach clearly in Hegel's attempt to show that such contrary categories as finitude and infinitude in fact imply each other. Kant's own argument on this point is weakened by the fact that he assumes that all determination occurs in terms of judgement. We are thus left with an opposition between a determinate field of representations and a pure indeterminacy, which is of course open to the kind of arguments Hegel deploys against both Kant and figures such as Hölderlin and Schelling who come after him.

In this regard, the French response to the post-Kantian tradition we have explored in this book can be seen as a return to Kant, and an augmentation of Kant. In rejecting the equivocation of determination and judgement, we open the possibility of the contrary determinations of judgement falling away to reveal an entirely different model of determination. To give a few examples, we see this in Bergson's *Time and Free Will*, where the contradictions between free will and determinism lead both models to fall away and reveal the nature of time as duration. We also see it in Merleau-Ponty's use of antinomy to simultaneously show the limitations of empiricism and intellectualism. It is particularly clear in the case of Derrida, who, insofar as he is dialectical, seems much closer to the transcendental dialectic than the speculative dialectic of Hegel, the contradictions we find in experience leading not to a higher synthesis, but to the recognition that the plane of presence is necessarily incomplete. Finally, Deleuze's opposition of determination by judgement and the pure undifferentiated abyss captures the dilemma of German idealism itself. In each of these cases, then, we find the reinstatement of Kantian arguments through the introduction of a non-representational model of thought. Of course, such an approach requires a rejection of Kant's model of thinking, and this occurs through a radicalisation of the Kantian dialectic itself. Thus, we find Bergson in his lectures on Kant telling us that Kant's mistake is to confuse duration with the representation of duration. Sartre will argue that consciousness is conflated with knowledge of consciousness, Merleau-Ponty that perceptions are conflated with representations of perceptions, Derrida that origins are conflated with representations of origins, Foucault that power is conflated with the representation of power, and Deleuze that thinking is conflated with the representation of thinking. In each case, we find a criticism of Kant of having himself in effect fallen for a paralogism where the representation of thinking is taken for thinking itself. Hence, that which cannot be represented and is nothing for the representation of thinking is seen as indeterminate.

We can note furthermore that the accounts of thinking we have looked at share the twofold structure of Kant's own account of transcendental illusion. On the one hand, they explain why judgement is taken to be the model of thinking, and on the other, they give reasons for the rejection of the representation of thinking in favour of their account of thinking. Invariably, this therefore involves an account of how the representation of thinking has its genesis in thinking itself. Given judgement's nature as involving the synthesis of atomic elements, an account of the genesis of judgement will almost inevitably involve the genesis of these atoms from a non-atomic field, in order to avoid circularity. This leads to the kind of dissociative logic we have seen throughout this work. We can further note, given the inability of judgement to explain the genesis of sense, that this pre-representational logic will itself be a logic of sense.

We have also seen that while we can and should recognise the influence of the 'three H's', Hegel, Husserl, and Heidegger, on the development of French philosophy, a focus on these figures occludes some of the most important development in the French tradition, which could equally be characterised as the attempt to develop a new logic of multiplicities. As such, we need to recognise that despite the explicit influence of Bergson on Sartre and Merleau-Ponty waning, for instance, the influence of many of Bergson's central intuitions are so embedded in their thought as to pass without comment. We can further note that shifting the ground to the interrelation of thinking and judging allows us to bring these thinkers into closer proximity than they have hitherto been seen. We can, for instance, see Sartre as more than a poor critic of Heidegger. Instead he is a philosopher who attempts to introduce a logic of multiplicities into phenomenology. We have noted that it is only late in his career that Derrida admitted his debts to Sartre, but we could also note that neither of the two traits Derrida attributed to presence, a logic of opposition and a search for pure origins, can be attributed to either Bergson or Merleau-Ponty, for both of whom, whether through the essential openness of the organism or the inherently contextual nature of determination, no pure origin is possible. Similarly, Foucault's assimilation of Merleau-Ponty to the empirical-transcendental doublet is rendered problematic by Merleau-Ponty's claim that perception precedes both the transcendental subject and the empirical object. We equally cannot claim that Deleuze's move to an asymmetrical synthesis of intensity is in itself justified against Merleau-Ponty's synthesis of transition. The question of the relation of thinking to its representation therefore gives coherence to the tradition, and shows how each of these projects can be seen as emerging from a shared problem that is still of central importance to us today.

As such, our response to the aporias that emerge from equating thinking with judging remains open. This work has provided a novel framework for understanding and evaluating the responses of these different accounts of the transcendental illusion of judgement, and bringing them into dialogue with each other. Naturally, a number of questions are left unanswered, and here we have merely cleared the ground for further projects by drawing out the importance of the interrelation of thinking and judging. In particular, we are left with the question of what an ethics would be for a thought that operates on the basis of an incommensurability between sense and judgement. Here I would like to suggest that the great precursor to the kind of explorations we have seen in this volume is Kierkegaard. When Merleau-Ponty lays out his account of objective thought as the reduction of the world to representation, he attributes this discovery to Kierkegaard (Merleau-Ponty 2012: 74). While we may say that Nietzsche is a key figure for those writing after the 1960s, Kierkegaard's influence is plain from the ethics of ambiguity of the existentialists to the theatre of repetition post-structuralists. Kierkegaard's claim, for instance, that Hegel's *Logic* presupposes the movement of thought without being able to explain it on the plane of the *Logic* itself (Kierkegaard 1980: 81) prefigures the kind of transcendental account of thinking we have seen from Bergson's theory of duration through to Deleuze's account of the image of thought. Kierkegaard's description of the *Logic* as an 'introverted openness' (1980:

81) describes the sense of a logic that is public but only on the basis of a characterisation of judgement that eliminates the possibility of a genuine encounter with the outside. Such an exploration of what a Kierkegaardian ethics, bolstered by the sophisticated arguments we have examined in this work concerning the relations of sense and judgement, would look like will have to wait for a future work.

Bibliography

Allison, Henry E. (2004) *Kant's Transcendental Idealism*. New Haven, CT: Yale University Press.

Allison, Henry E. (2015) *Kant's Transcendental Deduction: An Analytical-Historical Commentary*. Oxford: Oxford University Press.

Ameriks, Karl (ed.) (2000) *The Cambridge Companion to German Idealism*. Cambridge: Cambridge University Press.

Ansell-Pearson, Keith (1999a) 'Bergson and Creative Evolution/Involution: Exposing the Transcendental Illusion of Organismic Life', in John Mullarkey (ed.) *The New Bergson*. Manchester: Manchester University Press, 146–67.

Ansell-Pearson, Keith (1999b) *Germinal Life: The Difference and Repetition of Deleuze*. London: Routledge.

Ansell-Pearson, Keith (2002) *Philosophy and the Adventure of the Virtual: Bergson and the Time of Life*. London: Routledge.

Appel, Toby A. (1987) *The Cuvier-Geoffroy Debate: French Biology in the Decades Before Darwin*. New York: Oxford University Press.

Atkins, Peter (2010) *The Laws of Thermodynamics: A Very Short Introduction*. Oxford: Oxford University Press.

Bartky, Sandra Lee (2002) '"Catch Me If You Can": Foucault on the Repressive Hypothesis', in *'Sympathy and Solidarity' and Other Essays*. Lanham, MD: Rowman and Littlefield, 47–68.

Baugh, Bruce (1999) '"Hello, Goodbye": Derrida and Sartre's Legacy', *Sartre Studies International* 5 (2): 61–74.

Beiser, Frederick C. (2002) *German Idealism: The Struggle Against Subjectivism, 1781–1801*. Cambridge, MA: Harvard University Press.

Beistegui, Miguel (2010) *Immanence: Deleuze and Philosophy*. Edinburgh: Edinburgh University Press.

Bell, Jeffrey A. (1998) *The Problem of Difference*. Toronto: University of Toronto Press.

Bell, Jeffrey A. (2016) *Deleuze and Guattari's* What Is Philosophy? *A Critical Introduction and Guide*. Edinburgh: Edinburgh University Press.

Berendzen, J. C. (2009) 'Coping with Nonconceptualism? On Merleau-Ponty and McDowell', *Philosophy Today* 53 (2): 162–73.

Bergson, Henri (1946) *The Creative Mind: An Introduction to Metaphysics*, trans. M. L. Andison. New York: Wisdom Library.

Bergson, Henri (1990) *Leçons de psychologie et de métaphysique: Clermont-Ferrand, 1887–1888*. Paris: Presses universitaires de France.

Bergson, Henri (1991) *Matter and Memory*, trans. Nancy Margaret Paul and W. Scott Palmer. New York: Zone Books.

Bergson, Henri (1998) *Creative Evolution*, trans. Arthur Mitchell. Mineola, NY: Dover Publications.

Bergson, Henri (2008) *Time and Free Will: An Essay on the Immediate Data of Consciousness*. Mineola, NY: Dover Classics.

Berkeley, George (2009) 'An Essay Towards a New Theory of Vision', in Desmond M. Clarke (ed.) *Philosophical Writings*. Cambridge: Cambridge University Press, 1–66.

Bernet, Rudolf (1989) 'On Derrida's "Introduction" to Husserl's *Origin of Geometry*', in Hugh Silverman (ed.) *Continental Philosophy II: Derrida and Deconstruction*. London: Routledge, 139–53.

Borges, Jorge Luis (2000) 'John Wilkins' Analytical Language', trans. Eliot Weinberger, in Eliot Weinberger (ed.) *Jorge Luis Borges: Selected Non-Fictions*. New York: Viking, 229–32.

Bowie, Andrew (1993) *Schelling and Modern European Philosophy: An Introduction*. London: Routledge.

Brogan, Walter (1989) 'Plato's Pharmakon: Between Two Repetitions', in Hugh Silverman (ed.) *Continental Philosophy II: Derrida and Deconstruction*. London: Routledge, 7–23.

Burbidge, John W. (1981) *On Hegel's Logic: Fragments of a Commentary*. Atlantic Highlands, NJ: Humanities Press.

Burbidge, John W. (2006) *The Logic of Hegel's Logic*. Peterborough, ON: Broadview Press.

Buroker, Jill Vance (1981) *Space and Incongruence: The Origin of Kant's Idealism*. Dordrecht: Springer.

Čapek, Milič (1971) *Bergson and Modern Physics: A Reinterpretation and Re-Evaluation: Synthese Library*. Dordrecht: Reidel.

Carmen, Taylor (2014) 'Between Empiricism and Intellectualism', in Rosalyn Diprose and Jack Reynolds (eds) *Merleau-Ponty: Key Concepts*. London: Routledge, 44–56.

Carr, H. Wildon (1912) *Henri Bergson: The Philosophy of Change*. London: T.C. & E. Jack.

Catalano, Joseph (1974) *A Commentary on Jean-Paul Sartre's 'Being and Nothingness'*. London: University of Chicago Press.

Catalano, Joseph (2010) *Reading Sartre*. Cambridge: Cambridge University Press.

Caygill, Howard (2000) *A Kant Dictionary*. Oxford: Blackwell Publishing.

Cisney, Vernon (2014) *Derrida's Voice and Phenomenon*. Edinburgh: Edinburgh University Press.

Clisby, Dale (2015) 'Deleuze's Secret Dualism? Competing Accounts of the Relationship between the Virtual and the Actual', *Parrhesia* 24: 127–49.

Delanda, Manuel (2002) *Intensive Science and Virtual Philosophy*. London: Continuum.

Deleuze, Gilles (1984) *Kant's Critical Philosophy: The Doctrine of the Faculties*, trans. Hugh Tomlinson and Barbara Habberjam. Minneapolis, MN: University of Minnesota Press.

Deleuze, Gilles (1986) *Cinema I: The Movement Image*, trans. Hugh Tomlinson and Barbara Habberjam. London: Athlone Press.

Deleuze, Gilles (1988a) *Bergsonism*, trans. Hugh Tomlinson and Barbara Habberjam. New York; London: Zone.

Deleuze, Gilles (1988b) *Foucault*, trans. Sean Hand. Minneapolis, MN: University of Minnesota.

Deleuze, Gilles (1990) *The Logic of Sense*, trans. Mark Lester, with Charles Stivale. London: Athlone.

Deleuze, Gilles (2000) *Proust and Signs*. Minneapolis, MN: University of Minnesota Press.

Deleuze, Gilles (2004) *Desert Islands and Other Texts: 1953–1974*, ed. David Lapoujade, trans. Michael Taormina. Cambridge, MA: Semiotext(e).

Deleuze, Gilles and Félix Guattari (1987) *A Thousand Plateaus*, trans. Brian Massumi. Minneapolis, MN: University of Minnesota Press.

Deleuze, Gilles and Félix Guattari (1994) *What Is Philosophy?*, trans. Hugh Tomlinson and Graham Burchell. New York: Columbia University Press.

Derrida, Jacques (1981a) *Dissemination*, trans. Barbara Johnson. London: Athlone Press.

Derrida, Jacques (1981b) *Positions*, trans. Alan Bass. Chicago, IL: University of Chicago Press.

Derrida, Jacques (1984) *Margins of Philosophy*, trans. Alan Bass. Chicago, IL: University of Chicago Press.

Derrida, Jacques (1988) *Limited Inc*. Evanston, IL: Northwestern University Press.

Derrida, Jacques (1989) *Edmund Husserl's Origin of Geometry: An Introduction*, trans. John P. Leavey Jr. Lincoln, NE; London: University of Nebraska Press.

Derrida, Jacques (2005) *Rogues*, trans. Pascale-Anne Brault and Michael Nass. Stanford, CA: Stanford University Press.

Derrida, Jacques (2011) *Voice and Phenomenon*, trans. Leonard Lawlor. Evanston, IL: Northwestern University Press.

Descartes, René (1984) 'Meditations on First Philosophy', trans. John Cottingham, in John Cottingham, Robert Stoothoff, and Dugald Murdoch (eds) *The Philosophical Writings of Descartes, Vol. II*. Cambridge: Cambridge University Press, 1–398.

Descartes, René (1985a) 'Discourse on Method and Essays', trans. Robert Stoothoff, in John Cottingham, Robert Stoothoff, and Dugald Murdoch (eds) *The Philosophical Writings of Descartes, Vol. I*. Cambridge: Cambridge University Press, 111–76.

Descartes, René (1985b) 'Rules for the Direction of the Mind', trans. Dugald Murdoch, in John Cottingham, Robert Stoothoff, and Dugald Murdoch (eds) *The Philosophical Writings of Descartes, Vol. I*. Cambridge: Cambridge University Press, 7–78.

Descombes, Vincent (1980) *Modern French Philosophy*, trans. L. Scott-Fox and J. M. Harding. Cambridge: Cambridge University Press.

Dillon, M. C. (1988) *Merleau-Ponty's Ontology*. Bloomington, IN: Indiana University Press.

Dreyfus, Hubert L. and Paul Rabinow (1982) *Michel Foucault: Beyond Structuralism and Hermeneutics*. Hertfordshire: The Harvester Press.

Elden, Stuart (2017) *Foucault: The Birth of Power*. Cambridge: Polity Press.

Esposito, Joseph L. (1977) *Schelling's Idealism and Philosophy of Nature*. Lewisburg, PA: Bucknell University Press.

Feuerbach, Ludwig (1997) 'Towards a Critique of Hegelian Philosophy', in Lawrence S. Stepelevich (ed.) *The Young Hegelians: An Anthology*. Amherst, NY: Humanities Press, 95–128.

Fichte, J. G. (1982) *The Science of Knowledge*, ed. and trans. Peter Heath and John Lachs. Cambridge: Cambridge University Press.

Foucault, Michel (1978) *History of Sexuality, vol. 1*, trans. Robert Hurley. New York: Pantheon Books.

Foucault, Michel (1994) *Dits et écrits: 1954–1988*. Paris: Gallimard.

Foucault, Michel (2002a) *The Archaeology of Knowledge*, trans. A. M. Sheridan Smith. London: Routledge.

Foucault, Michel (2002b) *The Order of Things*. Abingdon: Routledge.

Foucault, Michel (2002c) 'Subject and Power', in James D. Faubion (ed.) *Essential Works of Michel Foucault 1954–1984, vol. 3: Power*. London: Penguin Books, 326–48.

Foucault, Michel (2002d) 'Truth and Juridical Forms', in James D. Faubion (ed.) *Essential Works of Michel Foucault 1954–1984, vol. 3: Power*. London: Penguin Books, 1–89.

Foucault, Michel (2002e) 'Truth and Power', in James D. Faubion (ed.) *Essential Works of Michel Foucault 1954–1984, vol. 3: Power*. London: Penguin Books, 111–33.

Foucault, Michel (2008) *Introduction to Kant's Anthropology*, trans. Roberto Nigro and Kate Briggs. Cambridge, MA: Semiotext(e).

Freud, Sigmund (2010) *The Interpretation of Dreams*, trans. James Strachey. New York: Basic Books.

Gardner, Sebastian (1999) *Kant and the Critique of Pure Reason*. New York: Routledge.

Gardner, Sebastian (2009) *Sartre's Being and Nothingness: A Reader's Guide*. London: Continuum.

Gardner, Sebastian (2015) 'Merleau-Ponty's Transcendental Theory of Perception', in Sebastian Gardner and Matthew Grist (eds) *The Transcendental Turn*. Oxford: Oxford University Press, 294–323.

Gasché, Rodolphe (1988) *The Tain of the Mirror: Derrida and the Philosophy of Reflection*. Cambridge, MA: Harvard University Press.

Gioli, Giovanna (2007) 'What Is Transcendental Empiricism? Deleuze and Sartre on Bergson', *Pli – The Warwick Journal of Philosophy* 18: 182–203.

Gunter, Pete (1987) 'The Dialectic of Intuition and Intellect: Fruitfulness as a Criterion', in Andrew A. Y. Papanicolaou and Pete Gunter (eds) *Bergson and Modern Thought: Towards a Unified Science*. London: Routledge, 3–18.

Gutting, Gary (1989) *Michael Foucault's Archaeology of Scientific Reason*. Cambridge: Cambridge University Press.

Gutting, Gary (2001) *French Philosophy in the Twentieth Century*. Cambridge: Cambridge University Press.

Guyer, Paul (1987) *Kant and the Claims of Knowledge*. Cambridge: Cambridge University Press.

Guyer, Paul (1992) 'The Transcendental Deduction of the Categories', in Paul Guyer (ed.) *The Cambridge Companion to Kant*. Cambridge: Cambridge University Press, 123–60.

Guyer, Paul (2000) 'Absolute Idealism and the Rejection of Kantian Dualism', in Karl Ameriks (ed.) *The Cambridge Companion to German Idealism*. Cambridge: Cambridge University Press, 37–56.

Han, Beatrice (2002) *Foucault's Critical Project Between the Transcendental and the Historical*. Stanford, CA: Stanford University Press.

Hass, Lawrence (2008) *Merleau-Ponty's Philosophy*. Bloomington, IN: Indiana University Press.

Hatzimoysis, Anthony (2010) *The Philosophy of Sartre*. London: Routledge.

Hayner, Paul Collins (1967) *Reason and Existence: Schelling's Philosophy of History*. Leiden: E. J. Brill.

Hegel, Georg Wilhelm Friedrich (1971) *Early Theological Writings*, trans. T. M. Knox. Philadelphia, PA: University of Pennsylvania Press.

Hegel, Georg Wilhelm Friedrich (1974) *Lectures on the Philosophy of History, Vol. 1*, trans. E. S. Haldane and Frances H. Simpson. New York: Humanities Press.

Hegel, Georg Wilhelm Friedrich (1975) *Aesthetics: Lectures on Fine Arts*, trans. T. M. Knox. Oxford: Clarendon Press.

Hegel, Georg Wilhelm Friedrich (1977) *Phenomenology of Spirit*, trans. J. N. Findlay and Arnold V. Miller. Oxford: Clarendon Press.

Hegel, Georg Wilhelm Friedrich (1986) *The Jena System, 1804–5: Logic and Metaphysics*, trans. H. S. Harris, John W. Burbidge, and George Di Giovanni. Kingston: McGill-Queen's University Press.

Hegel, Georg Wilhelm Friedrich (1989) *Hegel's Science of Logic*, trans. Arnold V. Miller. Atlantic Highlands, NJ: Humanities Press International.

Hegel, Georg Wilhelm Friedrich (1991) *The Encyclopaedia Logic, with the Zusätze*, trans. Theodore F. Geraets, Wallis Arthur Suchting, and Henry Silton Harris. Indianapolis, IN: Hackett.

Hegel, Georg Wilhelm Friedrich (1995) *Lectures on the History of Philosophy, 3 vols*, trans. Elizabeth Sanderson Haldane and Frances H. Simson. Lincoln, NE: University of Nebraska Press.

Hegel, Georg Wilhelm Friedrich (2002) *Philosophy of Nature, Vol. 1*, trans. M. J. Petry. London: Routledge.

Hegel, Georg Wilhelm Friedrich (2007) *Hegel's Philosophy of Mind*, trans. W. Wallace and A. V. Miller, rev. M. J. Inwood. Oxford: Oxford University Press.

Heidegger, Martin (1985) *Schelling's Treatise on the Essence of Human Freedom*, trans. Joan Stambaugh. Athens, OH: Ohio University Press.

Henrich, Dieter (1989) 'Kant's Notion of a Deduction and the Background of the First *Critique*', in Eckart Förster (ed.) *Kant's Transcendental Deductions*. Stanford, CA: Stanford University Press, 29–46.

Henrich, Dieter (2003) *Between Kant and Hegel: Lectures on German Idealism*, ed. David S. Pacini. London: Harvard University Press.

Hölderlin, Friedrich (1988a) 'Judgement and Being', in T. Pfau (ed.) *Friedrich Hölderlin: Essays and Letters on Theory*. New York: SUNY Press, 124–6.

Hölderlin, Friedrich (1988b) 'Letter to Hegel, Jena, January 26, '95', in T. Pfau (ed.) *Friedrich Hölderlin: Essays and Letters on Theory*. New York: SUNY Press, 37–8.

Horstmann, Rolf-Peter (2000) 'The Early Philosophy of Fichte and Schelling', in Karl Ameriks (ed.) *The Cambridge Companion to German Idealism*. Cambridge: Cambridge University Press, 117–40.

Houlgate, Stephen (2005) *An Introduction to Hegel: Freedom, Truth and History*. Oxford: Blackwell.

Houlgate, Stephen (2006) *The Opening of Hegel's Logic*. West Lafayette, IN: Purdue University Press.

Houlgate, Stephen (2013) *Hegel's 'Phenomenology of Spirit': A Reader's Guide*. London: Bloomsbury.

Hume, David (1978) *A Treatise of Human Nature*. Oxford: Clarendon Press.

Hume, David (2007) *An Enquiry Concerning Human Understanding*. Oxford: Oxford University Press.

Husserl, Edmund (1960) *Cartesian Meditations*, trans. Dorion Cairns. London: Nijhoff Publishers.

Husserl, Edmund (1982 [1913]) *Ideas Pertaining to a Pure Phenomenology and to a Phenomenological Philosophy*, trans. F. Kersten. The Hague: Nijhoff.

Hyppolite, Jean (1974) *Genesis and Structure of Hegel's Phenomenology of Spirit*, trans. John Heckman and Samuel Cherniak. Evanston, IL: Northwestern University Press.

Kant, Immanuel (1929) *Critique of Pure Reason*, trans. Norman Kemp Smith. London; New York: Macmillan; St Martin's Press.

Kant, Immanuel (1987) *Critique of Judgment*, trans. Werner S. Pluhar. Indianapolis, IN: Hackett Publishing.

Kant, Immanuel (1991) 'What Is Orientation in Thinking?', in Hans Reiss (ed.) *Kant: Political Writings*, trans. H. B. Nisbet. Cambridge: Cambridge University Press, 237–49.

Kant, Immanuel (1997) *Prolegomena to Any Future Metaphysics: That Will Be Able to Come Forward as Science*, trans. G. Hatfield. Cambridge: Cambridge University Press.

Kant, Immanuel (1999) *Correspondence*, trans. and ed. Arnulf Zweig, Cambridge: Cambridge University Press.

Kant, Immanuel (2002) 'What Real Progress Has Metaphysics Made in Germany Since the Time of Leibniz and Wolff?', in Henry Allison and Peter Heath (eds) *Theoretical Philosophy Since 1781*, trans. Peter Heath. Cambridge: Cambridge University Press, 337–424.

Kant, Immanuel (2004) *Metaphysical Foundations of Natural Science*, ed. and trans. Michael Friedman. Cambridge: Cambridge University Press.

Kant, Immanuel (2005) *Notes and Fragments*, ed. Paul Guyer, trans. Curtis Bowman, Paul Guyer, and Frederick Rauscher. Cambridge: Cambridge University Press.

Kant, Immanuel (2007) 'Anthropology from a Pragmatic Point of View (1798)', in Günter Zöller and Robert B. Louden (eds) *Immanuel Kant: Anthropology, History, and Education*, trans. Robert B. Louden. Cambridge: Cambridge University Press, 227–429.

Kearney, Richard (1998) *The Poetics of Imagining: From Modern to Postmodern*. Edinburgh: Edinburgh University Press.

Kelly, Mark G. E. (2013) *Foucault's History of Sexuality, Volume I: The Will to Knowledge*. Edinburgh: Edinburgh University Press.

Kelly, Michael R. (ed.) (2010) *Bergson and Phenomenology*. Basingstoke: Palgrave Macmillan.

Khurana, Thomas (2016) '"The Common Root of Meaning and Nonmeaning": Derrida, Foucault, and the Transformation of the Transcendental Question', in Olivia Custer, Penelope Deutscher, and Samir Haddad (eds) *Foucault/Derrida Fifty Years Later: The Futures of Genealogy, Deconstruction, and Politics*. New York: Columbia University Press, 80–104.

Kierkegaard, Søren (1980) *The Concept of Anxiety*, trans. Reidar Thomte and Albert B. Anderson. Princeton, NJ: Princeton University Press.

Koopman, Colin (2010) 'Historical Critique or Transcendental Critique in Foucault: Two Kantian Lineages', *Foucault Studies* 9 (September): 145–55.

Landes, Donald A. (2015) 'Between Sensibility and Understanding: Kant and Merleau-Ponty and the Critique of Reason', *The Journal of Speculative Philosophy* 29 (3): 335–45.

Larmore, Charles (2000) 'Hölderlin and Novalis', in Karl Ameriks (ed.) *The Cambridge Companion to German Idealism*. Cambridge: Cambridge University Press, 141–60.

Lawlor, Leonard (2002) *Derrida and Husserl: The Basic Problem of Phenomenology*. Bloomington, IN: Indiana University Press.

Lawlor, Leonard (2003) *The Challenge of Bergsonism: Phenomenology, Ontology, Ethics*. London: Continuum Press.

Lawlor, Leonard (2010) 'Intuition and Duration: An Introduction to Bergson's "Introduction to Metaphysics"', in Michael R. Kelly (ed.) *Bergson and Phenomenology*. Chippenham: Palgrave Macmillan, 25–41.

Lawlor, Leonard (2012) *Early Twentieth-Century Continental Philosophy*. Bloomington and Indianapolis, IN: Indiana University Press.

Lawlor, Leonard (2019) 'Jacques Derrida', *Stanford Encyclopaedia of Philosophy*. https://plato.stanford.edu/entries/derrida.

Leibniz, G. W. F. (1989a) 'The Principles of Philosophy, or, the Monadology', in Roger Ariew and Daniel Garber (ed. and trans.) *Philosophical Essays*. Indianapolis, IN: Hackett Press, 213–24.

Leibniz, G. W. F. (1989b) 'Samples of the Numerical Characteristic (1679)', in Roger Ariew and Daniel Garber (ed. and trans.) *Philosophical Essays*. Indianapolis, IN: Hackett Press, 10–18.

Leibniz, G. W. F. (1997) *New Essays on Understanding*, trans. and ed. Peter Remnant and Jonathan Bennett. Cambridge: Cambridge University Press.

Leibniz, Gottfried Wilhelm and Samuel Clarke (2000) *Correspondence*, ed. Roger Ariew. Cambridge: Hackett Publishing.

Locke, John (1975) *An Essay Concerning Human Understanding*, ed. Peter H. Nidditch. Oxford: Clarendon Press.

Longuenesse, Béatrice (1998) *Kant and the Capacity to Judge: Sensibility and Discursivity in the Transcendental Analytic of the* Critique of Pure Reason, trans. Charles T. Wolfe. Princeton, NJ: Princeton University Press.

Longuenesse, Béatrice (2007) *Hegel's Critique of Metaphysics*, trans. Nicole J. Simek. Cambridge: Cambridge University Press.

Lord, Beth (2012) 'Deleuze and Kant', in Daniel Smith and Henry Somers-Hall (eds) *The Cambridge Companion to Deleuze*. Cambridge: Cambridge University Press, 82–102.

Lovejoy, Arthur O. (1961) *The Reason, the Understanding, and Time*. Baltimore, MD: Johns Hopkins University Press.

Löwith, Karl (1991) *From Hegel to Nietzsche: The Revolution in Nineteenth-Century Thought*, trans. David E. Green. New York: Columbia University Press.

Lundy, Craig (2017) 'Tracking the Triple Form of Difference: Deleuze's Bergsonism and the Asymmetrical Synthesis of the Sensible', *Deleuze Studies* 11 (2): 174–94.

Magee, Bryan (2000) *The Great Philosophers: An Introduction to Western Philosophy*. Oxford: Oxford University Press.

Maker, William (1994) *Philosophy without Foundations: Rethinking Hegel*. Albany, NY: State University of New York Press.

Matherne, Samantha (2014) 'The Kantian Roots of Merleau-Ponty's Account of Pathology', *British Journal for the History of Philosophy* 22 (1): 124–49.

Matherne, Samantha (2016) 'Kantian Themes in Merleau-Ponty's Theory of Perception', *Archiv für Geschichte der Philosophie* 98 (2): 193–230.

May, Todd (2006) *The Philosophy of Foucault*. London: Acumen.

Maybee, Julie E. (2016) 'Hegel's Dialectics', *Stanford Encyclopaedia of Philosophy*. https://plato.stanford.edu/entries/hegel-dialectics.

McCumber (2014) *Time and Philosophy: A History of Continental Thought*. London: Routledge.

McQuillan, Colin (2010a) 'Philosophical Archaeology in Kant, Foucault, and Agamben', *Parrhesia* 10: 39–49.

McQuillan, Colin (2010b) 'Transcendental Philosophy and Critical Philosophy in Kant and Foucault: Response to Colin Koopman', *Foucault Studies* 9 (September): 145–55.

Merleau-Ponty, Maurice (1963) *The Structure of Behavior*, trans. Alden L. Fisher. Boston, MA: Beacon Press.

Merleau-Ponty, Maurice (1964a) 'Eye and Mind', in James M. Edie (ed.) *The Primacy of Perception*. Evanston, IL: Northwestern University Press, 159–92.

Merleau-Ponty, Maurice (1964b) 'The Primacy of Perception', in James M. Edie (ed.) *The Primacy of Perception*. Evanston, IL: Northwestern University Press, 12–42.

Merleau-Ponty, Maurice (1968) *The Visible and the Invisible*, ed. Claude Lefort, trans. Alphonso Lingis. Evanston, IL: Northwestern University Press.

Merleau-Ponty, Maurice (1993) 'Cezanne's Doubt', in Michael B. Smith (trans. and ed.) *Merleau-Ponty Aesthetics Reader*. Evanston, IL: Northwestern University Press, 59–75.

Merleau-Ponty, Maurice (2003) *Nature: Course Notes from the Collège de France*, ed. Dominique Séglard, trans. Robert Vallier. Evanston, IL: Northwestern University Press.

Merleau-Ponty, Maurice (2012) *The Phenomenology of Perception*, trans. Donald A. Landes. London: Routledge.

Moulard-Leonard, Valentine (2008) *Bergson-Deleuze Encounters: Transcendental Experience and the Thought of the Virtual*. New York: SUNY Press.

Mullarkey, John (1999) *Bergson and Philosophy*. Edinburgh: Edinburgh University Press.

Mullarkey, John (2006) *Post-Continental Philosophy: An Outline*. London: Continuum.

Norman, Judith and Alistair Welchman (2004) *The New Schelling*. London: Continuum.

Oksala, Johanna (2005) *Foucault on Freedom*. Cambridge: Cambridge University Press.

Patton, Paul (2000) *Deleuze and the Political*. London: Routledge.

Plato (1997a) 'Meno', trans. G. M. A. Grube, in John M. Cooper (ed.) *Plato: Complete Works*. Indianapolis, IN: Hackett Publishing, 870–97.

Plato (1997b) 'Phaedo', trans. G. M. A. Grube, in John M. Cooper (ed.) *Plato: Complete Works*. Indianapolis, IN: Hackett Publishing, 49–100.

Plato (1997c) 'Phaedrus', trans. Alexander Nehemas and Paul Woodruff, in John M. Cooper (ed.) *Plato: Complete Works*. Indianapolis, IN: Hackett Publishing, 506–56.

Plato (1997d) 'Republic', trans. G. M. A. Grube, rev. C. D. C. Reeve, in John M. Cooper (ed.) *Plato: Complete Works*. Indianapolis, IN: Hackett Publishing, 971–1223.

Richmond, Sarah (2007) 'Sartre and Bergson: A Disagreement about Nothingness', *International Journal of Philosophical Studies* 15: 77–95.

Rockmore, Tom (2011) *Kant and Phenomenology*. Chicago, IL: University of Chicago Press.

Romdenh-Romluc, Komarine (2011) *Routledge Philosophy Guidebook to Merleau-Ponty and the* Phenomenology of Perception. London: Routledge.

Rosen, M. (1982) *Hegel's Dialectic and Its Criticism*. Cambridge: Cambridge University Press.

Rosenberg, Harold (1994) *The Tradition of the New*. New York: De Capo Press.

Rouse, Joseph (2005) 'Power/Knowledge', in Gary Gutting (ed.) *The Cambridge Companion to Foucault*. Cambridge: Cambridge University Press, 95–122.

Sartre, Jean-Paul (1960) *The Transcendence of the Ego*, trans. Forrest Williams and Robert Kirkpatrick. New York: Hill and Wang.

Sartre, Jean-Paul (1965) 'Playboy Interview: Jean-Paul Sartre – Candid Conversation', *Playboy: Entertainment for Men* 12: 69–77.

Sartre, Jean-Paul (1967) 'Consciousness of Self and Knowledge of Self', in N. Lawrence and D. O'Connor (eds) *Readings in Existential Phenomenology*. Englewood Cliffs, NJ: Prentice-Hall, 113–42.

Sartre, Jean-Paul (1970) 'Intentionality: A Fundamental Idea of Husserl's Phenomenology', trans. Joseph P. Fell, *Journal of the British Society for Phenomenology* 1 (2): 4–5.

Sartre, Jean-Paul (1978) *Being and Nothingness*, trans. Hazel E. Barnes. New York: Pocket Books.

Sartre, Jean-Paul (2004) *The Imaginary*, trans. Jonathan Webber. Abingdon: Routledge.

Sartre, Jean-Paul (2012) *The Imagination*, trans. Kenneth Williford and David Rudrauf. Abingdon: Routledge.

Schelling, F. W. J. (2004) *First Outline of a System of the Philosophy of Nature*, trans. Keith R. Peterson. Albany, NY: SUNY Press.

Schelling, F. W. J. (2012a) 'Further Presentations from the System of Philosophy', in Michael G. Vater and David W. Wood (trans. and eds) *The Philosophical Rupture between Fichte and Schelling*. Albany, NY: SUNY Press, 206–26.

Schelling, F. W. J. (2012b) 'Presentation of My System of Philosophy', in Michael G. Vater and David W. Wood (trans. and eds) *The Philosophical Rupture between Fichte and Schelling*. Albany, NY: SUNY Press, 141–205.

Schmidt, James and Thomas E. Wartenberg (1994) 'Foucault's Enlightenment: Critique, Revolution, and the Fashioning of the Self', in Michael Kelly (ed.) *Critique and Power: Recasting the Foucault/Habermas Debate*. Cambridge, MA: MIT Press, 283–314.

Schrift, Alan D. (2006) *Twentieth-Century French Philosophy: Key Themes and Thinkers*. Oxford: Blackwell.

Smith, Daniel W. (2012a) 'Deleuze, Hegel, and the Post-Kantian Tradition', in *Essays on Deleuze*. Edinburgh: Edinburgh University Press, 59–71.

Smith, Daniel W. (2012b) 'The Doctrine of Univocity: Deleuze's Ontology of Immanence', in *Essays on Deleuze*. Edinburgh: Edinburgh University Press, 27–42.

Snow, Dale E. (1996) *Schelling and the End of Idealism*. Albany, NY: State University of New York Press.

Somers-Hall, Henry (2013a) *Deleuze's* Difference and Repetition: *An Edinburgh Philosophical Guide*. Edinburgh: Edinburgh University Press.

Somers-Hall, Henry (2013b) 'Deleuze's Use of Kant's Argument from Incongruent Counterparts', *Southern Journal of Philosophy* 51: 345–66.

Somers-Hall, Henry (2013c) 'The Logic of the Rhizome in the Work of Hegel and Deleuze', in J. Vernon and K. Houle (eds) *Hegel and Deleuze: Together Again for the First Time*. Evanston, IL: Northwestern University Press, 54–75.

Somers-Hall, Henry (2015) 'Feuerbach and the Image of Thought', in *At the Edges of Thought: Deleuze and Post-Kantian Philosophy*. Edinburgh: Edinburgh University Press, 253–71.

Stern, Robert (1990) *Hegel, Kant and the Structure of the Object*. London: Routledge.

Stern, Robert (2002) *Hegel and the Phenomenology of Spirit*. London: Routledge.

Stone, Alison (2005) *Petrified Intelligence: Nature in Hegel's Philosophy*. Albany, NY: SUNY Press.

Sturma, Dieter (2000) 'The Nature of Subjectivity: The Critical and Systematic Function of Schelling's Philosophy of Nature', in Sally Sedgwick (ed.) *The Reception of Kant's Critical Philosophy*. Cambridge: Cambridge University Press, 216–31.

Toscano, Alberto (2006) *The Theatre of Production: Philosophy and Individuation between Kant and Deleuze*. Basingstoke: Palgrave Macmillan.

Wambacq, Judith (2017) *Thinking between Deleuze and Merleau-Ponty*. Athens, OH: Ohio University Press.

Webber, Jonathan (2009) *The Existentialism of Jean-Paul Sartre*. London: Routledge.

White, Alan (1983) *Schelling: An Introduction to the System of Freedom*. New Haven, CT: Yale University Press.

Widder, Nathan (2009) 'John Duns Scotus', in Graham Jones and Jon Roffe (eds) *Deleuze's Philosophical Lineage*. Edinburgh: Edinburgh University Press, 27–43.

Widder, Nathan (2019) 'The Mathematics of Continuous Multiplicities: The Role of Riemann in Deleuze's Reading of Bergson', *Deleuze and Guattari Studies* 13 (3): 331–54.

Williams, James (2003) *Gilles Deleuze's* Difference and Repetition*: A Critical Introduction and Guide*. Edinburgh: Edinburgh University Press.

Wood, David (1988) '*Différance* and the Problem of Strategy', in David Wood and Robert Bernasconi (eds) *Derrida and Différance*. Evanston, IL: Northwestern University Press, 63–70.

Wright Henderson, P. A. (1910) *The Life and Times of John Wilkins*. Edinburgh and London: William Blackwood and Sons.

Zuckert, Catherine H. (1996) *Postmodern Platos: Nietzsche, Heidegger, Gadamer, Strauss, Derrida*. Chicago, IL: University of Chicago Press.

Index

For EU product safety concerns, contact us at Calle de José Abascal, 56–1°, 28003 Madrid, Spain or eugpsr@cambridge.org.

www.ingramcontent.com/pod-product-compliance
Ingram Content Group UK Ltd.
Pitfield, Milton Keynes, MK11 3LW, UK
UKHW020355140625

459647UK00020B/2486

* 9 7 8 1 0 0 9 0 4 8 6 3 7 *